DIVE THE ISLES OF SCILLY
AND NORTH CORNWALL

DIVE THE ISLES OF SCILLY AND NORTH CORNWALL

A DIVER GUIDE

Richard Larn and David McBride

Underwater World Publications

Above: A ship's officer's cap badge from the wreck of
the *Hollandia* (Site **31**).

Title page: One of the large bronze cannon recovered from the
wreck of the *Association* (Site **35**) is mounted on a wooden sea-
carriage and displayed as part of the Valhalla Collection on Tresco.

Front cover: Diver at 35m depth inside a side-light housing on
the *Italia*, off St. Agnes (Site **23**).

Although reasonable care has been taken in preparing this guide, the publishers and
authors respectively accept no responsibility or liability for any errors, omissions or
alterations, or for any consequences ensuing upon the use of, or reliance upon, any
information contained herein. Due caution should be exercised by anyone attempting
dives on any site herein described or indicated. The authors and publishers would be
glad to hear of any inaccuracies or any new relevant material. The reproduction by any
means in whole or part of any content of this book is expressly forbidden without the
written permission of Underwater World Publications Ltd.

Copy-editing by Susannah Wight

Maps drawn by Nigel Greenaway

Typesetting, editorial production and index by Martyn Yeo

Produced by DIVER Magazine

Published by Underwater World Publications Ltd,
55 High Street, Teddington, Middlesex, TW11 8HA

First published 2003

© Underwater World Publications Ltd 2003

ISBN 0 946020 33 7

Printed in the United Arab Emirates by Emirates Printing Press,
PO Box 5106, Al Quoz, Dubai

Contents

How to use this guide

This book is divided into fifteen areas. Eight cover the Isles of Scilly (the five inhabited islands, the Western Rocks and Seven Stones, and then the other rocks and islands) and seven cover North Cornwall (from Sennen Cove in the west to the Devon border in the north-east). The account of each area consists of an introduction followed by descriptions of the coastal dives and offshore sites. Detailed access and route information, wreck details, recommended launch sites and harbour information is given in each case. Appendix 1 contains useful addresses and phone numbers.

Dive site numbers are printed in bold type, and relate to the numbers shown on individual detailed maps. Depths are given in metres, distances in yards and miles. Ship tonnages are gross unless otherwise stated.

The information given was correct at the time this book was written, but change is inevitable and the authors and publishers would appreciate any corrections or updated information, which will be used (with acknowledgement) in the next edition of this book.

Unless specified otherwise, any references to Ordnance Survey maps are to the 1:50,000 Landranger Series.

Opposite: Porth Conger, St Agnes, Isles of Scilly, showing the slipway and quay. Tresco can be seen in the far distance.

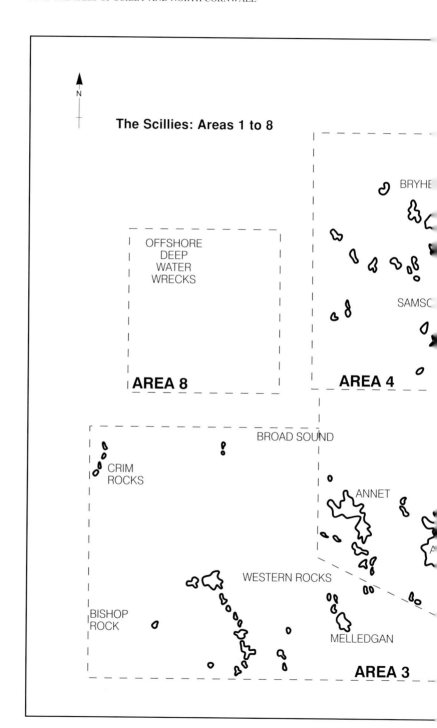

The Scillies: Areas 1 to 8

BRYHE

OFFSHORE
DEEP
WATER
WRECKS

SAMSC

AREA 8

AREA 4

BROAD SOUND

CRIM
ROCKS

ANNET

WESTERN ROCKS

BISHOP
ROCK

MELLEDGAN

AREA 3

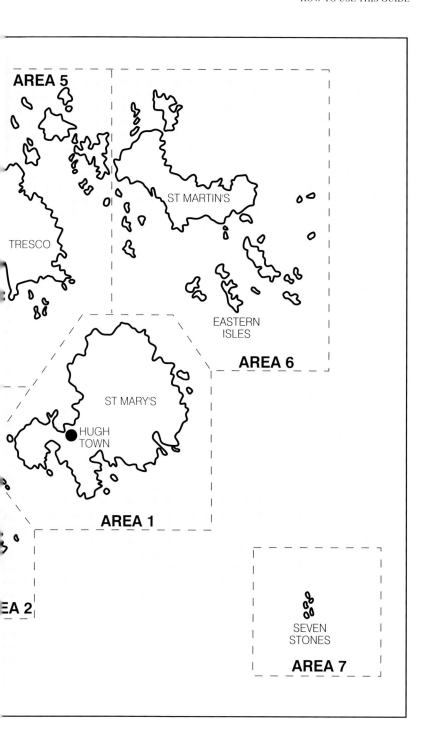

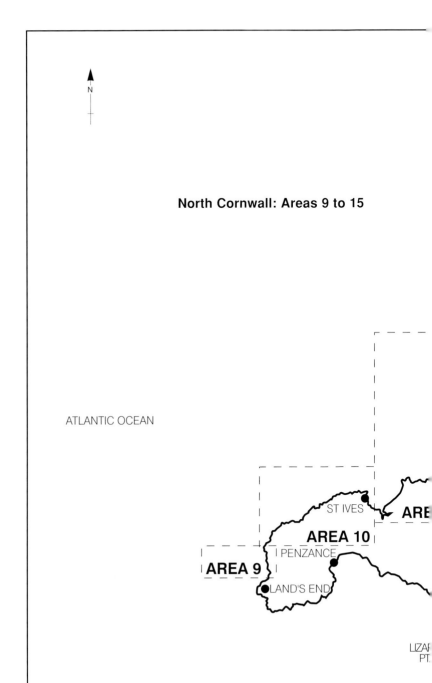

North Cornwall: Areas 9 to 15

ATLANTIC OCEAN

ST IVES

AREA 10

AREA 9

PENZANCE

LAND'S END

LIZARD PT.

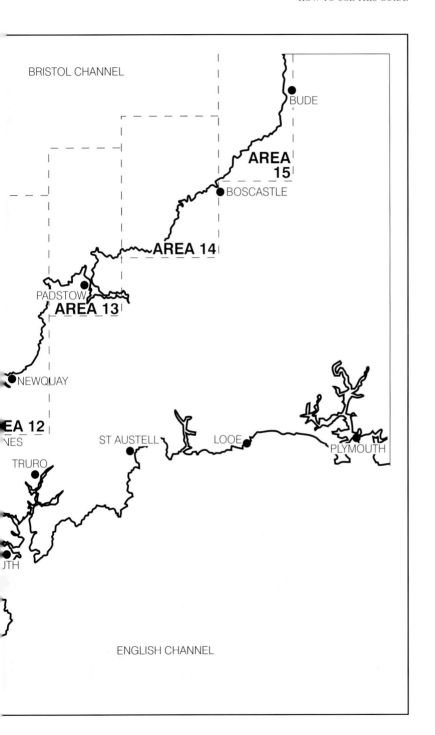

About the Isles of Scilly and North Cornwall

The Isles of Scilly comprise five inhabited islands, some 48 islets and hundreds of rocks spread out over some 63 square miles, 28 miles west of Land's End. The group is the peak of a submerged seamount, with individual islands, at one time joined together, now a series of granite outcrops separated by shallow sea. The islands are very low lying – the highest part of the main island, St Mary's, is only 57m above sea level – and when shrouded in fog or rain the entire group of islands merges into a background of heaving grey sea. This feature has been the most singular cause of shipwrecks here.

Deep water surrounds the Scillies and there are often depths of 73m within less than a quarter mile offshore, so that in places rock faces plunge vertically from the surface to 30m or more. Located at the junction of the Bristol and English Channels, there is a considerable tidal flow, but it seldom exceeds 3 to 4 knots, with reasonable periods of slack water. Between the individual islands the sea bed is predominantly sand with average depths of 3 to 9m. With no rivers and few fresh water streams, and swept by tides direct from the Atlantic, water clarity can be almost tropical; divers frequently comment on underwater visibility, which can exceed 35m.

Chambered burial mounds of the megalithic period survive on the islands, which are known to have been inhabited in the Bronze Age. Roman remains are evidence of the islands' occupation during the first century AD and they have remained permanently occupied ever since. The resident population of the islands at the time of writing is about 2,200 – of whom some 1,600 live on St Mary's, the main transportation terminal between the mainland and the islands. Visitors' vehicles are discouraged on St Mary's and prohibited on the other islands. However, several diving clubs regularly take vans across but no parking of vehicles, trailers or boats

Opposite: St Mary's Hugh Town harbour, with dive boats alongside.

7

is allowed on the quay, and it is necessary to make prior arrangements for anything sent in advance to be moved. Chris Jenkins of South'ard Engineering (tel./fax 01720 422539) offers to meet ferries and tow boats or trailers off the quay and leave them near the Rechabite slip. Sleeping vehicles, motor-homes or caravans of any type are strictly prohibited.

The climate on the Isles of Scilly is sub-tropical, due to prevailing south-westerly winds whose temperature is influenced by the Gulf Stream. Sea temperatures – around 11°C in winter, 14°C in summer – mean that diving without a wet-suit jacket can quickly lead to hypothermia; full wet or dry suits are advisable all year round.

North Cornwall

This guide covers the north coast of Cornwall from the Sennen Cove lifeboat station at Land's End to the north-east coast at Marshland Mouth near Bude. It can be a dangerous and inhospitable coast, subject to heavy ground-seas, an almost constant swell and exposed to strong winds, but summer months give underwater visibility of 20m, and often 25–30m.

The full potential of diving the north coast can be realised only when using a boat, as the best wrecks, rocks and islands are offshore; very few sites can be considered shore dives. However, there are few slip launch sites for diving boats, and you should be prepared to haul your inflatable over soft sandy beaches using a suitable four-wheel-drive vehicle; as yet there are no live-aboard diving charter vessels based on this coast.

St Ives, Newquay, Padstow, Rock and Port Gaverne are the best areas on which to base diving off North Cornwall as they are central to the entire coastline and have good facilities. Newquay, Padstow and Port Gaverne in particular offer easy access to many offshore islands, rocks, reefs and shipwrecks.

Travel

Roads The motorway routes into Cornwall are the M6 and M4. These merge at Bristol into the M5, which continues west to Exeter. From London, an alternative route is via the M25, M3 and A303. The A303 from the M25 is some 40 miles

---

MOTORING ORGANISATIONS

The main motoring organisations can be contacted as follows:

AA 24-hour breakdown service: tel. 0800 887766; from mobile telephones: 08457 887766; enquiries: 08705 444444

RAC 24-hour breakdown service: tel. 0800 828282; customer services: 08705 722722;

Direct Line Rescue – national coverage – 24 hours: 0845 2468 999

A30 Newquay – 8am to 5.30pm recovery service: 01726 860043

Godrevy Point, and the lighthouse on Godrevey Island.

shorter to Exeter than travelling via the M4 and M5; it is less congested than the motorways and has plenty of service stops. There is also the south coast route via Southampton and Dorchester (A27, M27, A31, A35) to Exeter. Resorts on the north coast of Cornwall can be reached by turning off the A30 at various points.

For those travelling from abroad, Cornwall can be reached by ferry direct to Plymouth from Roscoff (Brittany) or Santander (northern Spain). Plymouth offers access to Bodmin via the A38, where it links with the A30.

Travelling at peak holiday periods should be carefully planned. Otherwise, travelling to the South West should present no problems, but make allowances for delays when timing your journey, particularly since the ferry service to the Isles of Scilly normally makes only one crossing each day. There is no public transport to or from the islands by sea or air on Sundays, except in emergencies.

Many of the dive sites described in this guide require negotiation of high-sided narrow lanes, one vehicle width only, with infrequent passing places, and it is suggested that another vehicle not towing a boat or trailer should lead the way, to warn other road users that a longer vehicle is following.

Many launch sites offer limited or no parking facilities: please use the parking places mentioned in this guide and accept there will be few sites where you can leave your vehicle close to the water's edge or alongside a slipway.

THIS STONE MARKS THE PLACE
WHERE THE BODY OF
ADMIRAL OF THE FLEET,

SIR CLOUDESLEY SHOVELL,

WAS WASHED ASHORE
AFTER HIS FLAGSHIP, HMS ASSOCIATION
WAS WRECKED ON THE GILSTONE ROCKS
ON THE NIGHT OF 22ND OCTOBER 1707

Above: The memorial stone marking the site at Porth Hellick Cove where Sir Clowdisley Shovell is said to have been temporarily buried in 1707.

Top: The inscription on the plaque below the stone.

RAIL COMPANIES

Rail companies can be contacted as follows:

National Rail Enquiries (tel. 08457 484950; minicom service: 0845 605 0600; www.nationalrail.co.uk).

First Great Western Trains (tel. 08457 000125; group travel: 08457 413777; www.greatwesterntrains.co.uk).

Motorail (tel. 0845 601 0847; fax 08457 413776). Vehicles loaded at Paddington, to Penzance only (June to September only).

Virgin (tel. 08457 222333; textphone: 0845 744 3367).

Wales & West (tel. 0845 300 3005; textphone: 0845 758 5469).

Rail services There are services from London, the Midlands and the North to Penzance, the terminal for rail travel to Cornwall. Travel time from London is currently 5¼ hours and from Bristol 3½ hours. Seat reservations are recommended during the holiday season and on trains leaving Paddington on Fridays. See the information panel above.

Flights British Airways City Express operates to and from London Gatwick and Newquay and has four flights a day, every day throughout the year to the West Country (Newquay); for enquiries and travel information: tel. 0845 7733377 (24 hours). At the time of writing, this service was due to cease in October 2003.

Helicopter Helicopter flights to the Scillies depart from the British International Heliport outside Penzance. It is less than a mile from the rail and coach stations, and a private shuttle bus takes passengers and baggage between these stations, other local destinations and heliport. The heliport has a long- and short-term car park with an unloading area directly in front of the terminal entrance. Alternatively, the Harbour Garage, Coinagehall Street, Penzance (tel. 01736 366408; mobile 07799 694698) will keep your vehicle safe in a locked compound. You can arrange to have your vehicle collected from the heliport and looked after for an additional charge.

Baggage on the helicopter is restricted to 15kg per person, plus a small piece of hand baggage. It is advisable to book excess baggage well in advance; if the flight is full, the company may refuse to accept excess baggage, but will usually transport it on a later flight at excess baggage rates. Pressurised diving cylinders will not be accepted under any circumstances. An alternative method of transportation is to send your heavy diving equipment on the RMS *Scillonian III* ferry as unaccompanied baggage, which will be delivered to your accommodation for a nominal charge.

Flying time to St Mary's is 20 minutes, and certain flights land on Tresco en route, with as many as four direct flights a day to that island during the summer. Check-in time is at least 30 minutes before the flight. No charge is made for altering your reservation, and no charge for cancellation, provided this is made at least one hour before the scheduled flight time. For travel enquiries and tickets, and details of discounts for group travel, Late Saver Returns, Short Break Returns and Advance

Purchase discounts, tel: 01736 363871, fax 01736 332253. For late enquiries (on the day of departure), cargo, or excess baggage, tel: 01736 364296. Helicopter flights during the peak holiday period are frequently fully booked with a lengthy stand-by list, so you are advised to ring well in advance concerning availability and flight times, and make your booking as early as possible (B. I. H. St Mary's Airport: tel. 01720 422646 or agent K. Morley: tel 01720 422665).

Ferry The ferry *Scillonian III* sails daily on Monday to Saturday between late March and September and four days per week during October. There are no services on Sundays. The crossing takes approximately 2½ hours. The harbour has a car park and there are other privately operated secure car parks. One of these is the Harbour Garage (tel. 01736 366406); details of other garages can be obtained from the Isles of Scilly Steamship Company, Quay Street, Penzance TR18 4BZ (tel. 08457 105555).

Purchase tickets for your crossing from Isles of Scilly Steamship Company booking office at the entrance to the quay (tel. 01736 334220). Luggage must be left in containers – there is one for each destination island. Make sure you use the correct one, note its number, and clearly mark each item of luggage with your name, destination island and accommodation address; luggage labels are provided. Passengers are allowed two pieces of personal luggage, to a maximum combined weight of 25 kilos.

Brass and copper fittings salvaged from shipwrecks around the Isles of Scilly, awaiting disposal in the Queen's Warehouse, St Mary's. In the foreground are three condenser end plates and brass condenser tubes.

The harbour at Hugh Town, St Mary's.

Freight charges may apply to excess luggage, which must be booked and paid for in advance. Charges for trailers and boats vary by length (the ferry company does not place any restrictions on the overall weight of a boat and trailer, so that diving and other equipment can be packed inside). Boats and box trailers are often carried on the upper deck, so should be adequately covered against wind and weather, and any covers well lashed down.

Advanced booking is essential; cancellations are subject to a 15% penalty fee and a minimum of 48 hours' notice must be given on freight. Seats cannot be reserved, but the ferry has plenty of seating accommodation and there are a limited number of bunks and couchettes, also a cafeteria and bar. You are advised to arrive at least 30 minutes prior to sailing.

Information and tickets can be obtained by post or telephone from the Isles of Scilly Travel Centre, Quay Street, Penzance TR18 4BD (tel. 01736 334220). Enquiries about freight at Penzance (tel. 01736 366485) and on St Mary's should be addressed to the Travel Centre's office off Hugh Street, St Mary's (tel. 01720 424220) or the quay freight office (tel. 01720 424230; fax 01720 422192).

An additional freight service to the Scillies is available all year round, on Mondays, Wednesdays and Fridays via the MV *Gry Maritha*. Should a large group of divers consider going to the islands for more than a week, taking with them one or more inflatables and equipment, a cheaper option than sending equipment on the *Scillonian III* may be to hire a container to hold all the gear. Contact the Isles of Scilly Steamship Company's offices for freight charges, sailing dates and times.

Skybus An alternative means of reaching the Isles of Scilly is the Skybus service, run by the Isles of Scilly Steamship Company, from Land's End Airport. Flights can be booked through Isles of Scilly Travel, Penzance (tel. 08457 105555). A free shuttle bus service operates between Penzance railway station and Land's End

En route from Bristol to Padstow with a general cargo, the SS Venetienne struck Roscarrick Rock off Pentire Head on 24 January, 1883 but managed to get into the estuary before she sank near Hawker's Cove, leaving her masts and funnel showing. Her cargo was salvaged by divers, and the wreck was broken up where she lay for scrap.

Airport. Parking at Land's End is free, provided you reserve a space when booking your ticket. Flight time is about 20 minutes. Flights are also available daily direct to St Mary's from Newquay airport and from Southampton, Bournemouth, Bristol and Exeter via Newquay (between March and November only) (tel. 01637 860934); travelling this way could save you a great deal of time as British Airways offers flights from London Gatwick to Newquay, and by Ryanair from Stansted. Check-in time is 30 minutes prior to the flight at Land's End and 45 minutes at Newquay. Passengers are permitted 15kg luggage; excess is charged at 50p per kilo plus VAT, but may not be carried on the same flight or day. If travelling from Bristol and Newquay, call British Airways (tel. 08457 733377); Ryanair (tel. 0871 246 0000).

Skyrail This is an all-in travel package, which will take you from your nearest home railway station by train and then plane all the way to your accommodation on St Mary's. The package includes all transfers, rail and air travel, and insurance. Details are available through the Isles of Scilly Travel Centre (tel. 01720 424220).

Where to stay

There is plenty of accommodation in most of the Isles of Scilly and throughout North Cornwall, but advance booking is essential, particularly in the Scillies – an extremely popular holiday location – and is recommended in Cornwall during peak holiday periods. Be aware that there are no caravans for hire on the Isles of Scilly and camping or sleeping in tents is allowed only on the registered campsites. The Isles of Scilly Tourist Information Centre at The Hugh Street Tourist Centre, St Mary's, Isles of Scilly TR21 OJD (tel. 01720 422536; fax 01720 422049; e-mail TIC@scilly.demon.co.uk; www.simplyscilly.co.uk) produces a comprehensive free accommodation list.

Many pubs and inns in Cornwall offer evening meals and bed-and-breakfast accommodation and the following guides, though a few years old, are recommended: *The Complete Guide to Cornish Pubs* (David Guthrie, Half Pint Press, Erith, 1991 ISBN 0 9514450 0 6) and *Cornwall* (David Franklin and Paul Watkins, Golden Hart Guides, Sigwick and Jackson, London, 1983, ISBN 0 283 98912 2).

The Cornwall Tourist Board is at Pydar House, Pydar Street, Truro TR1 1EA (tel. 01872 322900; fax 01872 322895; www.cornwalltouristboard.co.uk) and will send free accommodation and tourist information. Note that accommodation on the coast is usually more expensive than accommodation inland. Details of accommodation for any particular area can be obtained from the appropriate local tourist information centres:

Bodmin (tel./fax 01208 76616)
Boscastle (tel./fax 01840 250010)
Bude (tel. 01288 354240; fax 01288 355769; e-mail budetk@visit.org.uk)
Camelford (tel./fax 01840 212954)
Hayle (tel. 01736 754399)
Newquay (tel. 01637 854020; fax 01637 854030; e-mail info@newquay.co.uk)
Padstow (tel. 01841 533449; fax 01841 532356; e-mail padstowtic@visit.org.uk)
Penzance (tel. 01736 362207)
Perranporth (tel. 01872 573368; fax 01872 573138; e-mail thevoice@dircon.co.uk)
Polzeath (tel. 01208 862488; fax 01208 869058)
St Agnes (tel./fax 01872 554150; e-mail stagnes.tic@stagnes.com)
St Ives (tel. 01736 796297; fax 017367 8309)
St Just (tel. 01736 788699)
Tintagel (tel./fax 01840 779084)
Truro (tel. 01872 274555)

The following numbers may also be useful:

Newquay Tourist Park (tel. 01637 871111)
Penwith District Council, Resorts Section (tel. 01736 62207)
Scilly online (tel. 01242 529509; fax 01242 228401;
www.scillyonline.co.uk/accomm.html)

The following places to stay are convenient for diving holidays:

Area 1

Garrison Farm Campsite, St Mary's (tel. 01720 422670)

Pelistry Farm, St Mary's (tel. 01720 422550) – 2½ miles from quay and harbour

Area 2

St Agnes Campsite (tel. 01720 422360)

Area 4

Bryher Campsite (tel. 01720 422886)

Area 6

St Martin's Campsite (tel./fax 01720 422888)

Area 9

Camilla House Hotel (tel./fax 01736 363771)

La Connings Country House (tel./fax 01736 762380)

Pendennis Hotel (tel./fax 01736 363823)

Kelynack Caravan and Camping Park (tel. 01736 787633)

Kenneggy Cove Holiday Park (tel./fax 01736 763453)

Mounts Bay Caravan Park (tel. 01736 710307)

Roselands Caravan and Camping Park (tel. 01736 788571)

Adanac (tel. 01736 871348)

Bay View (tel. 01736 871375)

Bosavern House (tel./fax 01736 788301; www.bosavern.u-net.com)

Boswedden House (tel./fax 01736 788733)

Harbour View (tel. 01736 871206)

Harbourview Flat (tel. 01736 731324)

Nanpean Barn (tel. 01736 788731)

The Old Success Inn (tel. 01736 871232; fax 01736 871457)

The Regent (tel. 01736 362946; fax 01736 332832)

Sennen Cove Hotel (tel. 01736 871275)

Sunnycroft (tel. 01736 871744)

Tredinney Farm (tel. 01736 810352)

Trevear Farm Cottages (tel. 01736 871205)

Area 10

St Ives Holiday Park, Polmanter (tel. 01736 795640; www.bob.org.uk)

Longships Hotel, Talland Road, St Ives TR26 2DF (tel./fax 01736 798180)

Bay View (tel. 01736 796469)

Trelawne Guest House (tel. 01736 794140)

Area 11

Atlantic Coast Holiday Bungalows (tel. 01872 552485;
www.chycor.co.uk /cottages/atlantic-holidays)
Woodlands Chalets (tel. 01872 553593)
Engine House Cottage (tel. 01379 640926)

Area 12

Crantock Beach Holiday Park (tel. 01637 871111)
Gull Rock Holiday Apartments (tel. 01872 573289)
Hendra Holiday Park (tel. 01637 875778; e-mail hendra.uk@dial.pipex.com)
Trevornick Holiday Park (tel. 01637 830531)
Perranova Guest House (tel. 01872 573440)

Area 13

Mariners Hotel and Guest House (tel. 01208 862312; fax 01208 863827)
South Winds Holiday Park (tel. 01208 863267; fax 01208 862080)

Area 14

Pencarmol Guest House (tel. 01840 250435)
Valency Guest House (tel. 01840 250397)
The Old Coach House (tel. 01840 250398; fax 01840250346; e-mail
parsons@oldcoach.demon.co.uk)
Wadebridge (tel. 01208 813725; fax 01208 813781)

Area 15

Old School Holiday Cottages (tel. 01840 230310; fax 01840 230612)
Atlantic View Bungalows (tel./fax 01288 361716)
Bude Holiday Park (tel. 01288 355955; fax 01288 355980)
Mornish Holiday Apartments (tel./fax 01288 352972)
West Point Guesthouse (tel. 01288 331594)
Court Farm (tel./fax 01288 361494; www.cornwall-online.co.uk/court-farm)
Wooda Farm Park (tel. 01288 352069; fax 01288 355258)

Dive planning

There are three ways of exploring the Isles of Scilly as a diver. The simplest is to book a place on one of the many dive charter vessels visiting the islands. If you take this option your transportation and accommodation problems will be taken care of, your dive skipper will know the area and where best to dive in differing weather conditions and the tides. However, as with many live-aboard dive boats, your diving will be limited to the sites the skipper chooses, dependent on sea conditions, tide and weather. Dive charter vessels usually offer up to two deeper dives every day, followed by a shallow dive, which make them suitable for the dedicated and serious sport diver.

The second option is to book with a local licensed dive boat skipper, who within reason will take you to sites of your choice. This option leaves you secure in the knowledge that the skipper is fully aware of local conditions, is registered, and not only knows the local waters but can also arrange for your cylinders to be collected, refilled and delivered back to the boat each day.

The third option is to take your own boat and trailer, which will give you total freedom to dive where and when you please. There are considerable dangers in taking this option because of potentially dangerous weather and tidal conditions, and your possible lack of knowledge of safe channels and the location of wreck sites and natural hazards. If you are visiting this area for the first time seek advice from the harbourmaster and local boatmen and note information about local weather conditions and decompression accidents. Times of local high water are posted daily on a board outside the harbourmaster's office on the quay at St Mary's. Divers with inflatables may be allowed to leave them on visitors' moorings, but it is essential that you book in advance. It is not advisable to leave any diving equipment in boats overnight and be warned that fuel is much more expensive on the islands than on the mainland.

Opposite: The harbour at St Ives.

Safety precautions

When operating off the Scillies and North Cornwall it is essential that your boat is well equipped, with VHF radio, GPS or DGPS, flares or other visual distress signals, paddles, an anchor with at least 3m of chain attached to a minimum 27m of rope, a reliable main engine, a "get-you-home" backup motor, spare fuel and a suitable tool kit with spare starter cable, plugs, and so on.

Make sure that someone ashore knows of your destination, who is on your boat, and your estimated time of departure and return. The majority of Coastguard lookouts and watch houses are now closed so also advise the MRCC at Falmouth by radio of your plans, then let them know of your arrival on site, departure and eventual safe return. A radio check before you go offshore is a sensible precaution anyway, since it not only confirms the working of your radio, but tells you whether or not you are in a "dead-spot" due to screening.

Weather

In the Scillies, the prevailing wind is from the south-west, and you cannot usually dive there between November and early March. Local boat owners do not put pleasure craft in the water until after 1 April. Usually the weather is unsettled until early May, with strong winds, but from then on diving conditions improve until early October.

The north Cornish coast is very exposed so when dive planning always take note of the wind direction and strength from a forecast. With the prevailing wind south-west, anything over Force 3 will restrict diving from Land's End to Trevose Head near Padstow, but Padstow Bay and the Stepper Point area will remain reasonably sheltered, as will the coast from there north to Tintagel. Should the wind be Force 4 or stronger from the west round to north-east it is unlikely you will be able to dive the north coast at all; if this is the case, consider seeking somewhere sheltered on the south coast. Fine weather usually brings easterly winds, which can create ideal diving conditions for the entire length of the north coast. More precise details have been included in individual areas.

Underwater visibility

There is little pollution around the Scillies, so underwater visibility is often excellent. Although storms sometimes stir up the sea bed, and spring or summer plankton bloom can make the sea appear thick or green, in even reasonably calm conditions visibility will be in excess of 12m around the perimeter rocks and islands, where the bottom can plunge away to considerable depths. The shallow waters between the islands have a sand bottom, which can also be stirred up by a heavy swell, but this will quickly return to almost crystal clear semi-tropical conditions.

The north coast of Cornwall can also enjoy excellent underwater visibility, often in excess of 20–25m, especially during a calm spell. Adverse wind and surface conditions generally return to normal quickly, and visibility will rapidly improve.

WEATHER INFORMATION

Weather forecasts for the Isles of Scilly and Cornwall are available as follows:

Radio

BBC Radio 4 long wave – shipping forecast daily at 0033, 0555, 1355 and 1750.

BBC Radio Cornwall (95.2 and 103.9 MHZ – Cornwall) (96.00 MHZ – Isles of Scilly) – general weather forecast after each news bulletin on the hour and also at 0610, 0645, 0845, 1030, 1230; shipping forecast 0645; tides at 0745; five-day forecast 0715 (www.bbc.co.uk/cornwall).

Met fax forecasts

General 24-hour shipping forecast: fax 09060 100441 (updated at 0030, 0600, 1400 and 1800 daily).

Two-day fax South-West region inshore forecast: tel. 09060 100458 (updated at 0700 and 1900 daily)

Two- to five-day fax Channel waters forecast: tel. 09060 100473 (updated at 0500 daily).

Five-day fax South-West region coastal forecast: tel. 09060 100412.

Four-day planners and charts: fax 09060 100470 (sea areas Finisterre and Sole), which includes the Isles of Scilly, or 09060 100473 (sea areas Fastnet and Lundy), which covers the north coast of Cornwall.

MetFAX helpline (tel. 08700 750075; fax 0870 750076; e-mail metfax@meto.gov.uk).

MetFAX marine two- to five-day forecast chart: fax 09060 100426.

A two-day MetFAX forecast is displayed on the Isles of Scilly harbour noticeboard along with tidal information, and it is recommended that you read this every day, since local conditions change very rapidly.

Telephone

To talk direct to a Met. Office forecaster: tel. 08700 767888.

Marinecall Select five-day forecasts by phone: tel. 09068 110010.

Marinecall South-West region (covers Lyme Regis to Hartland Point) two-day inshore forecasts: tel. 09068 500458.

English Channel two- to five-day forecasts: tel. 09068 500992 (updated daily at 8am).

National inshore forecasts: tel. 09068 500450.

Three- to five-day national forecast: tel. 0898 500450.

Local weather forecast: tel. 0898 500404.

Mobile phone SMS service – Vodafone only: 08700 767838; choose a one-off or regular update; order the product (Looe to Padstow, no. 4582) or (Padstow to Hartland Point, including the Isles of Scilly, no. 4583); end the call but leave your phone switched on in order to receive weather messages and regular updates. These are updated at 0001, 0500, 1100 and 1700. Charges are at the standard mobile rate. For coastal reports for Falmouth and Isles of Scilly, updated from 0300 at three-hour intervals: 08700 767838 4311.

Above: Crayfish, once prolific around the Isles of Scilly but now sadly in decline, are still to be found in deep water on the fringe reefs and rocks. Below: Many areas off North Cornwall have never been visited by divers, hence hand-feeding fish or catching them by hand is possible. This diver holds a wrasse briefly for the camera.

Charts

The new Small Craft Folio Chart SC 5603 Falmouth to Padstow (July 2000) includes the Isles of Scilly and much of the coastline of North Cornwall. Chart 5603-1 covers Penzance to the Isles of Scilly; 5603 covers Penzance to St Ives; Chart 5603-4 covers Pendeen to Penhale Point; Chart 5603-5 covers Newquay to Port Gaverne, with large scale inserts Newquay Bay, Padstow Bay and Port Isaac Bay, on which the Padstow and Camel Estuary insert is most useful; Chart 5603-8 covers the southern part of the Isles of Scilly, including the Western Rocks; Chart 5603-9 covers the northern part; Chart 5603-10 covers St Agnes, Gugh, St Mary's Sound and part of St Mary's island; Chart 5603-11 covers St Mary's Pool Tresco, Tresco Channel, St Helen's and Tean and Chart 5603-12 covers part of St Mary's, Crow Sound, St Martin's and the Eastern Islands. The set comes in a useful transparent PVC cover, suitable for boat use.

Large-scale Admiralty Charts for this area include Chart 34 (Isles of Scilly complete), 883 (the main inhabited islands in the group), 1148 (Land's End, Wolf Rock, St Mary's and St Martin's) and 2565 (Falmouth to Scilly, including Land's End and Wolf Rock).

Admiralty Charts may be purchased from various agents, including The Sea Chest Nautical Bookshop, Queen Anne's Battery Marina, Plymouth (tel. 01752 222012); Marine Instruments, Bosun's Locker, Upton Slip, Falmouth (tel. 01326 312414); Chart Distributors at Fowey (tel. 01726 833233) and Penryn (tel. 01326 74177) and Gibon-Kyne Gift Shop, Garrison Lane, St Mary's (tel. 01720 423081) who stock tide tables and the relevant Isles of Scilly charts, as well as books.

Fishing regulations

Cornwall and the Isles of Scilly have regulations similar to those for other parts of the country, with the exception of the minimum size for crabs and lobsters. There are also minimum sizes specified for crayfish, which at one time were plentiful around the islands, in particular, but now are seldom seen. The details are shown in the tables below and on page 24.

Crabs (across the broadest part of the back)	
Males	160mm
Females (berried females should never be taken)	140mm
Spider crabs (across the broadest part of the back)	120mm
Lobsters (rear of eye socket to end of body shell)	90mm
Velvet crabs	65mm
Crayfish (across the carapace)	110mm
Scallops (maximum width of shell)	100mm

Minimum sizes for shellfish.

Bass	37.5cm
Black bream	23cm
Blue ling	70cm
Brill	30cm
Cod	35cm
Conger eel	58cm
Dab	15cm
Flounder	25cm
Haddock	30cm
Hake	30cm
Herring	20cm
Lemon sole	25cm
Mackerel	20cm
Megrim	25cm
Mullet, grey	30cm
Mullet, red	15cm
Plaice	25cm
Pollack	30cm
Saithe	35cm
Sea bream, red	25cm
Shad	30cm
Skates and rays (from wing tip to wing tip)	35cm
Sole	24cm
Turbot	30cm
Whiting	27cm
Witch	28cm

Minimum sizes for fish.

Contact the Cornwall Sea Fisheries Officer (tel. 01736 369817) for further information, or County Hall (tel. 01872 322000).

The Isles of Scilly Marine Park

The Isles of Scilly constitute the largest of the UK's national Marine Parks. The protected area extends shoreward to include all the land continuously or intermittently covered by the sea at the highest tide. The marine plants and animals, and their habitats within the park, are of outstanding importance. Some species are unique and many are rare in British waters. Please do not collect or take marine specimens unless they are for genuine scientific study, and then only in the smallest quantity acceptable for your requirements.

The use of powered spearguns is totally prohibited anywhere within the Marine Park, but the traditional use of hand spears is permitted. Divers should try to cause the least possible disturbance when underwater, particularly when diving in the

*With the sea warmed by the Gulf Stream, marine life around Scilly can be an
underwater photographer's dream.
Above: Plumose anemones. Below: A carpet of colour on the sea bed.*

special areas on the east coast of St Mary's and off the south-east coast of St Agnes and Gugh. Many delicate species of sea fans, corals and sponges found here are very slow growing, and many tens of years of growth can be destroyed by the thoughtless actions of divers.

For further information contact the Isles of Scilly Wildlife Trust, Carn Thomas, St Mary's (tel./fax 01720 422153).

Restricted-access islands Breeding and nesting birds are especially susceptible to disturbance, and there are periods when restrictions are imposed on landing on certain uninhabited islands within the Marine Park. Annet, the Western Rocks, the Norrard Rocks, Stoney Island, Green Island and Menavaur (off St Helen's) are closed from 15 April to 20 August, except by written permit for scientific work. Furthermore, during the period 15 April to 20 July, the islands' boatmen operate a voluntary restriction on the landing of day trippers on the small island of Tean.

Activities not permitted on the islands land include camping, the use of metal detectors, shooting, barbecues or lighting of fires. Divers and diving boat operators are requested to keep away from rock ledges and reefs on which seals are basking, particularly the Norrard Rocks.

Shipwrecks

Isles of Scilly The Isles of Scilly represent something of a signpost to the English, Bristol and St George's channels, and once presented a fearsome barrier lying astride a 10-mile wide shipping approach. Almost 1,000 shipwrecks have been recorded in this area and undoubtedly many more occurred at night or in storms and so were unseen. The islands have claimed almost every type of sailing merchantman, East Indiamen, historic men-of-war, steamships, packet vessels and motor ships. The last wreck to date was the 3,083-ton container-feeder vessel *Cita* in March 1997 (Site **15**).

Many of these wrecks are of historic significance, particularly four warships of the Royal Navy lost on the same night in 1707, along with the famous Admiral Sir Clowdisley Shovell (Site 13). The wreck site of the flagship *Association* (Site 35) was found in 1967 by divers of the Royal Navy, which sparked off interest by other diving groups to search for long-lost treasure ships, resulting in the location of the Dutch East Indiaman *Hollandia* (Site 31), *Prinses Maria* (Site 36), the man-of-war *Colossus* (Site 68), and other important finds.

The most notorious area of the Scillies for wrecks is the Western Rocks, which are a remarkable collection of fearsome islands, reefs and submerged rocks. They hold the remnants of probably two-thirds of the 1,000 or so ships lost in the islands, including the German transatlantic liner *Schiller* (1875) (Site 40), the *Thomas W. Lawson* (1907) (Site 32), plus numerous steam and full-rigged ships, and six Dutch and English East Indiamen. The first lighthouse in Cornwall was built on St Agnes in 1679; it was only the second in the British Isles, the Western Rocks being already long synonymous with shipwreck and disaster.

Equally interesting and varied wrecks can be found all round the islands, including the *Cita* (Site 15), which drove ashore in March 1997 and whose accommodation and stern section lie off Newfoundland Point, Porth Hellick Bay. The Scillies are also an excellent base from which to explore the wrecks on the infamous Seven Stones Reef, two groups of rocks a mile in length, which rise up out of deep water and have claimed 71 known wrecks, including the tanker *Torrey Canyon* (Site 88) in 1967. Visiting divers should be aware that three wreck sites in the Isles of Scilly have been claimed by local "Salvors in Possession". These are the sites of the *Association* (Site 35), *Colossus* (Site 68) and *Schiller* (Site 40).

North Cornwall The north coast of Cornwall has some 2,300 wrecks. Exposed to such a long, inhospitable coastline, larger sailing ships and steamers were unable to find shelter in bad weather, and having either lost their sails or suffered mechanical failure, they would almost certainly be blown ashore and wrecked.

The armada of deep-sea home and foreign shipping that once navigated the Bristol Channel included a vast coastal trade in Welsh coal and Cornish copper. Many of the vessels carrying it were built and registered in the small ports of North Cornwall; when there was bad weather they were better equipped than larger boats to find shelter somewhere along this coast. The first lighthouse in the area was built on the Longships, off Land's End, in 1795, and the second on Lundy Island in 1820; at this time there were no lighthouses between Land's End and Hartland, a coastline of 96 miles. No wonder so many vessels were wrecked there.

Shipwrecks include dozens of iron and steel steamers and motor vessels lost under the cliffs, while offshore 20th-century wrecks lie in depths ranging from 17 to 60m, including a Royal Navy destroyer, HMS *Warwick* (Site 282); two Royal Navy submarines, the *L-1* (Site 121); and the *E-43*; the liner *Armenian* (Site 243) and many other interesting vessels. Other interesting vessels include four intact German U-boats, two from the First World War and two from the Second World War. They lie in 55 to 60m. One of them appears to have been rammed just aft of the conning tower and a small collier – possibly the vessel responsible – lies only 65ft away. Another U-boat, perhaps the *U-61*, has been found in 55m, her hatches open, her deck gun still mounted forward of the conning tower.

Decompression accidents

The procedure to be followed if there is a decompression accident is laid down in the booklet *Safe Diving Practices* compiled by the National Diving Committee of the BSAC:

Decompression sickness symptoms vary between those so sudden that immediate air evacuation to a chamber is vital, to those which may not become apparent for some hours. Some of these less dramatic symptoms, which may well be delayed, can be more serious and produce greater disability than the excruciating pain associated with a joint bend. Tingling and numbness are included in this category.

At sea Air embolism or severe decompression sickness symptoms, occurring at sea, require rapid transfer of the subject to a compression chamber, laid flat on their back and, if possible, with the administration of 100% oxygen. Being bounced, rapidly, in a small boat is almost certainly going to worsen the symptoms rather than help the situation. RAF or RN Search and Rescue helicopters will almost certainly be involved and the availability and use of VHF radio is essential.

HM Coastguard, although co-ordinating all rescues at sea, are not medically qualified to diagnose diving-related medical disorders and have to seek advice before activating a "Medivac" air evacuation. The Department of Transport and British Telecom International operate a Radio Medical Advisory Service through the BTI Coast Radio Stations.

If your radio has a "Duplex" operating system, with Coast Radio Station working frequencies, it is advisable to contact the nearest Coast Radio Station where you will be put in direct contact with a doctor, via a telephone link. There is no charge for this service. Once the doctor has given his advice, the Coastguard is in a position to follow up without delay.

If your radio does not have Coast Radio Station frequencies, or has a "Simplex" operating system, it is advisable to contact the Coastguard on Channel 16.

This may take longer, as the Coastguard will have to contact the doctor on your behalf. If the situation is serious enough a "Pan-Pan" call would be necessary.

On land If decompression sickness symptoms arise on land and they are serious, you are advised to dial 999 and ask for an ambulance, explaining the symptoms on the phone. If a helicopter is needed, the doctor will contact the Coastguard (if you are on the coast) who will co-ordinate the rescue. Inland, rapid transport with police escort, can be arranged by the medical emergency services.

With less dramatic symptoms, contact with a GP or hospital casualty department is advisable. Ensure you carry the Portsmouth Royal Haslar Hospital phone number (tel. 07831 151523) and ask for the Duty Compression Chamber Doctor, to enable the doctor concerned to get specialist medical advice. Transfer to the nearest available compression chamber, where necessary, will be arranged.

The procedure for cases in the Isles of Scilly is the same as if a casualty occurs on the mainland, the only difference being the distance to Plymouth's Diving Diseases Research Centre (DDRC) (tel. 01752 209999 8.30am to 5pm; 01752 261910 after hours). In certain weather conditions Cornwall's Flying Ambulance Service would not be allowed to fly the 22 miles over the sea to the Scillies, a task normally undertaken by either Navy or RAF search and rescue Sea King or Merlin helicopters, which have "all-weather" capabilities. Note the following emergency numbers: Health Centre St Mary's (tel. 01720 422628; fax 01720 423160) and St Mary's Hospital (tel. 01720 422392).

Other emergencies

The following information will be of assistance if you have to deal with any type of diving emergency in the Isles of Scilly or mainland Cornwall, if you wish to advise the authorities of your activity or boat movements, or if you simply want a current weather forecast.

HM Coastguard The Falmouth Marine Rescue Co-ordination Centre (MRCC) (tel. 01326 317575) is at Pendennis Point, Falmouth, and staffed 24 hours. It broadcasts

The Underwater Safaris diving school at Old Town, St Mary's is run by Mark Groves. The school is located on the waterfront behind Mark's cottage, which is named 'Nowhere'. The Old Town Gull Rock shows in the background.

weather forecasts on VHF Channel 67 at four-hourly intervals, after an initial announcement on VHF Channel 16, and at two-hourly intervals if wind speeds are likely to reach Force 6 or above. A local weather forecast can be obtained by telephoning the Marine Rescue Co-ordination Centre (tel. 01326 317575; fax 01326 318342) before going to sea.

Brixham Marine Rescue Service (tel. 01803 882704) carries out the same function as the Falmouth Marine Rescue Co-ordination Centre, and will respond to radio distress calls from Dodman Point to the east.

Very few Coastguard lookouts around the coast are staffed, except sometimes in bad weather, so no reliance should be placed on anyone maintaining a visual watch of a particular area or activity. However, all the inhabited Scilly Islands have an auxiliary Coastguard Rescue Team:

Isles of Scilly Coastguard Section Manager (tel. 01720 423322)

St Mary's Coastguard (tel. 01720 422651)

St Agnes Coastguard (tel. 01720 422139)

Bryher Coastguard (tel. 01720 422862)

Tresco Coastguard (tel. 01720 423056)

St Martin's Coastguard (tel. 01720 422246)

The Falmouth MRCC advises that diving boats should contact the Coastguard on Channel 16 on departure from shore, with details of the size of the party, the type of craft and the area in which diving will take place. They welcome such advance information since, in the event of an emergency, boats known to be in the area

The rugged shoreline at Polzeath, looking north towards Daymer Bay.

could be contacted and asked to assist. Diving boats calling the Coastguard on departure must advise them on leaving the diving area or on return to shore, otherwise they may be posted as overdue or missing, and an unnecessary air and sea search instigated.

Other useful telephone numbers:
BSAC Technical Support Dept: (tel. 0151 350 6262; e-mail technical@bsac.com)
Divers Alert Network (DAN): (tel. 01224 585747 in emergency or 0797 0821222, non-emergency).

Emergency services

The Police, Fire Brigade, Ambulance Service and Coastguard (including lifeboats) can be contacted through any public or private telephone free of charge by dialling 999 or 112. You will be asked which service you require, and be put in direct contact with them.

The local marine rescue centres can be contacted on VHF Channel 16, or by telephone as follows: Falmouth Marine Rescue Co-ordination Centre – tel. 01326 317575. Brixham Marine Rescue Services Centre – tel. 01803 882704.

It is also most important that an early radio call is made to the Coastguard Marine Rescue Co-ordination Centre if there is any concern for the safety of divers who have not surfaced within a reasonable time, or may have gone missing on the surface. It takes time for the rescue services to be alerted and assembled, and the Coastguard would prefer to have rescue services on standby and then stood down, than a last-minute call when a situation has deteriorated to the point of being serious. If a diver goes missing call the Coastguard immediately with the details – do not wait.

When diving in the Isles of Scilly, which have no compression facilities, the above advice is particularly relevant, since any Search and Rescue helicopter attending from RNAS Culdrose is unlikely to be on site for at least 45–60 minutes, and the nearest chamber is at Plymouth.

Radio information Always call for assistance on VHF Channel 16 as the Coastguard Marine Rescue Co-ordination Centres maintain constant watch on this channel. If it is a distress or urgency call, it will have absolute priority. If in a distress situation, when life is in grave or imminent danger, use the distress call MAYDAY MAYDAY MAYDAY followed by your name or the call sign of your craft, your present position and the nature of the problem.

If the situation is urgent, but no imminent danger to life exists – for example you have broken down, are drifting or have run out of fuel – call PANPAN PANPAN PANPAN followed by your name or the call sign of your craft, your present position and the nature of the problem. Continue to broadcast the message until an answer is received.

A new system to replace existing worldwide distress and safety communications, known as the Global Maritime Distress and Safety System, has been developed by the International Maritime Organisation. A free booklet, *Safety on the Sea – GMDSS Guidelines for Small Boat users in European Waters*, gives details of the system and is available from the Marine Safety Agency, Coastguard, Royal Yachting Association, Royal Life Saving Society, Royal National Lifeboat Institution or British Marine Industries Federation.

Emergency medical advice and assistance Coastguard rescue centres hold details of the emergency hyperbaric (compression) chambers in the area, and have access to 24-hour emergency transport and specialist emergency diving medical advice. If there is an emergency at sea off the Scillies contact the Marine Rescue Co-ordination Centre on VHF Channel 16; if on shore contact the St Mary's Health Centre, Buzza Road (tel. 01720 422628) or the hospital (tel. 01720 422392) or telephone 999 or 112 for the emergency services and ask for the Coastguard.

The Rachabite slipway at Hugh Town, St Mary's has free vehicle and trailer parking nearby, with no launching fees. There are also public toilets.

Cornwall has its own air ambulance service, but its helicopter is not equipped with winching facilities, and therefore has to land to pick up casualties.

Do not attempt yourself to organise the admission of a diver thought to be suffering from a bend or other compression problems to a compression chamber. The chamber may not be able to accept the patient, the necessary medical backup team may not be available, or an alternative chamber may be nearer, in which case valuable time could be saved. In the South West generally, all compression treatment will normally take place at the Diving Diseases Research Unit (tel. 01752 209999) at Derriford Hospital, Plymouth. You can call the Royal Hospital Haslar, Gosport (tel. 07831 151523) for advice from an expert in hyperbaric medicine, but admission to a hyperbaric chamber for treatment can only be authorised through the normal emergency channels.

The Military Remains Act

The Military Remains Act 1986 may in the future affect the wreck diver much more than at present. Its main purpose is to preserve the sanctity of "war graves" – the wreckage of military ships and aircraft thought to contain the remains of service personnel.

The wreckage of all military aircraft of any nation is automatically protected, but ships will have to be designated by the Secretary of State and will need a statutory instrument to do so. This means that ships to be identified as "war graves" will have to be named and approved by Parliament in the same way that ships to be protected as historic wrecks need a statutory instrument passed through Parliament.

There seems no doubt that those who passed the Act had little idea of the number of ships that could fall under its terms, such as a merchant ship with a Navy gunner aboard – was he among the survivors? – and as a result very few ships have been named under the Act. This does not mean that other wrecks are not covered by the general thrust of the Act and divers should therefore treat all possible "war graves" with total respect.

However, once a particular ship has been named, a diver commits an offence only by tampering with, damaging, moving, removing or unearthing remains, or by entering an enclosed interior space in the wreckage. The punishment on conviction of an offence is a fine. Nothing in the Act prevents the wreck diver from visiting the site, examining the exterior or even settling on the wreckage. An offence is only committed if the diver disturbs remains or enters a proper compartment of the wreck.

This is of course only a brief description, and serious wreck divers should study the Act itself. Your library or the Stationery Office Bookshop should be able to obtain a copy.

There are two Royal Navy vessels to which this Act applies on the north coast of Cornwall: the *ML-247*, wrecked in 1918, and the destroyer *Warwick* (Site 282), sunk in 1944. This destroyer lies in two parts, with her stern some distance west of the main forward section; both halves come under the Act.

The Merchant Shipping Acts

The Receiver of Wreck is responsible for the administration of the Merchant Shipping Acts of 1984 and 1906, which deal with wreck and salvage. It is a legal requirement that all recovered wreck (flotsam, jetsam, derelict or lagan – whether recovered within or outside United Kingdom territorial waters) is reported to the Receiver of Wreck.

Finders who conceal items are liable to prosecution, so any object – even if it appears to have no monetary value – should be declared as soon as possible. The Receiver of Wreck can then make a decision as to the future ownership of the property.

Wreck recovered from within United Kingdom territorial waters that remains unclaimed at the end of a statutory one-year period becomes the property of the Crown, and the Receiver of Wreck is then required to dispose of it. This may be through sale at auction, although in many instances the finder will be allowed to keep unclaimed items of wreck in lieu of salvage award. This, however, is at the discretion of the Receiver of Wreck, and each case is judged on its merits.

For further information contact: The Receiver of Wreck, The Coastguard Agency, Spring Place, 105 Commercial Road, Southampton SO15 1EG (tel. 01703 329474; fax 01703 329477).

The Protection of Wrecks Act

Divers who find a site that might be of historical, archaeological or artistic importance should leave everything as it is and report their findings, in confidence and as soon as possible, to English Heritage (or its equivalent in Northern Ireland, Scotland or Wales). If appropriate, the wreck can then be designated under the Protection of Wrecks Act 1973, in order to control activities on the site.

Designated sites may only be dived or items recovered if a licence for that purpose has been granted; failure to comply with this is an offence and can result in a fine. All recoveries from designated sites must be reported to the Receiver of Wreck, The Coastguard Agency, Spring Place, 105 Commercial Road, Southampton, Hampshire SO15 1EG (tel. 023 8032 9474; fax 023 8032 9477). Copies of the "Report of Wreck and Salvage" form (TCA/ROW-1) are obtainable from this address, the Curator of the Isles of Scilly Museum, Customs and Excise offices or Coastguard stations. For further information contact: The Secretariat of the Advisory Committee on Historic Wreck Sites, James Stevens, English Heritage, 23 Savile Row, London W1S 2ET (tel. 020 7973 3000; www.adu.org.uk).

If you want advice about who owns what, have an artefact you want identified, are looking for advice on treatment and conservation, or just general guidance, contact the Curator of the Royal Cornwall Museum, River Street, Truro (tel. 01872 272205), the Charlestown Shipwreck and Heritage Centre, near St Austell (tel. 01726 69897), the curator of the Isles of Scilly Museum (tel. 01720 422337), Richard Larn, Isles of Scilly (tel. 01720 423679) or David McBride (tel. 01720 423162).

In the Isles of Scilly there are three sites designated under the Act: the 3rd rate man-of-war *Eagle* (Site 42); an unidentified wreck of *c.*1545 on Bartholomew Ledge, the oldest wreck site found among the islands to date; and the 3rd rate man-of-war *Colossus* (Site 68). There are no protected wrecks off the north coast of Cornwall and only one World War Two Royal Navy wreck that falls within the Military Remains Act.

AREA 1:

St Mary's

St Mary's is 2¾ miles from east to west and 2½ miles from north to south. The highest point of land is at the northern end on Telegraph Hill (57m); otherwise the island is very low lying with no cliffs above 30m. There are two towns: Hugh Town, centred around the harbour and Porth Cressa, and Old Town, centred around Old Town Bay. Most of the island's facilities are in Hugh Town, where you will find the harbourmaster and services. During the summer the sea is clear but cold, and generally safe swimming conditions exist at all the beaches, except at Bar Point and Pelistry, where extreme caution must be exercised owing to strong tides. Nowhere in the Isles of Scilly will you find beach warning flags or lifeguards.

No diving is allowed within the confines of the quay and harbour, except by prior permission of the harbourmaster. It is also necessary to liaise with the harbourmaster should you wish to lay alongside one of the quays. The new quay is used extensively by passenger boats, and the RMS *Scillonian III* ferry and MV *Gry Maritha* have priority for berthing. Visiting craft should contact the harbourmaster on VHF Channel 16 during working hours to obtain permission to tie up alongside. Thoughtless blocking of landing steps and access ladders could lead to you being banned from the harbour. Fresh water and fuel is available on the quay, as are public toilets, a waiting room and public telephone. Showers and washing facilities are available next to the Harbourside Hotel.

As there are limited facilities on the islands, take care to avoid incidents that might require the assistance of emergency services. You are advised to liaise with the harbourmaster (tel. 01720 422768), to check times of high and low water and any known hazards or restrictions, and to inform him of your intended diving programme, the number of divers in your party and their names. Tell him by VHF radio when you depart and, later, when you return. It is a sensible precaution also to inform a third party ashore of where you will be diving, and your expected return time, as the harbourmaster's office may be closed after 5.30pm. There is no 24-hour visual or radio distress coastguard watch on the islands, and any emergency radio calls must be addressed to the Falmouth Marine Rescue Co-ordination Centre, some 60 miles away.

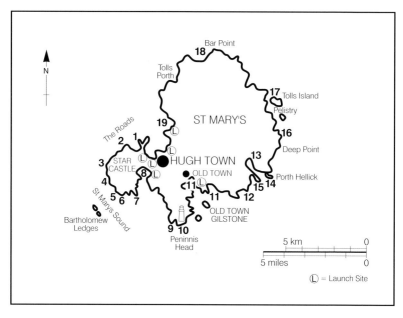

Dive sites in Area 1 (St Mary's).

Coastal dive sites

The majority of dive sites around St Mary's can be safely reached only by boat. Trailed boats can be launched free of charge from the Atlantic Hotel slipway in the centre of Hugh Town; the Rechabite slipway on The Strand, Town Beach, opposite the Man of War shop; at the northern end of Porth Cressa Beach, at the back of the old lifeboat house (with difficulty); at Porth Mellon, opposite the industrial estate; at Old Town Bay slipway and Porthloo. The Rechabite slip is the most practical, with unlimited free parking for a vehicle and trailer on the adjacent roads and public toilets at the head of the slipway. A four-wheel drive vehicle is essential for launching and recovery, as at any state of the tide other than high water you will have to cross flat, soft sand.

Many inter-island boats pass the Garrison Shore daily, often keeping close to the land in order to avoid the tide. Diving boats are advised to stay close to the rocks out of the shipping channel in St Mary's Sound and Roads, always to show a diving flag when divers are down and to use SMBs.

The following dive sites are all close inshore, many of them suitable for snorkelling or beginners; they are listed anti-clockwise around St Mary's from the main quay.

1 Rat Island and the Newman   Rat Island was detached until the new quay was built. The south-west side faces into a large sheltered bay, with many rock outcrops and sandy patches; this makes it an ideal 10m dive site for beginners. The shore continues to a rocky outcrop known as the Newman, where the water can be 15m deep and there is dense weed and much fish life. To the west of the Newman lies Woodcock Ledge, an outcrop rising from 19m. You will begin to feel the tide this far offshore, particularly on the ebb, when it can reach 2 to 3 knots.

2 Barrel of Butter and the Indipendenza   The Barrel of Butter rock outcrop is a short distance offshore, and dries to 16m. The 795-ton wooden barque *Indipendenza* of Genoa drove ashore here on 24 September, 1881, after leaving Bristol four days earlier for Rotterdam with a cargo of 1,200 tons of hides, animal horns and guano, and a crew of 14. Dense fog prevented the captain from taking any observations after leaving Lundy, and the crew navigated by dead reckoning until about 3am, when the pilot thought they were some 15 miles south-west of Scilly. The vessel struck heavily four times as she grounded on the Crim Rocks; she came off leaking badly, and the crew abandoned ship. Finding that the barque did not immediately sink they returned on board and set a course of east-north-east, but then either the crew became frightened or the vessel unmanageable and the *Indipendenza* was abandoned for a second time. Allowed to drift free through Broad Sound into St Mary's Road, she went ashore on the Barrel of Butter.

A mast and a large quantity of materials were saved, but her cargo was difficult to work, and only about 15 tons were recovered. This area is seldom dived and probably worth further exploration.

3 Steval Point and Rock   Steval Point is the most westerly part of St Mary's and is close to where the Garrison Shore Battery defences start. There are reports of two small iron cannon lying among the rocks in shallow water, which may have originated from the garrison or from a shipwreck. Steval Rock has the same rocky structure as the whole of this coastline and water depths are about 19m. There have been a number of wrecks here, the last being the temporary stranding of the Lowestoft steam trawler *Lord Haldane* on 20 March, 1929.

The Steval is best known for the wreck of the richly laden *Triumph*, which went ashore during the storm on 9 October, 1736. On passage from Jamaica to London with a cargo of rum, sugar and dye wood, the *Triumph* also carried £10,000 in gold coins. Many of the crew were drowned after jumping into the sea and attempting to swim ashore, while those who remained on board were saved. Some bags of gold were brought ashore and lives were lost in attempting to save the remainder, which was scattered among the rocks. No coins appear to have been found.

4 Conger Ledge and HM Tug Blazer   49.54.33N; 06.19.40W. From Steval Point, the Garrison shore heads south-east to Woolpack Point over some 600yds. The remains of the requisitioned Admiralty tug *Blazer* are close to Conger Ledge, which is about 200yds from Steval Rock. Built at Ayr, Scotland, the *Blazer* was employed as an examination vessel for neutral shipping in 1914. She was returning from the mainland when she got inside the Woolpack Rock, struck the shore and began to fill. As she foundered, half the crew got into the ship's boat; the remainder were left clinging to her mast and were later rescued. The wreck was relocated in 1966, when a number of live shells were found, as well as a great deal of brass and copper from the engine room. The wreck is very broken and has been heavily

The Serica was wrecked on 24 November, 1893 near the Woolpack, Garrison Shore, St Mary's (Site 6).

salvaged over the years, but makes an interesting shallow dive in 8m, the stern of the wreck standing 3m tall.

5   Serica Rock   Serica Rock lies some 200yds south-west of the shore, marking the edge of the shipping channel leading into St Mary's Sound. This is an interesting rock dive, with lots of fish life and strong tides, in 21m maximum.

6   Woolpack Point and the Serica   49.54 23N; 06 19 20W. The Woolpack is a large rock 150yds offshore from Woolpack Point, marked with an iron beacon. Because of the strong tidal flow over the rock, a wide variety of fish can be seen here, including bass and pollack. The whole area is worth searching for evidence of early shipwrecks, of which there are believed to be several.

   The bottom part of the steel screw steamship *Serica*, built in 1888 by Black, Hawthorn & Co Ltd of Sunderland, lies here in 10m. The London-registered, 2,652-ton vessel was on passage from Cardiff to Port Said with coal and a crew of 25 under Captain Sydney Smith. She had encountered bad weather in the Bristol Channel, and lost the tarpaulin covers from two holds, causing her main cabin to flood and everything abaft the bridge to be swept away. Incredibly, her captain was washed overboard twice, only to be flung back aboard by the sea both times. The steamship reached Scilly on 19 November, 1893, in a distressed condition. On 24 November, following repairs, the *Serica* left St Mary's at low water to continue her voyage, but struck this previously un-named rock, and sank 160yds north-north-west of the Woolpack beacon. She was immediately abandoned.

This is a very colourful and relaxing dive, provided slack tide is calculated correctly. The wreck lies in only 10m and is easy to locate, with little weed and large sandy patches. Just below and in front of the boiler lie a wooden hatch with covers still in place, and many interesting bits and pieces can be found. A long swim the length of her prop shaft will bring you to a three-bladed propeller standing upright.

7 Morning Point A short distance to the east of the Woolpack lies a reef of rocks stretching from Morning Point to the Wras and Biggal Rocks. Morning Point is where St Mary's sewer outfall enters the sea and, although the effluent has been treated, it is not a particularly pleasant place to dive. There are a number of iron cannon scattered in the shallows here, among which have been found lead and iron ingots from some long forgotten vessel.

One of the wrecks in the area was the French brigantine *Minerve* of St Malo, bound from Swansea to Cadiz with coal. She drove ashore in a south-westerly gale on New Year's Eve 1881; six of her crew were saved by the rocket apparatus, the seventh by a local boat, after which she went to pieces. Offshore from the Biggal, the bottom drops away to 27m to a flat, sandy sea bed.

8 Porth Cressa This sheltered bay reaches out from Porth Cressa Beach, and is an easy shore dive or snorkel. There are extensive rocky foreshores on both sides leading out to sea, with a large outcrop in the centre. The bottom is predominantly fine sand, but around the rocky areas you will find plenty of fish life and urchins.

9 Peninnis Head Peninnis Head is the most spectacular headland on St Mary's, marked by an automatic lighthouse, consisting of an extensive collection of vertical granite masses. The first of these is The Chair, 900yds from the beach at Porth Cressa. Other rock faces and islets are known as The Murrs, Inner Head, Monks Cowl, Pollard and the Outer Head. Of these the Inner Head is the most spectacular dive, where a sheer rock face plunges down almost vertically to a sandy bottom in 22m.

The remains of an unidentified wreck lie scattered in the sand, and over the years divers have uncovered lead sheathing, musket shot, copper fasteners, coins and other evidence of an early sailing vessel. The items recovered suggest an 18th-century wreck, possibly the vessel known to have been lost after hitting Nicholl's Rock. The brig *Criccieth Castle* was also lost here on 9 February, 1883. Carrying a cargo of guano from Fray Bentos to Liverpool, she had called at Falmouth for orders, and struck Peninnis Head in a Force 9 south-south-westerly gale.

Underwater visibility can be spectacular here, and frequently you can look up from the sea bed and see every detail of a boat on the surface.

10 Minnehaha 49.54.10N; 06.18.03W. The 158ft wooden barque *Minnehaha* was built at St Johns, New Brunswick, in 1857 and owned by Messrs Hughes of Menai. The Liverpool-registered vessel left Falmouth for Dublin, on passage from Callao with a cargo of guano. The weather deteriorated badly; soon a hard north-westerly gale was blowing. The vessel struck the south-east corner of Peninnis, near Big Jolly Rock. She thumped the rocks so hard that a large hole was made in her port bow. Within two minutes she was under water and those who had not been swept away took to the rigging. Captain Jones sprang into the sea and was last seen swimming for the shore. The mate led the remaining crew onto the rocks. The pilot was drowned, as was the captain of the *Minnehaha* and several members of the crew. Had they followed the mate's example and remained in the rigging until daybreak and low tide, all would no doubt have been saved.

Despite having been a wooden ship, a great deal of the upper-deck ironwork and chain remains, including one of the anchors and the windlass. This is an easy sheltered dive; wreckage goes off seaward into deep gullies at around 20m, with lots of tantalising but heavily concreted pieces of brass showing.

11 Old Town Bay and the Brodfield   Old Town Bay leads into the original main harbour and settlement on St Mary's. At the mouth of the bay lies one of two sets of rocks in the Isles of Scilly known as the Gilstone, this one drying at 3.3m at low spring tides. The other is the more infamous Gilstone Rock, which sank the *Association* and *Romney* in 1707. The Old Town Gilstone holds the remains of an armed transport vessel; the Rock and its ledges are swept by exceptionally strong tides, particularly on the ebb: take care when diving here.

Moving into the shallows between Gull Rock and Tolman Point, the sea bed becomes very shallow with a mixture of rock outcrops and sand. It is an ideal dive for beginners or snorkelling area, almost unaffected by tide and sheltered, where you will find flat fish, sea urchins and abundant rock life. East of Tolman Point the shoreline enters Porth Minick, where there is much metal debris in the shallows as this area was once an island rubbish dump.

The coastline from Porth Minick to Church Point is a tumble of rocks going off to 10m, covered in dense weed, which conceals the remains of the SS *Brodfield* under Blue Carn (at 49.54.35N; 06.17.38W) and two flattened steel containers from the MV *Cita*, lost just over half a mile away. The 3,567-ton *Brodfield*, registered at London and on passage from Le Havre to Barry in ballast, lost her way in fog and drove ashore on 13 November, 1916, without loss of life. Her remains can be found

Wrecked in fog on 11 May, 1917 while carrying a cargo of coal, the same night that the Italia was lost on St Agnes, the Lady Charlotte (Site 14) lies submerged off Porth Hellick. The more recent Cita wreck lies close to the reef on the right of this photograph.

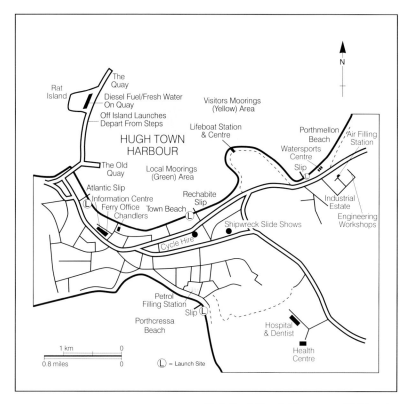

Detail of Hugh Town on St Mary's.

close inshore in as little as 3m, and many small non-ferrous pieces can be found among steel frames.

12   Giant's Castle   This is an Iron Age cliff castle and is a worthwhile area to dive, with large rock formations dropping off sharply to 45m, with no particular attractions other than marine life. The inlet leading to Porth Loggos, where the bottom shelves up rapidly from 30m to 3m and has the remnants of a wreck of 1771. There is some evidence suggesting that a larger shipwreck occurred here, as two enormous iron stockless anchors can be found in the sand near Church Porth.

13   Porth Hellick   Porth Hellick is a shallow sand and rock cove best known for its connection with Sir Clowdisley Shovell, the admiral on board the English man-of-war *Association*, lost among the Western Rocks in 1707. His body washed ashore in Porth Hellick the day after the wreck, where he was found still alive by an old woman. She is said to have murdered him for his jewellery, before burying him in a shallow grave above the tide line. We must assume that she mentioned her find

The last wreck on the Isles of Scilly to date, the container-feeder ship Cita (Site 15), lies stranded on the rocks at Porth Hellick after going ashore at full-speed at 3.30am on 26 March, 1997. All the crew were fast asleep and the vessel on automatic pilot with the radar alarm system switched off.

– but not the robbery – to others, since his corpse was exhumed and later conveyed to London where it was buried in Westminster Abbey.

14 Lady Charlotte 49.54.50N; 06.16.42W. Owned by the Redcroft Steam Navigation Co of Newcastle, this 3,593-ton British steamship had been built as the *Aphrodite* in 1905 by the Tyne Iron Steamship Building Company, Newcastle-upon-Tyne. She had been requisitioned as an Admiralty collier and was on passage from Cardiff to Alexandria with coal when she drove ashore in dense fog just outside the Newfoundland Rocks on 11 May, 1917. No lives were lost among the crew of 30, the men getting ashore in Porth Hellick using their own boats.

This dive is easily found, sheltered and memorable, and the best time to dive is one hour before high water or one hour before low water at St Mary's. The flattened wreck lies north-west to south-east with her bow to the north in 10m. The deeper end is the most interesting part, with two boilers showing in the centre of the ship and a spare propeller standing upright off to the starboard side. The stern is in 30m, where there are large winches and a massive steering quadrant and stern rails. Small quantities of her coal cargo still lie scattered between her plates, but the bulk has been salvaged.

15 Cita 49.54.43N; 06.16.40W. This is the most recent shipwreck on the Isles of Scilly. Built in Germany in 1977 as the *John Wulff*, the vessel's name was changed in 1983 to *Lagarfoss*, and again in 1996 to *Cita*. A bulk carrier-container feeder motor-vessel of 3,083 tonnes, she left Southampton on 25 March, 1997, for

42

Left: Children's clothing for Marks & Spencer, washed up on Porth Cressa beach following gales three years after the wreck of the container ship Cita (Site 35), which carried many thousands of such items.

Below: A cargo container salvaged from the Cita on Porth Mellon beach in March 1997, with empty gas cylinders, bales of tobacco and other items from the wreck.

Belfast, carrying 145 containers of general cargo. At 3.30am on 26 March, with only the First Mate on the bridge – sleeping – and her automatic radar alarm switched off, she drove ashore at full speed on Newfoundland Point in fog, assuming an immediate heavy list to starboard of some 30 degrees.

No distress call was made, but at 3.35am the Falmouth Maritime Rescue Co-ordination Centre received a request for assistance, and called out the St Mary's RNLI lifeboat. Seven crew members were taken off by lifeboat; the captain was airlifted off the wreck, which had by now assumed a 70 degree list and was in danger of capsizing.

Containers stacked three high above and below deck fell into the sea as their securing lugs broke. As residents and visitors to the island became aware of the nature of the *Cita*'s general cargo – which included car engines, batteries, cast iron, clothing and French wine – a free-for-all arose, with everyone helping themselves to what they could carry away. The local authorities were overwhelmed by the situation, and could only hand out wreck and salvage report forms and hope people would complete and return them! The *Cita* survived intact for 12 days then broke in two. Her bow section is on the rocks in 12m; her stern section, complete with machinery, accommodation and bridge fell to 30m, where it remains.

At the time of writing the stern of the *Cita* is still reasonably intact, although her stern and bridge area have separated, making for an exciting dive of all three parts of the wreck in a range of depths. The bridge structure rests on a sea bed covered in large boulders resting against a dropoff, in a sort of granite canyon; the bow

The beach and slipway at Old Town, St Mary's, photographed on a bleak winter's day following a gale that left the foreshore covered in seaweed.

stands 9m high in about 26m, facing seaward. The wreck's stern still holds a variable pitch propeller. Choose slack water to dive here as strong tides sweep across Newfoundland Point. The wreck is normally marked with a permanent buoy and a substantial mooring rope, made fast just forward of the bridge, making it easy for a boat to tie up.

16   Deep Point   49.55.15N; 06.16.26W. North-east of Porth Hellick Point there is a half-mile stretch of coast with relatively high cliffs to Deep Point, then another half mile to Tolls Island. The shoreline is broken rock right through to South Pelistry Bay passing Deep Point, where the rock face plunges off at a steep angle to 36m. At one point it is possible to look down a sheer rock face disappearing into the gloom with no bottom in sight. Historically, Deep Point was used for the disposal of unwanted motor vehicles and it is likely that you will find evidence of these on the sea bed.

17   Toll's Island   49.55.43N; 06.16.40W. Centred in Pelistry Bay, this is a large, overgrown rock island, which offers little more than interesting snorkelling, but has a long, white sand beach, which is popular with families. Observe the notices advising of the dangers of swimming at certain states of the tide: this is a very dangerous area and has tidal currents of up to 3 knots. Pelistry Bay is accessible from the shore via Pelistry Lane, and can be considered a shore dive, provided you have transport. The only known wreck here was the French lugger *Frère et Soeur*, driven ashore during the Great Blizzard of March 1891.

There are no further practical shore dive points until you reach Pendrathen, 1¼ miles further round the coast.

18   Pendrathen and Bar Point   49.56.12N; 06.17.58W. This site is reached by taking Telegraph Road to the highest point of the island, turning right past the Napoleonic Coastguard and Signal Station into Pungies Lane, then left into McFarland Down. It is recommended only for beginners as the area is very shallow; the broken foreshore extends some distance out to sea, and care should be taken with the tide off Bar Point. You may find evidence of the shipwreck of the brig *Rosherville* of London near Bar Point. On 3 March, 1855, she was bound for Jamaica with a cargo of rice, beer, wine and brandy, when she caught fire, burnt through her hawser and went ashore. From here the coast runs south-west, beneath the golf course, where you will find interesting iron remnants of shipwreck, from any one of a number of vessels. One was the French brig *La Maria Clara*, carrying timber, which was driven ashore on Carn Morval on 30 December, 1780; another the *Letitia Tennant* of Stromness, which broke her anchor chain in a hurricane and went ashore on Creeb Rock on 14 April, 1829.

19   Porthloo   49.55.18N; 06.18.40W. This is a large sandy bay bounded by Taylor's Island and Newford Island. It is permissible to leave a vehicle and trailer here free of charge, but launching an inflatable through the gap in the dunes is hard work as the sand is very soft. Accessibility and lack of strong currents make Porthloo an attractive beach for families, as it is devoid of boat traffic and you can combine swimming with snorkelling and shallow diving, but only at high water.

Several vessels have become total wrecks here. The French barque *Ticina* parted her anchor cable and drove ashore to become a total loss on 30 December, 1869, as had the barque *Express* 15 days earlier. An unusual class of ship lost here was the double-ended wooden steamship *Gem*, of Liverpool. Although only 118 tons, on 31 October, 1881, she was making the long passage from Holyhead to the Brass River in Africa, carrying 37 tons of coal as ballast. A serious leak was discovered, causing her to shelter, but later she continued, using paddle wheels when the wind was unsuitable for sailing. When she reached St Mary's Pool she was run ashore for repairs. On 21 November the *Gem* was moored to a buoy when she parted in a west-north-west gale and went on the rocks to become a total loss. A quantity of riveted iron plate and frames still survive among the shallow rocks.

South of Newford Island the coast passes through Shark Pit to Thomas Porth and Porth Mellon, both of which are popular sand beaches leading into safe shallow water, suitable for diver training and beginners. The *Friar Tuck* was wrecked on Newford Island at the height of a storm on 2 December, 1863. One of some 500 vessels at anchor in The Road, this full-rigged 662-ton ship, carrying a cargo of tea, cut away her masts after going ashore, but quickly filled. The crew was saved by various means, as were three small shiploads of tea, sails and stores, but large quantities of the cargo found its way into local hands. Her figurehead is in the Valhalla collection on Tresco, as are some Chinese geese, which are descended from those on board.

AREA 2:

St Agnes and Annet

St Agnes and Gugh lie ¾ mile south-west of Woolpack Point on St Mary's, across the Sound. Annet is an uninhabited bird sanctuary ¾ mile further west on the other side of Smith Sound, which separates the islands. St Agnes and Gugh together occupy roughly 1 square mile, the latter accessible only on foot at low tide. Surrounded by deep water, St Agnes lies at the head of the Western Rocks and its location is such that it is frequently cut off from St Mary's during bad weather. Men from St Agnes were usually the first to reach shipwrecks among the Western Rocks, and the island's history is full of tales of heroic rescues. The second oldest lighthouse in the British Isles was built here in 1680, eventually made redundant by the building of the Bishop Rock lighthouse on the Western Rocks.

The residents of St Agnes live mostly in the three town areas known as Higher, Middle or Lower, which cluster around the old lighthouse building. Annet is privately owned and is famous for its many Megalithic remains. The landing point is the quay at Porth Conger.

In the south-east corner of St Agnes, searching for beads on the foreshore at Beady Pool makes an interesting beach occupation. Their source and origin is unknown, but it is said that in the early 18th century a slave trading vessel bound for West Africa was wrecked in the cove, and that the beads, thought to be of Dutch manufacture, spilled out of the wreck and became buried in the sand. The museum on St Mary's and the Old Town Café have a number of beaded necklaces on display.

An intriguing possibility exists that there may be three large undiscovered French warship wrecks off St Agnes, to the south in deep water. Documentary evidence suggests that in February 1781 three men-of war, the *Conquerant*, *Le Priarus* and *Julie*, were sent to attempt a landing and capture of the Isles of Scilly at night. They met a gale off St Agnes and all three foundered, with no survivors. Reports suggests that three untouched 18th-century warships await location offshore, complete with their fixtures and fittings, including 192 cannon of which a number could be bronze. However, French navy records show that there were no warships

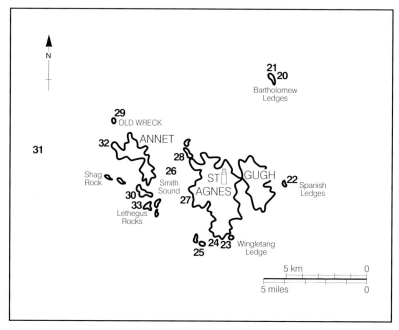

Dive sites in Area 2 (St Agnes and Annet).

named *Priarus* or *Julie* at the time, and that the *Conquerant* was probably broken up at Gibraltar, so it is possible that the reports of these wrecks are erroneous.

Several ships are recorded as having been lost on Gugh but no physical evidence has yet come to light. An unidentified ship was lost in 1771, probably on Cuckolds Ledge, and the Caernarfon schooner *Bolina*, carrying slates from Porthmadog to London, became a total wreck on 12 January, 1887. The coastline of this island from Porth Conger clockwise to The Cove offers only shallow water rocks and reefs, with excellent visibility and the species of marine life one would expect to find in these conditions.

None of the shipwreck sites around St Agnes can be reached from the shore; they must be considered as open water boat dives, several of them on the edge of deep water, and swept by strong tides. They are mostly concentrated in the south-west quarter of the island.

20 Bartholomew Ledges   49.54.20N; 06.19.50W. The Bartholomew Ledges lie in the main fairway of St Mary's Sound. They comprise two main rock outcrops and a shallow reef, and are marked by a permanent marker column. This is a fascinating shallow site, well known for its prolific marine life and underwater photographic opportunities; to get the best from your dive get below the kelp and slowly pull yourself across the bottom. On spring tides the site is swept by a current of 3 to 4 knots on the ebb, making it unsafe to dive, unless you drift dive the entire length of Bartholomew Ledges and North Bartholomew followed by a boat.

Two wrecks lie here: the steel-hulled French trawler *Magdeleine*, in 49.54.20N; 06.19.51W, and an early unidentified armed merchant vessel of around 1555, in 49.54.18N; 06.19.52W. The remains of the *Magdeleine* lie on the north-west side of Bartholomew Ledges, where she was wrecked during the evening of 3 June, 1906. This Boulogne-registered trawler had put into St Mary's Road the previous day. The trawler passed the wrong side of the Ledges' buoy and went aground, but the tide was high and she managed to get clear. On leaving the next day, the captain again took the *Magdeleine* on the wrong side of the buoy, struck the reef and she foundered two hours later. The wreck has been heavily salvaged, her engine having been removed by the Western Marine Salvage Company, but a considerable amount of iron work remains.

21   Bartholomew Ledge Wreck   This is the oldest known shipwreck site in the Isles of Scilly, designated a protected wreck and of historic importance. It was discovered in 1978, when some 60 boat-shaped lead ingots, each weighing around 80lbs, 5 tons of bronze bell fragments and other artefacts were recovered. The ship is believed to be a small armed Spanish or Spanish-Netherlands cargo vessel.

Six breech loading guns, a number of silver two-real coins dating from 1474 to 1555 and personal items have been found. A few lead ingots remain buried in the sea bed along with bell fragments, and a large "banded" gun lies concreted upright to a shallow reef. The names of at least seven other sailing vessels that have been wrecked on the Ledges are recorded, but no trace of them has been found. Good surface cover and SMBs are strongly recommended on this site because of the tide and proximity to the shipping channel.

The French trawler Magdeleine on Bartholomew Ledges, where she was wrecked on 2 June, 1906, having put into St Mary's to land an injured seaman. She lies on the same reef but some distance from the 16th-century protected wreck.

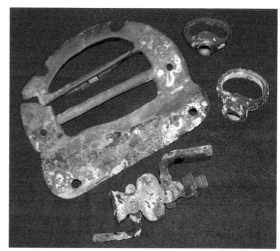

Above: Deck scupper plate, porthole fastenings and a machinery oil-cup fitting, found in the wreck of the SS Plympton (Site 25), which now lies upside down beneath the SS Hathor.

Above: Porthole from the wreck of the SS Italia on Wingletang Ledge (Site 23).

Right: Brass shell case from World War One, three 'tallies' from machinery spaces, and a speaking tube mouthpiece, also from the Italia.

The bow section of the SS Plympton (Site 25) on Lethegus Rocks on 22 July, 1906, following her partial capsize after going ashore. Two local boatmen and a visitor, engaged in 'wrecking', at the time she turned right over, were sucked down with the ship and only the visitor escaped.

22 Spanish Ledges 49.53.54N; 06.19W. About ¾ mile south-east of Bartholomew Ledges and at the entrance to St Mary's Sound lie Spanish Ledges, also marked with a buoy. Its distinctive bell tolls with the swell and can often be heard in Hugh Town. The Ledges lie 880yds from Gugh Island, at the edge of a large shallow area of rock and sand. Diving in the fairway is not recommended as large vessels enter and leave St Mary's Road via this Sound at all times of day, and the area has 2 knot tides.

The ledge itself is not normally visible, but at low water springs it is only 1m below the surface, dropping away to 15m and a sand bottom. Inside the bell buoy, at roughly 49.53.40N; 06.19.10W, some 15m north of Round Rock, the remains of a container from the *Cita* wreck were recently located, its contents being china soap dishes, toothbrush holders and beakers.

23 Italia 49.52.52N; 06.20.18W. This armed Italian-registered 2,792-ton steamship drove ashore in dense fog during the same night that the SS *Lady Charlotte* was wrecked near Porth Hellick, St Mary's, 3 miles to the east. Built as the *Gulf of Florida* in 1891, by Hawthorn Leslie, Newcastle-upon-Tyne, she was carrying coal from Cardiff to Toronto with a crew of 63. She drove ashore on Wingletang Ledge and the inhabitants of St Agnes were unaware of the wreck, as the sound of escaping steam and her siren were thought to be coming from the *Lady Charlotte* wreck.

The *Italia* is an excellent dive for beginners and experienced alike, and lies trapped in a sheltered, steep, sloping gully, her stern in 13m, her bow in 45m. She remains reasonably intact, despite heavy salvage, during which most of her engine room fittings were removed. The cargo of coal spilt out down the rocks and lies scattered around the wreck's bow section, where you will find her sidelight housings, handrails and anchors covered in marine growth, which make for excellent photography.

Above: This small wooden tub of petroleum is a relic from the Thomas W. Lawson wreck (Site 32) and is on display in the Isles of Scilly Museum.

Below: The gold medal awarded by President Theodore Roosevelt of the United States to William Cook Hicks, a Trinity House pilot living on St Agnes who risked his life saving three crew from the wreck of the Thomas W. Lawson.

You are recommended to start your dive amidships, going deep down to the bow in some 45m, where you will be subject to quite a lot of tide, then work your way back up to the shallows, exploring as you go. Her stern gun was salvaged in 1966.

24 Horse Point   At least two, if not three containers from the wreck of the *Cita* drifted on the tide and went ashore in the bay between Horse Point and The Beast, on the most southerly point of St Agnes. This is an area in which you can frequently dive among seals; there is a cascade of large rocks and boulders dropping off into deep water.

25 Lethegus Rocks, the Plympton and the Hathor   49.53N; 06.20.40W. These rocks are best known for two large steamship wrecks, which offer spectacular diving in a range of depths to 46m. Here you will find the remarkable coincidence of two wrecks actually piled one upon the other like broken toys.

Local divers examining the propeller and shaft of the SS Plympton (Site 25) at 30m.

The first ship to sink was the SS *Plympton* of London, owned by the Commercial Steamship Company, which was carrying maize from Rosario, Argentina, to Falmouth in 1909. Having received orders to discharge at Dublin, the *Plympton* encountered dense fog in the Channel. She struck the Lethegus Rocks, filled and was abandoned, her crew of 24 and one passenger landing on St Agnes. The ship capsized before her cargo could be salvaged, drowning a Scillonian trapped in the accommodation.

Eleven years later, on 2 December, 1920, the 7,060-ton German SS *Hathor* sank across the wreck of the *Plympton* at the base of the Lethegus Rocks. Built in 1912 at Geestemunde and registered at Hamburg, the *Hathor* had been interned in Chile. On release, she was overhauled, only to break down near the Azores. While under tow of two tugs, she was abandoned in a gale off the Isles of Scilly after the hawsers parted. With the tow reconnected, the crew returned on board, but the *Hathor* became unmanageable in a severe storm and the tow was slipped half a mile off St Agnes. The St Mary's lifeboat was launched and found the ship with both anchors down, but dragging, with only five officers on board, the remaining crew having taken to the boats. The *Hathor* eventually drove ashore and sank with all her cargo.

Over the years the wrecks of the *Plympton* and *Hathor* have intermingled, with the huge stern section of the *Plympton* upside down, still holding its three-bladed propeller. Wreckage lies criss-crossed with masts and derricks, and the stern of the *Hathor* remains intact and upright in 40m.

26   Smith Sound   Iron cannon lie in a general depth of 11 to 15m on a rock bottom with sandy patches somewhere in Smith Sound and are believed to have come from the wreck of the fireship *Firebrand*, lost in October 1707 during the same night that the *Association, Eagle* and *Romney* were lost.

Porth Conger, St Agnes, showing the slipway and quay.

Carrying a cargo of beans and cotton-seed, the Newcastle registered Earl of Lonsdale accidentally steamed between the islands of St Agnes and Annet in dense fog on 8 June, 1885 and was wrecked under Troy Town, St Agnes (Site 27).

27   Earl of Lonsdale   49.53.25N; 06.21.22W. This 1,543-ton iron steamship was on passage from Alexandria to Portishead, carrying a cargo of beans and cotton seed, when she drove ashore a short distance off Troy Town in thick fog at 2am on 8 June, 1885. The steamship's lookouts had already sighted breakers ahead of the vessel, and the captain ordered the engine to be stopped just as she struck a rock, causing her bow to swing to port; then she struck for a second time. As the fog thinned, a glimmer of artificial light was seen, which turned out to be the St Agnes lighthouse. Slowly the ship filled with water and settled down just to the north of Menglow Rock, where the crew abandoned ship.

The wreck was sold to Vasey & Company of Newcastle, who removed most of her machinery, after which she was heavily salvaged by the old Western Marine Salvage Company of Penzance. The ship's remains make an interesting shallow, but heavily weeded dive, and small souvenirs are still to be found jammed between the rocks.

28   Burnt Island   Periglis Bay is north of Troy Town and offers safe shallow shore diving, with an abundance of marine life, including large numbers of Atlantic grey seals. The main rock outcrop north of Periglis and the old St Agnes lifeboat house and slipway is Burnt Island, with various offshore rocks. There are no known shipwrecks or particularly interesting dive sites north of St Agnes, but many of the named rocks suggest a shipwreck connection, and a rummage in places where others seldom dive may well reveal evidence of some forgotten incident.

29   Old Wreck Rocks and buoy   Some 530yds north-west of the Haycocks, off Annet, is a set of rocks known as Old Wreck, marked offshore by Old Wreck buoy. This was assumed to be the site of a wreck, but no evidence of any loss here was found until 1998, when a magnetometer search 300yds north-east of the Old Wreck buoy showed a strong anomaly. A number of dives revealed a single-cylinder steam engine standing upright among a small amount of scattered iron plating, but no boiler and little else. It would appear these are the remains of a very early steamship; the depth is about 23m, the sea bed small rocks with shale-sand-filled gullies.

30   Annet, Hellweathers and Melledgan   Between St Agnes and the Western Rocks, the last main island of any size is Annet, with Hellweathers, Isinvrank, Brothers and Melledgan as offshoot rocks to the south. Annet is a bird sanctuary, and there are periods when restrictions are imposed on landing here and on certain other uninhabited islands. Annet and Melledgan are closed to the public from 15 April to 20 August except by written permit. Breeding and nesting birds are especially susceptible to disturbance, and divers are particularly asked not to take

One of two bronze military mortar guns found on the wreck of the Hollandia (Site 31), carried as part of her valuable outward bound cargo.

With her stern under water, the Liverpool barque River Lune became a total wreck in Muncoy Neck, Annet, in July 1879 (Site 33).

inflatable boats close inshore here during the closed period. This is also an area favoured by seals, which abound, basking on the rocks at low water.

31   Hollandia   49.53.38N; 06.23.52W. This is one of the more famous treasure wrecks of Scilly. The *Hollandia* was a Dutch East Indiaman belonging to the Amsterdam Chamber, heading for Batavia in 1743 carrying 129,700 guilders in silver coin. She was on her maiden voyage with 246 crew and soldiers, as well as 30 passengers. She is thought to have struck the Gunners in Broad Sound during the night of 13 July, 1743, steered towards St Agnes light, only to founder in 30m near George Peter's Ledge, west of Shag Rock, Annet.

She lay undiscovered until 1971 when the wreck was located by Anthony Lonsdale, enabling a diving team led by Rex Cowan to explore her remains. Recoveries were spectacular, consisting of a large number of lead ingots, many thousands of silver Spanish-American pillar dollars and ducatons, bronze cannon, swivel guns and military mortars, as well as hundreds of items of cargo. The wreck is spread over 440yds, with some 40 iron cannon and anchors remaining. A number of small items from the wreck are on display in the museum on St Mary's; others are in the Rijksmuseum, Amsterdam. Unauthorised diving on this site is prohibited.

32   Thomas W. Lawson   49.53.38N; 06.22.55W. The largest shipwreck in this area, the 5,218-ton, 395ft *Lawson*, was a gigantic steel schooner. Built by the Fore River Engineering Company of Quincy, Massachusetts, in 1902, her seven enormous steel masts carried a total of 25 sails, requiring 40,612 square feet of canvas. The ship's dead-weight cargo capacity was 7,500 tons, her overall

These strings of beads have been made up from all the varieties that can be found at Beady Pool. They can be seen at the Old Town café on St Mary's, and there are further examples in the Isles of Scilly Museum.

displacement 10,000 tons. The *Lawson*'s build was such that she carried every possible mechanical aid, enabling her to be worked with a crew of just 18.

The *Lawson* left Philadelphia for London under Captain Geoffrey Dow on 20 November, 1907, carrying 2¼ million gallons of kerosene, valued at £40,000. Bad weather made for a difficult Atlantic crossing, and by the time the *Lawson* sighted the Isles of Scilly not one of her boats remained intact, and only six serviceable sails remained on her masts. By 13 December the she was off course and well inside the Bishop Rock, virtually embayed within the Western Rocks. She anchored in Broad Sound in a north-westerly gale and shortly before dusk the St Agnes lifeboat was launched to her assistance. Captain Dow refused the offer of help, but reluctantly accepted the services of a pilot. The St Mary's lifeboat also arrived, returning to her station with orders to telegraph Falmouth for tugs. The pilot agreed to burn a flare should the services of the lifeboat be required during the night.

Watchers on shore noticed that between 2.30 and 2.50am the schooner's lights vanished, but as no flares or distress signals had been sighted presumed all was well. In fact the *Lawson* had already become a total loss, daylight revealing her upturned hull and a mass of floating wreckage around Annet and St Agnes. A local gig put out, bringing back one injured seaman and, on a second trip, found Captain Dow and his engineer alive on Hellweathers. It seems the rest of the crew took to the rigging after the ship parted her cables and as the wreck fell on her side across Shag Rock everyone was catapulted into the sea.

The wreck now lies in shallow water in two parts, almost 440yds apart, her bow section to the north-east of Shag Rock, her stern to the south-west, both in depths varying from 8 to 18m. The site is covered in dense weed and is safe to dive, little affected by tide. Huge sections of the double bottom survive, with six steel masts and yards off to one side. Spectacular underwater photographs have shown sunlight penetrating the *Lawson*'s frames as divers swim through sections of the lower holds, tank-tops creating an underwater ceiling. The area is worth exploration as interesting relics continue to be seen.

Other sailing ship wrecks here are the *Financier*, lost at the back of Annet on 5 September, 1783, on passage from Charleston to London with rice, indigo and tobacco; the *Nancy*, sailing from Jamaica to London with rum, sugar and fustick, lost on the Brow of Hellweathers the same day; or the *Providencia*, travelling from St Andero to Bristol with wool valued at £10,000, lost on Hellweathers on 2 October, 1821.

33   River Lune   49.52.52N; 06.22.08W. In this iron barque, on passage from L'Orient to Ardrossan in ballast, Captain West was navigating by dead reckoning because of fog when the Second Mate reported rocks ahead less than a ship's length away. Within 10 minutes of striking Isinvrank Rock in Muncoy Neck with her port side on 27 July, 1879, she filled and was abandoned. The crew later returned to the vessel in an attempt to save personal belongings, but found the barque's stern underwater in 11m and left for a second time; she became a total wreck. Her remains today are very shallow and covered in weed.

Other wrecks around the island of Melledgan include an unidentified vessel on passage from the Bay of Honduras to London with mahogany, lost in 1733; another sailing vessel, believed to be Dutch, carrying wine and paper, lost on the Biggal of Melledgan in 1760; and the brig *Charlotte* of Sweden, wrecked on Melledgan Rock on Christmas Day, 1848.

AREA 3:

The Western Rocks

The Western Rocks is the name for the area west of Melledgan and Annet, as far out as the Bishop and Crim Rocks. It is one of the most spectacular diving areas in Britain, particularly at low water, when hundreds of rocks and islets are exposed, offering countless diving sites. The Rocks are uninhabited and comprise some 6½ square miles of formidable and dangerous seas, with strong tides and unpredictable conditions. There are many hundreds of known shipwrecks here and probably exciting discoveries yet to be made. The Western Rocks are extremely scenic, with many species of fish, shellfish, molluscs, corals and weed, and an abundance of grey seals. Water depths vary from extremely shallow to 37m, while around the southern and western edges of the seamount the sea bed plunges to 73m.

The lighthouse on the Western Rocks was built on the Bishop Rock, completed in 1887, and is now fully automatic.

WARNING The exposed nature of the Western Rocks is such that diving is frequently impossible or inadvisable, and you should be aware that during an average year diving is possible on only some 28 days. One of the best indicators of the sea conditions on the outer Western Rocks is the amount of broken water on the extreme western end of Newford Island Rocks or reef on the northern side of St Mary's harbour. If there is any broken water – *no matter how little* – on these rocks it means that it will be very rough and uncomfortable out towards the Bishop, and even a small amount of white water means the Western Rocks are undiveable.

There are so many places to dive among the Western Rocks that only the major wreck sites are described here. Local dive boats can take you to many others.

34   Gorregan and Pednathise Head   Gorregan is the first of the Western Rocks and one of the largest, on which the French steam fishing trawler *L'Authie* of Boulogne was lost on 11 October, 1909. Built in 1899 and carrying a crew of 15 she had sailed with a defective compass and log. She drove ashore in fog, losing her propeller on the rocks, and became a total loss.

Opposite: The Bishop Rock lighthouse, completed in 1887, with St Martin's Diving Services boat Morvoren in the foreground.

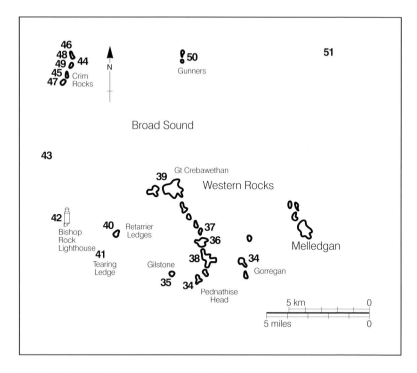

Dive sites in Area 3: The Western Rocks.

Pednathise Head is well known for deep water, strong tides and four shipwreck sites, commencing with Old Bess Rock to the north, which dries at low water. Here you can find evidence of an armed sailing vessel, possibly the man-of-war *Romney*, but still unidentified, in the shallows on the north-west side. The remains of two French fishing vessels can be found in 3m: the 246-ton *Jean Gougy* of Fecamp, lost on 24 February, 1970; and the 50-ton St Malo-registered *Enfant de Bretagne*, which broke up on 13 February, 1977.

If you dive deep on the south face of Pednathise, starting at 17m and going off to 40m, you will find the wreckage of the 2,626-ton Greek steamship *Antonios* (at 49.51.42N; 06.24.12W), which is known to have gone down on 8 December, 1912. Its wreckage washed ashore on St Agnes and items found included an oar marked *Greta Holme* (her previous name) and the lid of a medicine chest bearing the same name engraved on a brass plate. The St Mary's lifeboat searched the Western Rocks in vain for signs of the wreck or survivors, and it was presumed at Lloyd's that she had gone down offshore and hence was recorded simply as "missing". It was not until 1968 that the remains of the *Antonios* were found in 45m on a steep rocky slope.

A scattering of iron cannon can be found deeper still, which are probably associated with the shallow cannon site off Black Rock. This shallow, second dive, a short distance from Daisy in 10 to 15m, gave up a lot of gold coins and an astrolabe of around 1550 in the 1980s. Take care here as depths plunge into deep water.

35 Association   49.51.45N; 06.24.30W. This is possibly one of the best known historic wreck sites in Britain. The *Association* was part of a fleet of 21 English men-of-war, on their way home from Gibraltar to Portsmouth, that blundered into the Western Rocks at about 8pm on 22 October, 1707. Although the largest warship in the fleet was the 1st rate, 96-gun *Royal Anne*, Admiral Sir Clowdisley Shovell chose the 2nd rate, 90-gun *Association* as his flagship, which carried a crew of 680. Unsure of their position at the entrance to the English Channel, Admiral Shovell believed they were further south than they actually were. Three smaller vessels at the head of the fleet, the *Lenox*, *Valeur* and *Phoenix*, were ordered to proceed to Falmouth for convoy duty, leaving the larger vessels without any smaller ships ahead of them to warn of danger.

The yacht *Isabella* and the 3rd rate *Orford* had narrow escapes, as did the *Royal Anne*, which cleared the rocks by less than a ship's length; the 2nd rate *St George* struck the Gilstone Rock but was lifted clear by the swell. The fireship *Firebrand* also struck the Gilstone Rock, and then staggered away to the south-east to sink between St Agnes and Annet. The *Association* went ashore on the south side of the Gilstone Rock where she was lost. Four warships were wrecked: the *Association*, the *Eagle*, the *Romney* and the *Firebrand*, with a total death toll of 1,450 or thereabouts. See Site **13** for details of how Sir Clowdisley Shovell lost his life.

Early salvage attempts to recover guns and treasure from the wrecks were largely unsuccessful, and this national tragedy faded into history until 1964 when one of the authors led a Royal Navy diving team to the islands to search for the *Association*, which was successfully located in 1967. The first finds were a 9ft bronze cannon and 4,000 Reis, Portuguese gold coins. The Isles of Scilly Museum has a large collection of *Association* artefacts on display and one of her large bronze cannon is mounted on a wooden sea-carriage as part of the Valhalla figurehead collection on Tresco island.

Although not a protected wreck site, Scillonian Divers are "salvors in possession" and diving here is not permitted without their agreement. A number of High Court injunctions served on visiting divers have been upheld in the past, and you are advised to stay clear, unless you have their permission.

36 Prinses Maria   49.52.19N; 06.23.54W. The 1,140-ton *Prinses Maria* was a Dutch East Indiaman of the Zeeland Chamber. In February 1686, armed with 46 cannon and carrying a crew of 250, she was on passage from the Texel to Batavia with general cargo and a large quantity of treasure in the form of silver specie. She struck the rocks just north of Santaspery Neck and sank in 12m on a sandy bottom. The value of her treasure was such that James II sent the royal yacht to participate in her salvage, and when the Dutch owners petitioned for the treasure to be returned he denied its existence.

Details of the vessel's loss had almost been forgotten when, following the successful location of the Indiaman *Hollandia*, Rex Cowan employed divers to search for the *Prinses Maria*, which was located in 1973, only a short distance off Silver Carn. Extensive air-lifting of the sand covering the wreck revealed hull timbers and iron cannon as well as artefacts, and large numbers of silver Real coins were recovered, but no gold specie.

The wreck uncovers of its own accord, and 20ft beams and lengths of deck planking lie exposed most of the time, offering photographic opportunities or the possibility of finding artefacts if you dig deep enough.

37   Thames   49.52.23N; 06.24.10W. Built in 1827, the *Thames* was a very early packet paddle-steamer registered at Dublin, travelling regularly between Dublin and London. Carrying a general cargo, 26 crew and 36 passengers, she struck Jacky's Rock, less than 440yds north-west of Rosevear Island at 5am on 4 January, 1841. Captain James Grey mistook the St Agnes light for the Longships, navigating his ship past the Gunners and through Broad Sound,

Shortly before the *Thames* went aground a very heavy sea broke over her, which extinguished her single boiler, and suddenly she was without power. Distress rockets were fired, and small boats from St Agnes put out to the wreck, the larger island boats being pulled up high and dry above low water. Sixty lives were lost in the wreck. James Deane, a famous early diver, was employed to carry out salvage, after which her remains lay undisturbed until relocated in 1976. Wreck remains consist of iron sections and shards of pottery among the weed, rocks and sand, in depths as little as 1.8m. There are also many iron fittings concreted to the rocks. Examples of crested china from the wreck are on display in the museum on St Mary's, and in the Charlestown Shipwreck and Heritage Centre.

38   Rosevean and Rosevear   North of the Outer Gilstone lie a semi-circle of rocks and ledge, which are a natural ship trap. At the lower end are the two large islands of Rosevean and Rosevear, separated by Rosevear Neck. Early unidentified wrecks are known to have taken place here in 1730, 1752 and 1762 but almost no details are recorded. The first vessel was carrying wine from the Canary Islands; the captain and another survivor remained lashed to a rock on Rosevean for three days and nights before rescue. The wreck of 1752 was a Dutchman carrying cotton from which there were no survivors, and the 1762 incident a French vessel from which six men survived out of a crew of 18.

Other wrecks in the immediate area were the East Indies packet vessel *Nancy*, which struck the Outer Gilstone then Rosevear Island; the sloop *Mary*, lost on 20 March, 1819; and the Plymouth schooner *Solace* sailing from Lisbon on 27 April, 1839. Another vessel homeward bound from the Far East was the Rotterdam-registered barque *Nickerie*. Carrying coffee and sugar from Samarang to Holland, she struck a rock just south-west of Rosevear on 21 November, 1843, when her captain thought he was well east off the English coast. Eight crew drowned, leaving eleven men clinging to wreckage, and only two survived to be rescued.

The largest of the steamship wrecks here was the London-registered, 325-ton *Sado*, sailing from Oporto to Liverpool with wine, wool, oranges, minerals, eggs, 30 cattle, a crew of 20 and four passengers. She drove ashore in fog on the ledge of Rosevear Island and immediately filled with water. The wreck lies close to where the paddle steamer *Thames* was lost in 1841.

The island of Rosevear bears evidence of habitation, having been a base camp in 1852 when the second Bishop Rock lighthouse was built. Among the huge granite rocks are remains of the French steam trawler *Cité de Verdun*, which drove ashore on 21 March, 1925. The ship's two painted nameboards can be seen in the Atlantic and Mermaid pubs on St Mary's. In the shallows west of Rosevear, on

Rosevear Ledges, a large bronze gun was found by divers in 1968, which bore the same French marks as those recovered from the wreck of the *Association*.

39   Round Rock and Crebawethan   The most northerly of the obstructions in this long reef chain is Round Rock, where the remains of the 200-ton Liverpool wooden schooner *Douro* lie at 49.52.53N; 06.25.08W. She was wrecked on 27 January, 1843, on passage to Oporto and west Africa with a cargo described as "baled goods, armoury and brass stops". She struck Round Rock in fog and went down with all hands, only six bodies and her figurehead being recovered. Located by divers in the early 1970s, the "brass stops" proved to be thousands of brass manillas, bracelet-type tokens used in the African slave trade, which can still be found among the rocks.

Little and Great Crebawethan and Crebawethan Neck cover a considerable area of rocks and ledges, much frequented by seals, and have a long history of shipwreck. The *Zeelilie* was part of a large fleet of Dutch East Indiamen homeward bound from Batavia to Zeeland, escorted by a Dutch frigate, when near St Helena in the South Atlantic they were surprised by an English fleet of warships and captured. The *Zeelilie* was taken as a prize by HMS *Sceptre*, a 3rd rate man-of-war, and escorted to Limerick, where the ship was searched for valuables and a British prize crew put on board. She then sailed for London on 11 October, 1795, but at night ran onto "the most western rocks of the islands". She became a total wreck, with the loss of 25 lives, and took to the bottom a vast quantity of tea, valued at 716,139 Dutch florins or £140,000, and over 3 million pieces of Chinese porcelain, weighing 200 tons.

These silver napkin rings from the wreck of the Schiller (Site 40), are each marked with a place number and bear the crest of the German Transatlantic Steamship Company.

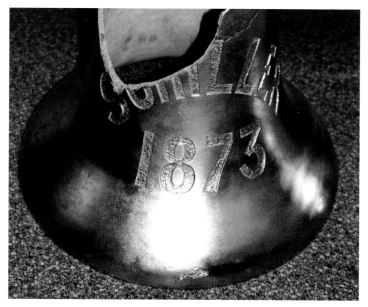

Above: The bell from the German liner Schiller (Site 40).

Below: Pottery shards from the wreck site of the steam packet Thames, lost near Jacky's Rock (Site 37).

The *Zeelilie* was part of the last convoy of Dutch East India Company ships from the Far East before that vast trading organisation went into liquidation in December 1795. On the north side of Little Crebawethan can be found some 30 iron cannon, five or six of which are trapped under huge boulders at the head of a gully in 4m. Further out are the remains of iron anchor flukes and shanks, suggesting this is where the *Zeelilie* struck before being washed over the rocks into the encircled pool to the south-east. Here, in a general depth of 10 to 12m, amid small rocks on a sandy bottom, lie thousands of small porcelain shards.

Other Indiamen known to have been lost among the Western Rocks and as yet not definitely located include the English Company's 450-ton *Phoenix*. The vessel was lost on 11 January, 1680, homeward bound with a valuable cargo of white pepper and cloth. Much of her pepper and textiles were sold by auction on St Mary's, and her remains may well lie near Menglow Rock, in Smith Sound.

The *Royal Oak*, another English East Indiaman, was lost on 18 January, 1665, reported to have driven between two outcrops where she foundered within 15 minutes. Her crew were rescued. More recent undiscovered wrecks include the snow *Pownall*, which was lost on Crebawethan on 16 October, 1759, carrying whale oil, sugar, tar, turpentine and staves. The full-rigged, 349-ton *Amelia*, armed with six 12-pounder cannon, on passage from Demerara to London, was lost on the same rocks on 31 August, 1810. Included in her cargo of sugar, rum, cotton and coffee was a box of silver bars and another box of dollars, which were never recovered. Other Crebawethan wrecks include the schooner *Minerva* of St Ives, lost on 13 October, 1836; the 3,004-ton steamship *Castleford*, carrying a general cargo and cattle, which drove onto the reef on 8 June, 1887, and the Admiralty auxiliary trawler *Carbineer*, put ashore on Crebawethan Point to save the lives of her crew after having struck the Crim Rocks during World War One.

40 Schiller 49.52.10N; 06.25.40W. Homeward bound from New York to Hamburg, this 3,421-ton German Transatlantic Steam Navigation liner, built in 1873 by Napiers at Glasgow, was passing the Isles of Scilly in fog when she got inside the Bishop Rock and struck Retarrier Ledges on the north side at night on 7 May, 1875. Double lookouts had been posted and Captain Thomas had reduced her speed to 4 knots. After going ashore the *Schiller*'s distress rockets and signal-guns were mistaken by people on St Agnes as the customary signals made by liners as they passed the Bishop Rock, and incredibly the keepers of the lighthouse were unaware of the wreck. Finding no help forthcoming from the shore, the crew attempted to launch the ship's two remaining serviceable lifeboats The 101 crew and 254 passengers were far more than her boats could possibly accommodate, and huge seas and a heavy list soon took its toll of lives. At dawn, a Sennen Cove fishing boat saved seven men, after which a fleet of Scillies boats and the packet steamer *Lady of the Isles* appeared and took off survivors. Of the 355 persons on board, only 43 survived. Many Scillonian boatmen were employed in recovering the bodies of drowned crewmen and passengers, several of whom were buried on St Mary's.

As well as a general cargo, 250 bags of mail and other valuables, the *Schiller* had on board $300,000 in American gold 20 dollar coins. It took a whole year for the first "standard" divers of the Western Marine Salvage Company of Penzance to recover almost all the elusive treasure. The salvors also recovered cargo and fittings.

The authors of this guide are legal salvors in possession of the wreck, which is marked with a buoy to that effect. Visiting divers are asked to request permission to dive the site (tel. 01720 423162), and to surrender any finds to the salvors. These will be declared to the Receiver of Wreck, and eventually put on display in St Mary's Museum.

The remains of the *Schiller* are scattered across Retarrier Ledges, mostly broken iron frames and pieces of machinery lying bridge-like on top of large boulders, going down to 27m, including her rudder and three-bladed iron propeller.

WARNING The site can only be dived at slack water, and there is a dangerous down-flow of very strong tide on the ebb, which can take you off the ledges down to 46m without warning. Several divers have suffered this un-nerving experience and been swept away from their boat to surface half a mile away with their air supply exhausted.

41 Eagle 49.52.14N; 06.26.30W. Lost on 22 October, 1707, at the same time as the *Association* was wrecked on the Outer Gilstone, the *Eagle*'s cannon site on Tearing Ledge was at first thought to be the remains of the 4th rate man-of-war *Romney*, but recent investigation of the number and size of the cannon has proved almost conclusively that it is the 3rd rate *Eagle*. The Gostelo map held in the British Museum shows the *Eagle* as being lost on the Crim Rocks and the *Romney* on Tearing Ledge, but it is now generally accepted that this is incorrect. The 1,099-ton *Eagle* carried 70 cannon and swivel guns, and a crew of 440 sailors, of which there were no survivors.

The wreck site is very spectacular, with at least 61 cannon scattered the length of a long rock gully in a general depth of 30 to 35m, lying south-east to north-west. Two clusters of cannon can be found at the extreme ends of the site, with one whole and one broken anchor. On top of Tearing Ledge, in very shallow water, are six 24-pounder cannon with concreted cannon balls. The ship's bell, dated 1701, was raised by divers in 1967 and is on display in the museum on St Mary's. Large numbers of 4,000 reis gold coins, English and Spanish silver have been recovered, and the site is believed to contain many more. It is currently a protected wreck site and must not be dived without a licence.

42 Bishop Rock 49.52.20N; 06.26.41W. At the extreme western edge of the Western Rocks, the Bishop Rock is centred on a reef measuring some 880yds north–south and 440yds east–west. Around the reef the sea bed drops away

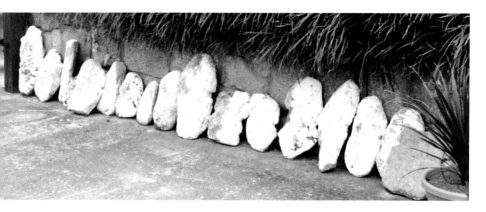

Top: This corroded bronze bell was recovered from the deep cannon site off the Crim Rocks (Site 45).

Above: Heavily corroded silver coins recovered from the unidentified cannon site on the west side of the Crim Rocks.

Opposite: A collection of stone anchors on display at Old Town Bay.

69

The first material from the wreck site of the Association (Site 35) was located by a team of Royal Navy divers and declared to the then local Receiver of Wreck in July 1967.

sharply to 48m with deep and shallow gullies. On the south-east side in depths ranging from 15 to 35m there is evidence of the original iron framed lighthouse, which collapsed into the sea in 1850. Additionally, the assorted debris of almost 150 years of occupancy by lighthouse keepers will be found strewn down the slope into deep water. As with Retarrier Ledges, there is a strong down-flow of tidal current here, which can push you down to the sea bed, but the Bishop is a remarkable and spectacular dive.

43   Falkland   About ¾ mile to the north-west, at roughly 49.52.50N; 06.28.00W, lie the remains of the four-masted, 2,867-ton, Liverpool iron barque *Falkland*, built in 1889 by W. H. Potter & Sons for the Palace Shipping Company Ltd. On 22 June, 1901, while on passage from Puget Sound to Falmouth for orders with grain, she hit the Bishop and sank in 44m.

Another victim of the Bishop Rock was the early 600-ton packet paddle-steamer *Brigand*, carrying 200 tons of coal and patent fuel from Liverpool to London. Fitted with a 200hp, two-cylinder simple engine, she had been specially built for the Liverpool–Bristol trade. Her lookouts sighted St Agnes' lighthouse during the early hours of 12 October, 1842, then shortly afterwards she struck the Bishop. Saved from sinking immediately by her four watertight bulkheads, there was just time for her 27 crew to take to the boats before the steamer sank, 7 miles from where she struck, in 82m.

The remains of the 5,695-ton SS *Western Front*, a Seattle-registered steamer built in 1917 for the United States Shipping Board, sailing from Jacksonville to London carrying 7,000 tons of naval stores, lie near the *Brigand* wreck. Fire was discovered in a hold when she was some 20 miles west of the Bishop. By the time the St Mary's lifeboat *Elsie* had reached her and rescued 40 of the crew from their boats, the blazing ship had drifted to within 7 miles of the Western Rocks. See Site **118**.

A more recent find, in August 1999, was the German submarine *U-681*, which is described at Site **110**.

44 Crim Rocks 49.53.50N; 06.27.10W. Crim Rocks are the most westerly group of rocks in the Isles of Scilly, extending from North Rock over a distance of

The SS Castleford, bound from Montreal to London with 460 cattle, went ashore on Crebawethan in the Western Rocks, in fog on 8 June, 1887.

880yds to another Tearing Ledge, not to be confused with that near the Bishop Rock. A number of the Crim Rocks show at low water, and diving here is generally an experience not to be missed. To the west of Peaked Rock a long series of flat granite ledges drop away to 37m, then to 55m, down to a sand and shingle sea bed; on these shelves crayfish are frequently to be found, usually at depths below 23m. The visibility out here so far from land can be in excess of 30m. Although the site is over 5 miles from Hugh Town Harbour, and frequently undiveable in any sort of heavy swell, it is well worth a visit if the conditions are favourable.

45   Cannon Site   49.53.43N; 06.27.24W. When first located in 1969 by crayfish divers working the Crim Rocks, this wreck was assumed to be the remains of the 4th rate man-of-war *Romney*, lost on 22 October, 1707, at the same time as the *Association*. The Gostelo map, which indicates the *Romney* was wrecked here, is now believed to be in error, as the size and number of cannon suggest a much older and smaller vessel, still unidentified. Some 15 or 20 cannon lie scattered across the sea bed and other remains have been found, which suggest she was a man-of-war.

WARNING Great care is necessary when diving this site as a strong down-flow of tide has taken many divers down to more than 50m before they were able to make their way back to the surface.

46   Hind   49.53.50N; 06.27.10W. The *Hind* was an early 6th rate English man-of-war, armed with eight cannon and built in 1655 at Wivenhoe. The ship is believed to have been lost in the centre of the Crim Rocks on 4 December, 1668. There are a number of small cannon sites on the Crim, which may be from the *Hind*. At the base of Peaked Rock on the west face of the Crim, off to the north-west and in 60m, lie the remains of a wooden wreck, whose beams, hatch covers, windlass, chain and anchors are laid out flat on the sea bed, clearly visible on a remote TV camera lowered to the sea bed in 1998 by David McBride.

47   Custos   This Liverpool-registered, full-rigged 400-ton ship was carrying a valuable general cargo, outward bound from Liverpool to Bonny, when she struck the Crim Rocks at 2am on 28 August, 1856, and sank within 10 minutes. Her crew took to the boats and landed on St Agnes. An inquiry into the loss revealed that Captain Daniel Shaw had been drunk for three days prior to the wreck. The boat's cargo included muskets, casks of gunflints, four bags of manillas and other items. As far as is known, this wreck has yet to be located.

48   Thornliebank   49.53.58N; 06.27.03W. The 2,105 ton, full-rigged *Thornliebank* was built at Glasgow in 1896, by Russell & Co Ltd and registered at Glasgow. She was carrying nitrate of soda from Pisagua to Falmouth when she hit Zantman's Rock towards the north end of the reef on 28 November, 1913. The St Agnes lifeboat answered her distress rockets and towed the survivors in their own boat back to St Mary's. In 1989 a visiting diver found the ship's bell bearing her name. The wreck now consists only of a scattering of steel plates and frames, but divers report having seen a windlass, anchors and cable in the shallows.

49   Susanna   49.53.57N; 06.27.03W. Another victim of fog, this steel full-rigged ship was en route for Falmouth carrying nitrate from Iquique, when she struck the Crim Rocks on 14 October, 1913. Her crew of 22 took to two boats and rowed

A grey Atlantic seal basking on the Eastern Rocks.

around in the fog until 5.30am the following day, when they fell in with two Sennen Cove fishing boats who piloted them to St Mary's. Since then the remains of the *Susanna* have been identified in 10m, her rudder, which is complete, lying in 30m.

50   Broad Sound, North Channel and the Gunners   Although seldom used by large vessels today, Broad Sound and the North Channel offer a westerly approach to St Mary's Road and Admiralty Charts still indicate appropriate bearings and landmarks. The Gunners are notorious for having caused the wreck of the *Hollandia* in 1743, which struck here only to founder nearer Annet. In the same way, the *Ardencraig* was lost after striking the Crim Rocks. The exposed position of the Gunners suggest that it must have claimed its fair share of ships, but no wrecks have been found around it to date.

51   Ardencraig   Another steel full-rigged ship, the *Ardencraig* sailed from Melbourne and called at Queenstown in southern Ireland for orders early in 1911; she was instructed to proceed to Calais to unload her cargo of wheat. Shortly after sailing she met with fog and struck the Crim Rocks on 8 January. When it was found she had 9ft of water in the hold her boats were lowered, but at that moment a wave lifted her off the rocks into Broad Sound when she was immediately abandoned. The St Agnes lifeboat arrived shortly afterwards and took off the crew. The *Ardencraig* sank in a position given roughly as 49.55.20N; 06.23.30W, west of Peaked Rock in 44m, but she is difficult to find even using a magnetometer. This is an exciting and challenging dive, the wreck lying on one side in deep, clear water, her masts disappearing into the gloom across the sea bed. It is important to calculate the time of slack water here as tidal streams are strong.

The slipway at Periglis Cove, once used by the St Agnes lifeboat, with St Agnes church in the background.

AREA 4:

Bryher and Samson

Across St Mary's Road from the Garrison lies the double-humped uninhabited island of Samson, and further to the north the sparsely inhabited island of Bryher. Just 1½ miles from north to south and less than ¾ mile wide, the northern end of Bryher is covered in Bronze Age remains and there was once an Iron Age cliff castle on Shipman Head. Bryher has some spectacular scenery, especially at this northern end. The recognised landing place is the old granite quay or the newer Anika Rice pier in the town. From the latter, it is an easy walk to the only Bryher shop, a small general store with post office and bakery, and the Hell Bay Hotel.

To the west of Bryher lie islands and rocks notorious for shipwrecks, which offer divers eight excellent sites, particularly on Scilly Rock, Maiden Bower and Steeple Rock. The only identifiable wreck site on Bryher can be found in Hell Bay where the *Maipu* was lost.

52 Maipu 49.57.47N; 06.21.37W. The *Maipu* was a Liverpool-registered 594-ton barque carrying saltpetre and nitrate of soda from Iquique to Hamburg. Built by Cammell-Laird at Birkenhead in 1865, the *Maipu* was 165ft with a beam of 27ft. She was sailing by dead reckoning in dense fog on 27 July, 1879, when Captain Thomas Wheeler ordered a depth sounding, which showed 60 fathoms (110m). Later that night, the vessel struck the coast in Hell Bay, close to the narrow channel separating Bryher Island from Shipman Head and became fast. The wreck later swung round on the tide, so that her stern was ashore. A line was passed to the rocks by which means some of the crew landed on Bryher, the remainder electing to remain on board with the captain.

The loss of the *Maipu* was attributed to fog and the lack of a foghorn or lighthouse on the island; within 16 days the ship had gone completely to pieces. This is a very shallow dive either from a boat or the rocks, and large sections of iron plates and frames can be found among the boulders.

53 Toledo 49.55.32N; 06.23.58W. As with so many wrecks around the Isles of Scilly, fog engulfed this 2,843-ton steamship, built by J. L. Thompson of Sunderland in 1882, when she was near the Bishop Rock in 1898. Feeling his way by dead reckoning, Captain John Wishart reduced speed, but during the afternoon of

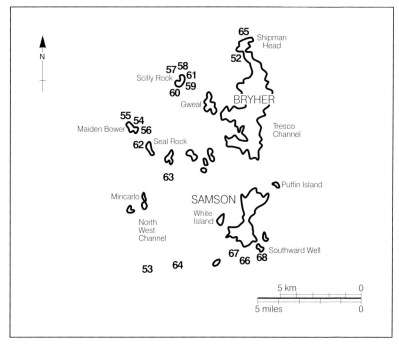

Dive sites in Area 4: Bryher and Samson.

20 August struck Steeple Rock on the edge of the North Channel. The Second Engineer saw her boilers lift in their mountings, after which the engine room began to flood at the rate of a foot a minute. Many of the crew took to the boats clad only in night attire before the *Toledo* rolled over and sank, bow first, in 42m.

The divers of Trinity House, who surveyed the wreck, reported that she was a navigational hazard, as her masts were only 6m below the surface, so she was dispersed by explosives. Today the wreck lies in a general depth of 50m south-west of Steeple Rock, standing 3m proud of the sea bed.

54   Zelda   49.56.50N; 06.23.30W. Less than 32 hours into her maiden voyage, this Liverpool-registered 1,338-ton steamship was carrying a general cargo from her home port to Palermo, when she ran into fog on 15 April, 1874. With sails set on both masts and travelling at full speed, she plunged straight into Maiden Bower Rock, having just missed Little Maiden Bower.

Standard divers worked on her for many weeks, recovering cotton, lard, oil, copper, tin and steel rails. The wreck can be found in a gully between the two parts of Maiden Bower, her stern pointing north with her propeller in 9m, her bow in 27m. The wreckage may well be mixed up with that of the wooden sailing barque *Osvetitel*, an Austrian ship carrying barley from Ibrail to Falmouth. She hit Maiden Bower on 14 July, 1816, also in fog.

55 Brinkburn 49.56.50N; 06.23.36W. The rusting remains of this 3,229-ton steamship lie almost parallel to and a little north and west of the wreck of the *Zelda*. After leaving Galveston in the United States for Le Havre on 22 November, 1898, the crew of the *Brinkburn* saw no sign of land until her lookout reported breakers ahead on 15 December. Fog had caused Captain James Martin to reduce speed to 2½ knots, but she went ashore. Her crew abandoned ship in their own boats, remaining close to the wreck until the following day and had every intention of going back on board to collect their belongings, but by early morning she had already sunk. Later, her bow section broke away and bales of cotton began to float out, causing the Liverpool Salvage Association to arrange for the Western Marine Salvage Company of Penzance to recover the cargo as soon as possible.

The wreck of the *Brinkburn* lies almost at right angles to the *Toledo*, the wrecks being only 60ft apart. Her massive engine block stands upright in 10m and you can swim down the centre of the site following her propeller shaft to 30m, with wreckage scattered widely on both sides.

The barque Maipu, wrecked stern-first in Hell Bay, Bryher on 27 July, 1879 in fog.
Sections of her plating and hull lie in the shallows here (Site 52).

56 Cannon sites   49.56.49N; 06.23.30W and 49.56.48N; 06.23.37W. A number of iron cannon have been found on the sea bed between the wrecks of the *Brinkburn* and the *Toledo*, and another site on the western side of Maiden Bower suggests yet another old wreck, but neither has been identified.

57 Scilly Rock   Directly west of Bryher's Shipman Head Down and some ¾ mile offshore lies Scilly Rock and its attendant Bann Ledge, South and North Cuckoo, Sharp Rock, Murr Rock, Biggal and East and Westward Ledges. With an average depth of 15m, the sea bed drops to 22m and then 45m and is an area of strong tides. Before 1970, Scilly Rock was a favourite haunt of crayfish divers, who frequently made huge catches on one tide: you may be lucky enough to see one. There are wreck sites on all four sides of Scilly Rock and it is an area you can happily explore all day without decompression.

58 Isabo   49.57.28N; 06.22.50W. This 6,827-ton Italian steamship (formerly the *Iris*) drove ashore on the Biggal in fog during the afternoon of 27 October, 1927. A Bryher coastguard heard her siren and escaping steam and called the lifeboat. The *Isabo* was also assisted by 18 Bryher residents who were alongside the wreck in gigs before the lifeboat arrived! Twenty-eight of the crew of 38 were saved by local boats and the lifeboat, in appalling conditions, and the people of Bryher, the boatmen and lifeboat crew received money, medals and certificates from the owners, the Italian government and the RNLI.

  The wreck has been well salvaged and flattened by the sea over the years, but much of it can still be recognised, lying on the north side of the seaward point of Westward Ledge. The wreck starts in 20m, with an almost sheer drop to 48m, and a torch is essential as it is a very dark dive.

59 Eric Rickmers   49.57.20N; 06.22.45W. This full-rigged steel ship, registered at Bremerhaven, was on passage from Bangkok to Bremen with a cargo of rice when she struck Scilly Rock at 9pm on 25 October, 1899, in fog. Her crew remained on board for 4 hours, then took to their boats as her hold slowly filled, boatmen from Bryher guiding them to the shore. The ship settled down quickly, leaving only her topmasts above water, and eventually went to pieces. The wreck lies in 20m on the south-east corner of Scilly Rock on South Cuckoo, her masts collapsed and with many deck fittings exposed.

60 Parame   49 57 28; 06 22 42W. A French barque registered at Redon, the *Parame* was wrecked close to the *Eric Rickmers* and only hours later, having taken an identical course for Scilly, which caused her loss on the same side of Scilly Rock on 26 October, 1899. The *Parame* was on passage to London from Trinidad and met the *Erik Rickmers* on 25 October, 1899, and the two ships sailed together until they became separated in fog. Later that night the *Parame* became trapped among rocks, which was where local boats found her the next morning; she was afloat but on her beam ends, her cargo of coconuts and rum spilling out of her holds. Captain Jeanno, his crew of ten and all their belongings were saved and landed on Bryher. The barque sank in 8m, and little or no salvage work was carried out. Today the *Parame*'s riveted plates lie just 65ft south-west of the *Eric Rickmers*.

61 Minnehaha   49.57.20N; 06.22.40W. The *Minnehaha* was a 13,443-ton liner of the Atlantic Transport Company, which went ashore in fog at 12.50am on 18 April, 1910. She was sailing from New York to Tilbury Docks, carrying 171 crew,

A diver hovers at 30m depth over the wreck of the SS Brinkburn (Site 55), its huge engine block and cylinders standing silhouetted in the background.

61 passengers, general cargo and 243 live steers. Captain Leyland thought his ship was 6 miles south of the Bishop Rock, when she slid gently ashore on to the rocks at 6 knots. Tugs were requested to help refloat her, but in the meantime the crew were dropping her cargo into the sea.

The cargo included new Ford V8 motor cars, grand pianos, sewing machines, brass-fronted cash tills, crated machinery, carpets and steers, 200 of which were roped to gigs and landed safely on Bryher. The ship was successfully refloated on 11 May when, escorted by three tugs and four salvage vessels, she made Falmouth under her own steam. Many hundreds of interesting relics have been found over the years, but you will need to hunt deep among the rock crevices.

62 Sussex 49.56.32N; 06.23.13W. This 2,795-ton steamship, registered at London, on passage from Baltimore, Maryland, to London carrying a general cargo and cattle, was expecting to pass some 20 miles south of the Isles of Scilly, but unfortunately her master's dead reckoning was inaccurate, and at 2am on 17 December, 1885, she struck Seal Rock, off Maiden Bower, in fog. A boat from Bryher went out to her, its occupants informing Captain Robert Robinson of his position and offering to lead the ship's lifeboats to safety. The *Sussex* broke up on 5 January, 1886, but not before 302 bags of flour, 60 cases of canned goods, 12 pails of lard and 2 bales of leather were landed; of the 250 head of cattle on deck, only 24 were saved after being landed on Gweal.

The wreck lies about 150ft to the west of Seal Rock in 5 to 13m. Occasional brass portholes can still be found, but even in these shallow depths the tide can be fierce, and it is recommended you visit the site only at low water slack tide.

An animated model of the Colossus (Site 68), built for the Charlestown Shipwreck Centre by Richard Larn, shown here in its display case.

63   Delaware   49.56.17N; 06.23.02W. The *Delaware* was a Liverpool-registered 3,243-ton steamship, which has become part of local history, as the rescue of her Chief Officer and Third Mate, the only survivors of 44 crew, was considered the bravest of the many lifesaving incidents around Scilly. Early on 20 December, 1871, Bryher pilots sighted a large steamship in distress, battling against a severe north-westerly gale, which was pushing the vessel towards Mincarlo and Tearing Ledge. On board, her shaft bearings began to overheat and the engine had to be stopped for 20 minutes. The cargo in the third hold shifted and the steamship took on a severe list. A huge wave washed away the ship's entire bridge structure, then successive seas caused her to fill and she sank. Watchers on Bryher immediately prepared the pilot gig *Albion* for sea and rowed through mountainous seas towards White Island. They found First Officer McWhinnie and Third Officer Jenkins and then searched the island, fruitlessly, for other survivors.

The wreck is easily found in a general depth of 11 to 28m on a sloping shelf of rock covered in marine life. Her engine and boiler stand proud of her flattened plates; this is a pleasant dive at a comfortable depth with minimal tide.

64   Empire   The *Empire* was a wooden paddle steamer, registered at London, on passage from Greenock to Bordeaux carrying coal, when she struck Peaked Rock on 26 November, 1860 during a severe gale. A number of Bryher and St Agnes boats went to her assistance, including the 30-ton *AZ* and the 25-ton *Gem* pilot

Below: A 28pdr iron cannon ball, with attached concretions and a copper barrel hoop, from the Colossus site on Southward Well, south of Samson (Site 68).

Foot: A lead gun apron, designed to be secured by cord lashings over the touch-hole of a cannon to keep out water, a sounding lead, pulley sheaves and other small artefacts from the wreck site of the Colossus.

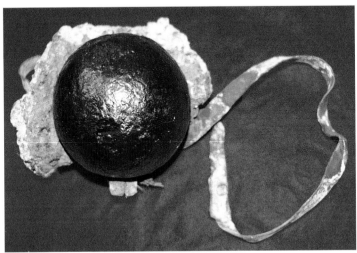

A view of Bryher from the moorings on Tresco.

cutters, but found the wreck with her lifeboats already in the water, the vessel sinking shortly after in 18 to 20m. The exact location of the *Empire* remains uncertain and it is generally accepted that this wreck has probably never been found, but it is possible that she floated awash towards St Agnes and is the unidentified site near Old Wreck buoy (Site 29).

65   Shipman Head   49.57.58N; 06.21.30W. The northernmost point of the island of Bryher consists of a large, rocky headland, rising some 18 to 24m out of the sea. It offers many interesting gullies, caves and inlets to explore. This was once the site of an ancient cliff-top castle and there may be Bronze or Iron Age implements lying in the shallows. The area is shallow and heavily weeded in summer, subject to a tidal stream of up to 1¼ knots. There are remains of wreck on the south-west side.

66   Southward Well   49.55.20N; 06.20.48W. Southward Well is a large, rocky area south of the island of Samson. It extends almost from Southward Well Point east to Tar Barrel Rock, and holds two particularly interesting shipwreck sites, both well known historically. The area can be subject to tide of up to 1½ knots, particularly on a spring ebb, but does not present any real hazard on the flood.

67   Little Western   49.55.00N; 06.21.00W. Built in 1858 at Renfrew, this small cargo passenger ship was used by the West Cornwall Steamship Company as a ferry between St Mary's and Penzance. Captain Francis Hicks and his crew of six had completed the passage from Penzance to St Mary's on 6 October, 1872, when at 3pm they were informed that the French brigantine *Jane* was in trouble 7 miles south-west of the Bishop Rock. Presumably having expectations of a lucrative salvage award should they be able to tow her to safety, the *Little Western* left St Mary's at 5.30pm with her full crew, a clerk from the company office and a boatman. On reaching the *Jane* they found two pilot-cutters already in attendance, and were told that their services were not required. They turned back, going close in around St Agnes to miss the tide, then up towards St Mary's Road where, in the dark, the weather fine and clear, the *Little Western* drove ashore on the rocks. Lighters and a tug were sent out from Penzance in an attempt to refloat the ship, but they failed and she became a total loss during December gales.

The ground seas on Southward Well have completely demolished the wreck's iron hull, but a great many small brass and copper items remain wedged between rocks, or part buried in the shallow, sandy bottom. As the area makes an interesting dive, and is intermingled with the wreck of the *Colossus*, it is well worth a long swim among the boulders and beneath the kelp fronds.

68 Colossus 49.55.15N; 06.20.55W. This 1,703-ton British 3rd rate man-of-war, armed with 74 cannon and carronades, was homeward bound from the Mediterranean and Lisbon for Portsmouth when bad weather forced her to seek the shelter of St Mary's Road on 10 December, 1798. On board were Captain George Murray, a crew of some 500, the body of Admiral Lord Shuldham encased in a lead coffin disguised as a large wooden crate, and Sir William Hamilton's second collection of ancient Etruscan and Greek pottery. The reason for the concealment of the Admiral's body was an incurable superstition among sailors that carrying a corpse on board would bring bad luck – which unfortunately proved all too true.

After anchoring in the Roads, the man-of-war slowly dragged her anchors across the sandy bottom, the watch on deck being sent aloft to strike her topmasts to reduce the windage, but at 4pm her main bower cable parted. She continued to drag in the dark until 8pm when she struck Southward Well, fell over on her beam ends, broke in two and quickly became a total wreck. At first light, local boats put out from all the islands and her crew were taken off, with only one casualty. Later, the Admiral's coffin was recovered, along with most of the ship's stores, spars, rigging and sails, and a small part of Hamilton's cargo.

The *Colossus* is a protected wreck site. Rare wooden carvings have been uncovered, including a 3m neoclassical warrior, part of the ship's port-quarter stern decoration. During September 2001 the Advisory Diving Unit from St Andrew's University spent several weeks on site in order to establish the size and importance of the find, now considered of international importance. In 2002 the figure was lifted at the expense and effort of Mac Mace, a Bryher commercial diver, and it is now in a freshwater holding tank on Tresco, awaiting decisions about ownership, conservation and eventual display to the public. Four 32-pounder iron cannon were also uncovered, still protruding through their original gunports, low down on her port side.

Many interesting items have been found on this site and recent finds by local divers are on display in St Mary's Museum. When conservation treatment is completed it will include the wooden bed of a 32-pounder gun carriage into which has been deeply carved the name *Colossus* and a serial number. Examples of pottery and other relics from the wreck can also be seen in the Charlestown Shipwreck Centre, including an animated model of the wreck, built by Richard Larn. The main collection of pottery shards is held by the British Museum. Many iron guns have been recovered over the years, some now serving as bollards on the quay.

AREA 5:

Tresco, St Helen's, Round Island and Tean

Tresco, the second largest island in the Scillies, is leased from the Duchy of Cornwall and run as a private estate. Passenger helicopters land there, and it is possible to fly direct to or from Penzance. The Valhalla Collection on the island includes many fascinating relics from shipwrecks, mostly wooden figureheads from vessels lost around the islands or found floating at sea, as well as ship-name and trailboards and other ornamental examples of ship carving. There is also a bronze 28-pounder cannon of French origin, with the word Vigo engraved on its breech, a relic captured by Sir Clowdisley Shovell at the battle of Vigo Bay, recovered from near the *Association*.

The area covered by this section holds a number of interesting shallow dive sites, but only two shipwrecks of any importance or size, although reference will be made to other vessels yet to be found.

69   Tresco Channel   Turning south past Shipman Head takes you into Tresco Channel, a narrow waterway 1½ miles long, the northern end of which is an anchorage used by medium-sized boats and visiting yachts. It has a very rough, rocky bottom, with a minimum depth of 7m opposite Hangman Island, from where it becomes very shallow, drying out completely at low spring tides. Even using an inflatable craft, great care is necessary when passing through Tresco Sound and over Tresco Flats at low water. Tresco Channel is so sheltered that it makes an ideal place for a live-aboard diving vessel to anchor overnight and has the advantage that you can land either at Bryher quay or New Grimsby harbour on Tresco.

On the eastern side of Tresco Channel, a short walk from the end of New Grimsby quay, is the New Inn, a popular public house and restaurant and a little

Opposite: A diver examines a winch drum on the deck of the wreck of the SS Mando. This is a shallow dive, and always interesting to explore (Site 71).

further up the hill a general store and post office. A feature of the shallows of Tresco Sound is the remarkable quantity and range of pottery shards to be found lying in the sand, which can be gathered snorkelling, or simply by waiting for low water and beachcombing.

70   Poleire   49.58.05N; 06.21.05W. Built as the MV *Marius Nielsen*, this 1,599-ton, 280ft motor vessel went ashore on Little Kettle Rock at the entrance to Tresco Channel in dense fog on 15 April, 1970, under its new name. Commanded by Captain Coulouris Gerasimos, with a crew of 15, she was carrying a cargo of zinc concentrate from Foynes to Gdynia. The boat struck the rocks off Gimble Point, and sent out a radio distress signal giving her position as near the Bishop Rock. The St Mary's lifeboat was launched at 4.43am, but wasted much time searching the wrong area, and it was 6.35am before the wreck was located. In the meantime, the motor launch *Faldore* of Bryher, having heard the *Poleire*'s siren, found the wreck and took off all the crew. By 3 August the *Poleire* was abandoned by the owners as a total loss. Gales have reduced her to a heap of scrap steel, but she still makes an excellent-shallow water dive.

Dive sites in Area 5: Tresco, St Helen's, Round Island and Tean.

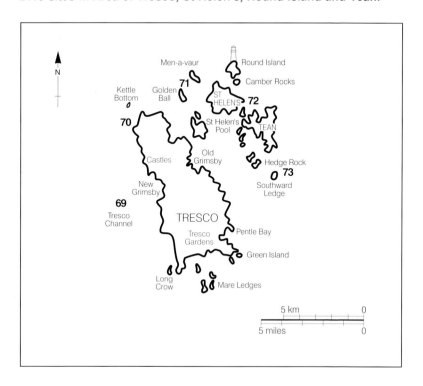

Above: Divers exploring the wreck of the MV Poleire, shortly after it sank in April 1970 on Kettle Rock, at the northern end of Tresco Channel (Site 70).

Right: The builders' name plate of the Poleire was recovered in May 1970.

71   Mando   49.58.27N; 06.20.15W. This 7,176-ton steamer was built as the American Liberty ship *Stepas Darius* and launched in October 1944. In 1947 she was sold out of service and on 21 January, 1955, was under the Panamanian flag carrying 9,000 tons of coal from Hampton Roads to Rotterdam when, some 120 miles west of Scilly, she suffered engine failure. She continued to drift towards the islands as frantic efforts were made to repair her machinery. When less than half a mile offshore from the Men-a-vaur Rocks, she was sighted by the Round Island lighthouse keepers who called out the St Mary's lifeboat, which took the survivors to safety. The *Mando*'s remains have long since been flattened by the sea, but

The Panamanian Liberty ship Mando (Site 71) was wrecked on Golden Ball Bar on 21 January, 1955 carrying a cargo of coal.

nevertheless there are always interesting areas to explore and items to find. The location is very exposed; it is a popular 10m shallow dive when the wind is in the south or south-east, and is unaffected by tide. You can swim the length of the wreck's propeller shaft and tunnel down to 30m.

72 Round Island, St Helen's, Tean and the Northern Rocks Round Island marks the northern extremity of the Isles of Scilly and holds one of the islands' three lighthouses. It rises steeply out of 15 to 30m, and has a number of ledges on the north face that fall away into some 73m. Built to extend the coverage of the Bishop Rock and Peninnis Head lighthouses, particularly in fog, Round Island lighthouse was erected at the same time as the Bishop lighthouse was increased in height, the work being completed in 1887. Diving around the island is an interesting experience, as the steep slope dropping off into deep water is littered with discarded items thrown into the sea by keepers for over a century. Access to the island can be gained using the steep set of steps cut into the rock on the south-east corner; the lighthouse, now automated and outbuildings will be locked, but this is an interesting area to explore, with terrific photo opportunities, especially around dawn and sunset.

Above: Tresco Channel (Site 69), looking north from New Grimsby Quay.

Below: The harbour and slipway at New Grimsby.

Early sailing ships used St Helen's Pool as an anchorage. Although the sea around this uninhabited island and Tean is very shallow, with large areas of sandy bottom and literally dozens of rock outcrops, it is interesting shallow snorkelling ground, with a proliferation of marine life and fish. Pottery finds indicate that the island was occupied from the 1st to 4th centuries AD, and three 2nd-century Roman coins as well as a bronze brooch and scraps of samian ware have been found here.

73   Annie F. Conlon   49.57.35N; 06.18.24W. This American three-masted schooner, carrying a cargo of lubricating oil, was attacked by a German submarine that fired several shells into her and then made off. Although badly disabled, the 591-ton vessel remained afloat and was towed into Crow Sound by a tug, where she fell over on her beam ends on 3 October, 1917. Partially emptied of her cargo, she was moved from near Guther's Island and beached about 100yds north-west of Broad Ledge, 400m south-west of the south-east end of Tean Island. Occasionally her timbers are uncovered by sand movement, but little else remains.

AREA 6:

St Martin's and
the Eastern Isles

This area covers the inhabited island of St Martin's, the small offshore White Island, and the series of rocks that make up the Eastern Isles. St Martin's is L-shaped, 1.7 miles from east to west and 0.6 miles at its widest point. There is a resident population of about 60, living in Higher, Middle or Lower Towns. The largest of these is Higher Town, only a short distance from the all-weather landing point at New Quay. There is another landing place at Lower Town, which is private: ask permission at the hotel before using it. There are a number of white sandy beaches, particularly Par Beach at Higher Town Bay. The coastal path round the island offers a full day's walk with opportunities of sighting rare seabirds, seals basking on the rocks, many antiquities and spectacular scenery.

75 Deep Ledge and Tide Rock 49.58.52N; 06.18.43W. East of Round Island, the Deep Ledge lies slightly further seaward than Tide Rock, the latter drying some 2.4m at low tide. They are a good marker for this spectacular dive site, offering a steep drop-off down to 73m. There is a considerable tidal flow over the ledges of up to 3 knots, so take great care when diving – SMBs are essential. White Island lies further east and can be reached on foot from Pernagie Point on St Martin's at low water only; you are warned that many visitors have been stranded on the island when cut off by the fast incoming tide.

76 Aksai 49.58.50N; 06.17.22W. The wreck of the Russian steamer *Aksai* lies next to Baker Rock. The ship went ashore in fog on 2 November, 1875, while carrying a cargo of coal from Cardiff to Odessa. The local packet steamer went to her assistance and took off Captain Boltine and his crew of 39, landing them at St Mary's. That same day the wreck took a heavy list to starboard and commenced to break up. The wreck lies with her bow to the south, her stern in 21m.

77 Tobasco and St Martin's Bay 49.58.37N; 06.17.15W. Only a short distance from the wreck of the *Aksai* are the remains of the 215-ton French barquentine

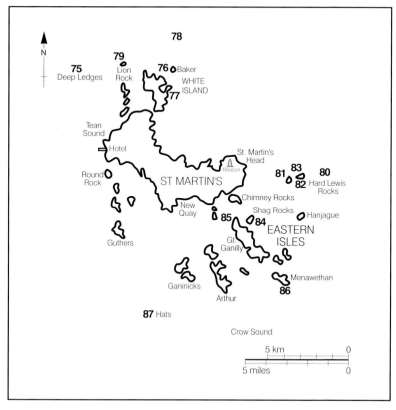

Dive Sites in Area 6: St Martin's and the Eastern Isles.

Tobasco, which went ashore shortly after midnight on 24 March, 1879. A new vessel, she carried a cargo of coal and bottled beer on passage from Greenock to Bordeaux, under Captain Jean Jules Dusson, and with a crew of eight. She was less than ¾ mile offshore when the lookout saw waves breaking on the rocks; despite attempts to steer clear, she struck heavily. Some of the crew took to her boat; the remainder clambered ashore over the rocks. The master later admitted that he had mistaken the Seven Stones light for that of Trevose Head, and when they struck White Island thought he was still near Land's End!

The wide sweep of St Martin's Bay and the north coast of the island from Pernagie Point to St Martin's Head offer very safe and sheltered diving in any conditions other than north or north-easterly winds. There are numerous rocks and ledges worth exploring and several unrecorded wrecks. In 1790 the sailing vessel *Elizabeth* of London, carrying salt from Alicante, was seen offshore with her mainmast and rigging overboard and trailing astern; it is said that she drifted right around the Scillies three times before going ashore on St Martin's. On 19 January,

1830, the 121-ton London brig *Hope* mistook the St Martin's daymark for the St Agnes lighthouse in fog and struck a rock on the north side of the island somewhere in the Bay. Two boats got away from this wreck, but all in the first boat were killed or drowned when the brig's mainmast collapsed across them before they could get clear of the wreck. The other boat managed to reach the shore safely. Of the cargo, 175 casks of palm oil, 450 elephants' tusks, 1,000 silver dollars, seven boxes of gold dust weighing 9,355gm each and some pepper was recovered. What percentage of the entire cargo this represented is unknown, but ivory survives well in salt water and if any tusks were left in the wreck some – probably worm-eaten by now – may remain trapped among rocks.

78   Embiricos   56.59N; 06.16.50W. This is a deep-water wreck off White Island, which can only be reached using mixed gas as it lies in 70m. The *Embiricos* was an Andros-registered 1,946-ton Greek steamship, which in fog and heavy rain struck either Deep Ledge or John Thomas Ledge at 4.30am on 6 February, 1892. Captain Lukisias and his crew of 22 attempted to get the vessel afloat again using her engine, but without success. Fifteen of the crew got into the starboard boat and landed on St Martin's. Less than 15 minutes after they had left the ship, her masthead light disappeared as she slipped off into deep water and sank. Later, another four members of the crew were picked up and it was deduced that only three crew and three passengers had been lost. Other wrecks in the vicinity include the Dutch schooner *Alida*, of Veendam, sailing from Swansea to Tarragona with patent fuel, lost off White Island while attempting to reach St Mary's with a bad leak.

79   Palinurus   49.58.55N; 06.18.04W. The first indication that the islanders of St Martin's had of this wreck was the bellowing of frightened cattle in the fields, the noise made by the wind in her torn sails alarming the animals on 27 December, 1848. Captain Gorl and a crew of 17, sailing from Demerara to London with a general cargo consisting mostly of spirits, had gone ashore near Lion Rock in a north-easterly gale. There were no survivors.

80   Hard Lewis Rocks   49.57.53N; 06.14.40W. Three-quarters of a mile east of St Martin's Head lies a series of rocks, which rise from 55 to 64m and dry at 3.7m

The new quay on St Martin's, with St Martin's Hotel in the background.

at low spring tides. They offer spectacular diving in a range of depths. There are three wrecks on Hard Lewis, two of which are quite easy to find, but the sailing vessel *Juno* (see below) is more difficult, lying off to the west in 17 to 21m.

81   Juno   49.57.55N; 06.14.53W. This is the first of two ships that foundered after going ashore in early January 1797. The 330-ton *Juno* was a wooden barque, built in London in 1782, on passage with a general cargo from London to Africa and the West Indies, presumably on the recognised "slave trade triangle". The wreck was found by accident when Steve Burrows of St Mary's came across the site in 1970. A diving expedition surveyed the area in December that year, locating five anchors, six iron cannon, and assorted iron and lead round shot; many items were recovered, most of which are now on permanent display in the Charlestown Shipwreck Centre, Cornwall.

The *Albion* was a 104-ton brig, built at Yarmouth, which had carried a crew of ten when she disappeared off Scilly on the same night as the *Juno*. Exactly where she went down is not known.

82   Gilmore   49.57.53N; 06.14.32W. This 535-ton wooden barque, sailing from Southampton to Quebec in ballast under Captain Duff, with a crew of 18, struck the rocks, filled and went down by the stern in less than five minutes on 12 April, 1866.

83   King Cadwallon   48.57.56N; 06.14.32W. This is the only steamship wreck on the Hard Lewis Rocks. After leaving Barry Docks for Naples, with 5,032 tons of coal, Captain George Mowat and his crew of 26 were plagued with fog all the way through the Bristol Channel; by the time they were in the vicinity of the Scillies, they were lost. The *King Cadwallon* went ashore just clear of the highest point of the Hard Lewis, at 5am on 22 July, 1906. The crew took to the boats, leaving the wreck to settle close to the remains of the *Gilmore*. The shattered remains of the ship can be found in 19 to 40m, her stern and very prominent steering quadrant covered in jewel anemones.

84   Gomes V   49.57.20N; 06.15.10W. The remains of a Portuguese steamship can be found on the north-east side of Shag Rocks, close to Irishman's Ledge.

These items were all recovered from the wreck site of the Juno (Site 80). The photograph shows a galley hearth brick, pulley sheaf, sounding lead, and three triangular pan weights

Above: The only Russian steamship lost in the Isles of Scilly, the Aksai was wrecked on White Island, at the back of St Martins on 2 November, 1875 (Site 76).

Below: The coal-laden SS King Cadwallon, of Glasgow, wrecked on Hard Lewis in the Eastern Isles on 22 July, 1906 (Site 83).

Built in 1882 at Grangemouth as the SS *Strathcarrow*, she was carrying 629 tons of coal from Cardiff to Oporto when she got among the Eastern Isles in fog, sinking to the east of Great Ganilly. In 1888 divers working for the Western Marine Salvage Company recovered steam winches, anchors and cable and deck fittings. The Dundee Salvage Company was initially contracted to save the vessel, but their survey found her bottom plates extensively damaged. Now most of the wreck lies buried in sand, in a general depth of 6 to 12m.

The prominent St Martin's Head daymark, sited 56m above sea level, stands alongside the now derelict signal station building, which was in use up until the late 19th century.

85   Earl of Arran   49.57.18N; 06.15.48W. Nornour holds the remains of a packet paddle steamer, once part of the important lifeline between the Isles of Scilly and Penzance, lost on 16 July, 1872. The *Earl of Arran* had left Penzance on her normal run at 10am for St Mary's, carrying eight crew, 100 passengers, mail and general cargo. On reaching the islands, Captain Richard Deason was concerned that they might miss the tide over Crow Bar, which would either delay their arrival or force them to go round St Mary's to get into the Sound. On board the packet was Stephen Woodcock, a Scillonian-hobbler-cum-local pilot, who said he knew a short cut between the islands, which would save 20 minutes. The captain allowed Woodcock to take charge of the vessel, but she struck Irishman's Ledge and began to fill, then ran ashore on the north-west side of Nornour. By mid-afternoon all the passengers, luggage and stores had been saved and two days later the wreck broke in two, the owners receiving only £1,000 compensation from the insurers owing to the manner in which she had been lost.

The ship's complete engine was salvaged by the Western Marine Company of Penzance, but her boiler still shows at low water, and there are bottom plates scattered in the shallows. A Board of Trade inquiry found the *Earl of Arran*'s captain guilty of neglect by allowing a passenger to take charge of his ship, hence causing its loss, and his certificate was suspended for four months.

86   Menawethan and HM Forester   49.56.37N; 06.14.42W and 49.57.18N; 06.16.57W. On the southern side of Menawethan, just to the north of Crow Sound approach, a single iron cannon lies in less than 6m. When found in 1968 it was thought to be one of the guns thrown overboard by the 6th rate man-of-war *Forester*. Research has since revealed that this 229-ton warship, built at Chatham Dockyard in 1832, was outward bound from Plymouth to Africa when she put into the Isles of Scilly on 12 February, 1833. A west-south-westerly gale got up causing both anchor cables to part and the ship drifted onto Cruther's Point, St Martin's, where her foremast was cut away, which brought down part of her mainmast. The ship's stores were landed on St Martin's, and her crew threw ten guns overboard, enabling her to be kedged off next day. On 30 February the wreck was towed away to Plymouth and returned to service following repair. In all the accounts of the *Forester*'s stranding, there is no mention of her guns being recovered – presumably they still remain on the sea bed.

87   Setiembre   49.56.19N; 06.16.56W. In Crow Sound, less than 440yds north-east of the Channel buoy, off Innisidgen Island, lies a ship's boiler, which partially dries and is a reminder of the Spanish steamer *Setiembre*, which went aground on 26 March, 1911. Registered at Bilbao, and on passage from Porman to Maryport with a cargo of iron ore, she carried a crew of 24. Having struck the Hats, serious hull damage caused her to flood and she was abandoned as a total wreck and sold for £95.

Also in Crow Sound, north-east of Tolls Island at 49.56.06N; 06.16.33W, lie the remains of the French chassemarée *St Vincent*, which sank on 6 December, 1839, while carrying barley. Her wooden hull often shows above the sand level – her stem, frames and planking around the bow still copper sheathed. Her windlass sits 10ft back, and she makes an excellent second dive in 20 to 25m.

AREA 7:

The Seven Stones

The Seven Stones lie approximately 7 miles north-west of St Martin's Head and 16 miles from Land's End, occupying about ¾ square mile. They are marked by an automatic lightship, which lies 2 miles to the west. The rocks can protrude above the surface at low spring tides and the Pollard Rock and Flat Ledge break at most states of low tide, from around 50m. The sea area between the lightship and the mainland is a very busy shipping channel divided into two lanes with vessels travelling north nearest to Land's End, and those going south keeping close to the lightship; there is a separation zone between them of 2 miles. This is an area for experienced divers only. You will be rewarded by the underwater terrain and spectacular scenery, with a wide range of depths, marine life and excellent underwater visibility.

WARNING Great care is needed if you make your way to the Seven Stones from Whitesand Bay, near Land's End, as this journey entails crossing two shipping channels, and small craft and inflatables are likely to be out of sight of land for some time before reaching the lightship area. There is considerable tide over the Seven Stones, particularly on the ebb, and much caution is required, especially if surface visibility decreases.

Until 1967 the Seven Stones Reef enjoyed a quiet notoriety among seafarers, as hardly any divers visited the area, and it was only the loss of the super-tanker *Torrey Canyon* on 18 March, 1967, that brought the area to the attention of the general public.

Fourteen known steam or motor vessels have been lost on the reef, and a further eight or nine close to it but in deep water; the wrecks of some 50 sailing ships are recorded as having been lost here.

Opposite: Broken into three pieces by the action of the sea, the bombed and burnt-out hull of the tanker Torrey Canyon *lies abandoned as a total constructive loss in early April 1967 on the Seven Stones Reef (Site 88). She was the largest and most damaging shipwreck in terms of oil pollution ever to happen in British waters.*

88   Torrey Canyon   50.02.30N; 06.07.45W. At the time of her loss the *Torrey Canyon* was one of the largest tankers in the world, carrying 119,328 tons of crude oil when, north-bound from the Persian Gulf to Milford Haven, she hit the Pollard Rock in broad daylight and good visibility at 8.50am on 18 March 1967. Built in 1959 by the Newport News Shipbuilding and Dry-dock Company, USA, the 974ft, 61,236 ton tanker carried a crew of 36 under Captain Pastrengo Rugiati, and was fitted with two steam turbines driving a huge bronze propeller. The Seven Stones lightship No. 19 was still manned in 1967, and her crew fired rockets and repeatedly flashed her warning signals. A nearby fishing trawler informed Land's End radio of the accident and the *Torrey Canyon* transmitted a Mayday distress call. The St Mary's lifeboat was launched, two SAR helicopters took off from RNAS Culdrose on the Lizard, and several ships in the area closed in on the casualty.

The *Torrey Canyon* had impaled herself on the largest of the Seven Stones, tearing a 610ft-long gash in her starboard-side hull plating. Eight and a half days later, having survived three attempts to refloat her, two gales and an internal explosion, the tanker broke into three pieces, spewing out her remaining cargo of dark brown oil. This created an oil slick measuring 18 by 2 miles, which eventually came ashore on the south coast of Cornwall, creating the worst oil spill contamination ever experienced in the British Isles. The slick continued to expand until it measured 30 by 8 miles, and the stench of oil was evident as far inland as Truro, almost 30 miles away.

With the three broken sections of the wreck still holding almost a third of the tanker's original cargo, the government took the decision to set her on fire and burn off as much of the oil as possible.,She burned for two whole days, leaving a tangle of steel with very little showing above water. In 1982 her entire forepart, still intact, was refloated and converted into an oil storage barge, and two blades of her huge propeller were removed by divers using explosives, one blade being accidentally lost off Padstow.

Dive sites in Area 7: The Seven Stones.

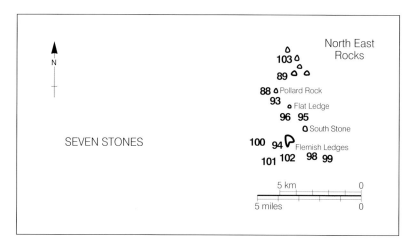

*Rations from one of the Torrey Canyon's lifeboats, which
washed ashore on the Isles of Scilly.*

The wreck lies spread out over a vast area in depths ranging from 14 to 27m and there are countless steel plates and frames scattered across the sea bed overgrown with weed; it is impossible to explore the entire wreck in a week of diving.

89 Three warships and two barques Location not known. The earliest recorded wreck on the Seven Stones was the *Primrose*, a 6th rate, 22-gun, English man-of-war, which was operating with the *Mayflower* in a search for two Spanish frigates cruising in the area in March 1656. The *Mayflower* lost her main topmast in heavy weather and, while Captain Sherwin of the *Primrose* was on board the *Mayflower* making arrangements to provide Captain Brown with a spare mast and spars, the master of the *Primrose*, through inattention, allowed the vessel to drift ashore on the reef. Although refloated, she was leaking badly and eventually sank in 109m, drowning 19 people.

Another early wreck here was the man-of-war *Revenge*, lost on 30 November, 1674, with only two survivors out of a crew of 17, followed almost a 100 years later by the 14-gun, 272-ton sloop *Lizard*. Built at Bursledon on the River Hamble in 1744, she went down with the loss of Captain Siffon and over 100 men on 27 February, 1748. The three warships between them carried some 66 cannon, and some or all of these probably survive somewhere on the Seven Stones Reef.

The first of several barques lost here was the *America*, of St John's, New Brunswick, lost in fog on 2 February, 1854. She carried a cargo of guano, or bird droppings, a common fertiliser. She was followed six years later by the Sunderland-registered wooden barque *Punjab*, which was carrying 300 tons of wool and hides from Algoa Bay to Amsterdam when she struck the reef on 14 September, 1860. Six years later, on 25 April, 1866, another Sunderland barque, the *Cibana* was lost. Although the wreck has never been identified, carrying a cargo of coal, iron and mining gear, she should be an easy target for location by magnetometer.

90 Nelson   Location not known. A 549-ton barque, registered at North Shields, with a cargo of lead and iron ore from Aguilas to the Tyne, the *Nelson* should also present a large target for a magnetometer search, although her hull was timber. Built in 1844, she struck the South Stone of the reef in dense fog on 7 October, 1870. She sank within 15 minutes, taking with her three men. The survivors managed to reach the nearby light-vessel in their own boat before they were taken off by a pilot boat and landed at Penzance. A nameboard from the wreck was washed ashore as far away as Bude.

91 Primos   Location not known. Registered at Bilbao, this Spanish barque was on passage from Havana to Greenock with a cargo of sugar. She was at anchor in Falmouth for 20 days awaiting instructions about discharge, then left on 22 June, her master having refused to take on board a pilot. In thick weather, the barque ran ashore at 7 knots when she struck the South Stone of the reef on 24 June, 1871.

The hull of the 6,369-ton general cargo motor ship Fantee, abandoned and with a broken back lies submerged on the Seven Stones on 6 October, 1949 (Site 101). Part of her cargo consisted of hardwood logs, which were later recovered by divers, towed to St Mary's and landed at Porth Mellon.

The crew of eleven launched the longboat but it was allowed to drift away, its painter not having been made fast. The only other boat was the captain's gig, but it capsized after 10 minutes. The only survivor managed to stay afloat by clinging first to a floating hen-coop for over an hour, and then to the ship's figurehead, which kept him afloat for several more hours until picked up by a pilot-gig from St Martin's. The figurehead is now in the Valhalla collection on the island of Tresco.

92   Rydall Hall   Location not known. The *Rydall Hall* was one of many full-rigged ships lost in deeper water around the reef. She was carrying a general cargo on her maiden voyage from Liverpool to San Francisco and was taken in tow by the packet vessel SS *Queen of the Bay*, but she got too close to the reef on 20 April, 1874, and struck an outlying rock.

93   Barreman   50.02.20N; 06.00.48W. The remains of this 1,452-ton, iron, full-rigged ship of Glasgow, which was carrying coke, bricks and general cargo from the Tyne to San Francisco, are now believed to lie buried beneath the wreck of the *Torrey Canyon*, as she too struck the Pollard Rock and foundered in fog and heavy seas on 9 July, 1887. The wreck was not discovered until two days later when fishermen saw a large mast sticking up out of the sea. The *Barreman* was identified by a piece of canvas attached to a yard, which was clearly marked with the name of a Greenock sailmaker and the year 1884. A nameboard, a white painted boat and other wreckage were later found ashore in Mounts Bay.

94   Brighouse   50.01.14N; 06.07.45W. Built as the *Wyvern* by Palmers and Co Ltd in 1864, the 952-ton *Brighouse* was fitted with a two-cylinder compound engine, a single boiler and screw. This was the first steamship wreck on the Seven Stones, which struck in dense fog on 12 December, 1887, and foundered. She was carrying a cargo of pit-props from Bordeaux to Cardiff when she went down. Captain Tregurtha and his 15 crew were saved, reaching the lightship in two boats.

95   Chiswick   50.02.15N; 06.07.27W. On passage from Cardiff to St Nazaire, this London-registered steamer, built in 1871 at Newcastle-upon-Tyne by C. Mitchell, Low Walker and Company, was carrying a cargo of coal when she ran ashore on the Seven Stones in fine weather on 5 February, 1891. It was high tide, so all the rocks were covered. Captain Hughes ordered his crew of 19 on deck and had the boats lowered, then put her engine to full astern. She came off the rocks very quickly, backed off into deep water, then settled so quickly by the bow that the captain informed the crew it was "every man for himself". Most of the men rushed below for lifejackets, and were in the accommodation when the steamer lurched to starboard and sank, taking down all the boats except one. Eight survivors clung to this for almost 10 hours, until rescued by the crew of the lightship.

96   Camiola   50.02.12N; 06.07.48W. Having sailed from Barry Docks, this Newcastle-registered 2,262-ton steamer, carrying coal for Malta, ran aground during the night of 1 October, 1892. The officer on watch ordered her engine to be stopped immediately, but the duty engineer failed to respond quickly enough, and she drove further onto the Seven Stones, opening up an already large hole in her hull. Both lifeboats proved difficult to launch and it was with great difficulty that they were got into the water without loss of life among the 24 crew.

97 Heathmore Location not known. On passage from Bilbao to Glasgow with a cargo of iron ore, this Liverpool-registered 1,864-ton steamer, built in 1883, struck the Seven Stones Reef on 5 July, 1897, in fog. She floated off and foundered at 8pm the same day in deep water, along with her cargo of iron ore. As far as is known the wreck has never been located.

98 Wendur 50.00.14N; 06.00.45W. The *Wendur* was a four-masted steel barque of Glasgow, which was on passage from Port Pirie to Plymouth and Swansea carrying 2,600 tons of wheat, when she struck the Reef on 12 March, 1912. She sank so quickly that her upper deck was awash before her master could issue a single order.

99 Seapoint Approx. 50.01N; 06.01W. The *Seapoint* was a London-registered 593-ton steamship, built in 1899 by S. McKnight and Company Limited, at Ayr, Scotland; she had a 104hp two-cylinder compound engine and one boiler. On 28 December, 1917, she was carrying a cargo of coal from Newport to Rouen, when she sprang a leak and foundered in heavy weather, possibly as much as 4 miles off to the south-east of the Seven Stones. The crew of 14 were all saved. As far as is known her wreck has not been found.

100 HMS Pincher 50.01.14N; 06.07.45W. One of the more interesting wrecks yet to be found on the Seven Stones was a Basilisk-class destroyer of the Royal Navy, one of 27 such ships completed, built in 1910 by Denny & Company, at Dumbarton, Scotland. Armed with one 4-inch and three 12-pounder guns, she also carried a 2-inch anti-aircraft gun and two 21-inch torpedo tubes. She drove ashore on the Seven Stones in fog on 24 July, 1918, her steam turbines driving her at full speed – about 24 knots. Her crew of 96 escaped in their own boats or on liferafts

A builder's name plate found attached to the wreck of the Romanian fish factory ship MV Rarau (Site 103) is dated 1955, but as the ship was built at Gdansk, Poland in 1972 this plate is something of a mystery.

A recent wreck on the Seven Stones was the Romanian fish factory-ship MV Rarau, which went ashore in fog on 29 September, 1976 (Site 103). She carried a crew of 84.

and, despite several magnetometer searches of the reef in recent years, her wreck has yet to be found. It is believed to lie off to the west in deeper water.

101   Fantee   50.01.14N; 06.07.45W. Built as the *Penrith Castle* in 1929, by Cammell-Laird Company Ltd at Birkenhead, Liverpool, on 6 October, 1949 this 6,369-ton general cargo motor ship was on passage from Matadi and Amsterdam to Liverpool, carrying a cargo consisting of palm kernels, palm oil, cocoa, rubber, cotton, coffee beans, copra and mahogany logs and other exotic hardwoods. The ship drove ashore in fog and subsequently broke her back. The crew of 53 was rescued.

Roy Mitchell of St Mary's obtained salvage rights and raised most of the hardwood logs that remained trapped in the wreck or lay on the sea bed in the 1980s. These were towed to St Mary's where they were sawn up. The wreck is very broken with remains of plates and frames jammed among huge rocks in around 40m.

102   Punta   50.02.14N; 06.07.45W. Built as the *Coolana*, this ship's name was changed in 1952 to *Fair-Med*, then *Punta*, when she was finally registered under the Panamian flag. The *Punta* was carrying phosphate rock from Bougie to Portishead when she drove ashore in dense fog on 22 July, 1955. Captain Mathiassos, his wife, the 23 crew, two stowaways and some animals were taken off the wreck by the St Mary's lifeboat, leaving the vessel to break her back three days later and sink in 28m.

103   Rarau   50.02.45N; 06.07.18W. The youngest wreck on the Seven Stones to date was a Romanian 2,681-ton, stern-trawling, fish-factory motor vessel, which went ashore in fog on 29 September, 1976. Registered at Constanza, she had been built at Gdansk in 1972 and was owned by the Romanian Ministry of Industry and Food. She carried a crew of 84. After the wreck, salvors from the Isles of Scilly went on board to save as much electrical and navigational equipment on the bridge as possible, but the captain protested vigorously and initially prevented any equipment from being removed. Then one of the salvors produced a couple of copies of *Playboy* magazine and the Romanians were happy to exchange these for anything on board! The wreck went completely to pieces, and now lies scattered in a general depth of 9 to 25m.

Her bell and builder's nameplate have been recovered, but there is something of a mystery here, since the details on the recovered builder's name plate do not agree with the history of the vessel. The name plate suggests that she was built in Abo, Finland in 1955 but she was in fact constructed in 1972 by Stoczina Gdanska at Gdansk in Poland – so is this a souvenir plate from a previous vessel named *Rarau*?

AREA 8:

Offshore deep water wrecks

The deep water targets included in this section extend up to 30 miles offshore from St Martin's daymark, and generally lie in excess of 50m; hence they can only safely be reached using mixed-gas diving techniques. Deep diving is not currently supported by any Isles of Scilly diving operators, as they are without nitrox or heliox charging facilities, but some mainland dive boat operators have provision for this.

104 Unidentified   49.40.08N; 06.27.36W. An unidentified wreck, possibly a submarine, believed to be 197ft, which lies in a general depth of 102m. It lies orientated east-south-east to west-north-north but appears to stand very little above the sea bed.

105 Unidentified   49.45.16N; 05.59.57W. There is another unidentified, decaying shipwreck lying in 90m, at 213 degrees, 13½ miles from the Wolf Rock. It is about 215ft, orientated south-south-east to north-north west, with a high point amidships. It was investigated by the salvage company Risdon Beazley in 1976.

106 Briardene   49.46.07N; 06.12.15W. The *Briardene* was a 2,701-ton British steamship, registered at Truro, carrying a general cargo from New York to London when she was shelled and captured by the German submarine *UC-19*. Her crew of 27 abandoned ship, after which the enemy vessel placed four explosive scuttling charges below decks, which sent the *Briardene* to the bottom on 1 December, 1916. The wreck lies in a general depth of 92m, orientated north–south, and gives a good magnetometer signal. She appears to have broken in two, the larger portion being some 400ft long.

107 Beechpark   49.47.32N; 06.14.53W. The *Beechpark* was a Newcastle-registered 4,763-ton collier carrying a cargo of coal and coke from the Tyne to Port Said when she was torpedoed and sunk by the German submarine *UC-75* on

2 August, 1917. With a least depth of 77m to the top of the wreck, she lies in a general depth of 90m, orientated north-east to south-west and gives a good electronic signal.

108   Headlands   49.48.28N; 06.33.54W. This wreck lies only about a mile south of the Isles of Scilly in a general depth of 93m, with a least depth of 81m. The 2,988-ton steamship, carrying a cargo of flints and mineral ore, was on passage from Burriana to Bristol and Swansea when on 12 March, 1915, she was torpedoed by the German submarine *U-29*. The steam packet *Lyonnesse* took her in tow and was about a mile south-east of the Bishop Rock when she sank at 8pm. She lies with her bow to the north-east, her stern portion apparently flattened.

109   U-683   49.52N; 06.31W. This Type VIIC German U-boat, commanded by Kapitänleutnant Gunther Keller, was depth-charged by HMS *Wild Goose* and HMS *Loch Ruthven* on 12 March, 1945, and sunk with all 49 crew. As far as is known, this wreck has not been found.

110   U-681   49.52.26N; 06.38.38W. Another Type VIIC German submarine, commanded by Oberleutnant zur See Werner Gebauer, the *U-681* ran aground on the Western Rocks on 11 March, 1945, while trying to enter St Mary's Road to attack a number of vessels at anchor. She suffered considerable damage to her hull and propellers and a fuel tank was ruptured, which caused fuel and oil to pour into her control room to a depth of 1m. She surfaced but was spotted by a US Navy Liberator bomber, which made two attack runs dropping a total of eight depth-charges. The explosions caused even more leaks, and the *U-681* crew were ordered to abandon ship. Eleven of the crew of 38 went down with the vessel. The wreck was found not far from the Bishop Rock in 1999 by divers operating from the diving tender *Mentor*; they confirmed her identity and recovered a rubber dinghy and pair of leather coveralls. The wreck is said to lie in a general depth of 70m, orientated north-east to south-west, the hull intact apart from a large hole in the starboard side.

111   HMS Decoy   49.52.45N; 06.03.00W. The HMS *Decoy* was a 275-ton D-class destroyer, built in 1894, armed with one 12-pounder and three 6-pounder guns and three torpedo tubes. The 185ft ship was lost on 13 August, 1904, following collision with the 550-ton HMS *Arun* west of the Wolf Rock. The wreck of a small warship has been located in this area standing 3m above the sea bed, and a 6-pounder Hotchkiss gun was raised by Risdon Beazley during salvage work in 1976, the manufacturer's plate marked with the year 1893. The wreck lies in a general depth of 77m on a flat sandy sea bed, partially collapsed.

112   U-247   49.53.56N; 05.49.55W. On 1 September, 1944, when some 3 miles from the Wolf Rock, the frigate HMS *St John* obtained a strong underwater contact and attacks were co-ordinated between that vessel, HMS *Swansea* and HMS *Port Colborne*. Depth-charge explosions caused a large quantity of oil to float to the surface, and further depth-charges were dropped directly over the target, which was now clearly visible on her echo sounder. The type VIIC submarine *U-247* was destroyed, with all 52 crew. The wreck was identified by the documents, clothing and equipment that floated to the surface. The remains lie in a general depth of 74m and stand some 6m above the sea bed.

The Bishop Rock lighthouse keepers had a grandstand view of the destruction of the
SS Western Front, after she caught fire offshore while carrying naphtha, resin and
turpentine. Of 5,696-tons and registered at Seattle, by the time the St Mary's lifeboat
had taken off forty of her crew, she had drifted to within seven miles of the Western
Rocks and finally sank on 11 July, 1921 in 110m (Site 118).

113   Mar Cor   49.54.12N; 06.29.19W. A 3,257-ton Italian steamship, registered
at Genoa, was laden with coal from Cardiff to Dakar when she was stopped by the
German submarine *UB-32* on 9 June, 1917. After her crew had abandoned ship,
she was torpedoed and sunk. The wreck lies in a general depth of 82m west of the
Isles of Scilly, orientated north-east to south-west. Sonar traces suggest she is in
two parts.

114   Horsa   49.55.08N; 06.23.18W. This Liverpool-registered 1,163-ton barque
left Bluff Harbour, New Zealand, in December 1892 carrying 1,450 tons of oats,
tinned meat and wool. She was 10 miles off Round Island light on 4 April, 1893,
when she twice missed stays attempting to clear the Hard Lewis Rocks and went
ashore in Bread and Cheese Cove, St Martin's. The SS *Lyonnesse* passed a tow
rope to the wreck and managed to get her out to sea, but she was abandoned 21
miles south-west of the Bishop Rock. Although the wreck has been dived and
identified, her location is a little uncertain; she is believed to lie much closer to the
Bishop Rock.

115   Unidentified   49.55.15N; 06.23.51W. This is believed to be the wreck of a
2,000-ton steamship, fitted with a cast-iron propeller and a triple expansion steam
engine with one boiler. Divers report large quantities of collapsed hull standing
about 3m above a sand and gravel sea bed.

116 HMS Monarch Location not known. This 22,500-ton Dreadnought battleship of the Orion class, built by Armstrong and launched on 30 March, 1911, was scuttled as a target off the Isles of Scilly for underwater detection trials by the Royal Navy on 20 January, 1925. A huge wreck, 545ft long with a beam of 88ft, she carried numerous anti-aircraft guns. This wreck is not a war grave and would be well worth finding.

117 U-480 49.51.47N; 06.06.45W. This Type VIIC German submarine was detected by frigates of the 3rd Escort Group when heading home to Brest and destroyed by depth-charges dropped from HMS *Duckworth* and HMS *Rowley*. Sufficient wreckage floated to the surface to confirm that the submarine had been destroyed, with all 48 crew.

118 Western Front 49.50.00N; 06.45.00W. On 11 July, 1921, this American steamship, registered at Seattle, built in 1917 for the US Shipping Board by Skinner, Eddy Corporation, was sailing from Jackonsville to London with 7,000 tons of naval stores when she caught fire some 20 miles off the Bishop Rock. The St Mary's lifeboat *Elsie* took some hours to reach her and take off 40 of the crew, the SS *British Earl* saved the remainder. By now the wind and tide had taken the burning ship to within 7 miles of the Bishop lighthouse, where she sank.

Sennen Cove

Details of the launch sites and other facilities at Sennen Cove can be found in *Dive South Cornwall*, but updated information about certain restrictions on divers using the area is given here. Sennen Cove makes a good base for exploring the offshore reefs and rocks around Land's End, especially the Longships. It has a wide sweep of flat, shallow sand, with a long beach; at low water large areas of shallow rock are exposed in little more than 6m, which make it ideal for beginners and snorkellers. Sennen Cove has three main car parking areas: at the top of the steep hill that runs down to the sea, at the bottom of the hill, and at the far end of the cove, beyond the lifeboat station. All charge a fee. Facilities in Sennen Cove are very good and there is plenty of accommodation nearby. There are three slipways in the cove, but sport divers are not allowed to use the harbour. If you wish to launch here, use the public slipway adjacent to the car park at the bottom of the hill. You are advised to walk to the Round House just beyond the lifeboat station and ask for permission. The recommended concrete slipway, maintained in good condition, leads to a flat, sandy beach some ¾ mile long; any westerly wind usually causes heavy surf, which can make launching difficult.

It is worth visiting the lifeboat station (tel. 01736 871222), which has eleven service-boards listing the rescues made from the station, during which a total of around 380 lives were saved up to the end of 2002.

Coastal dive sites

There are several wrecks in Whitesand Bay. To the north, on Gwynver Beach, parts of the wreck of the barque *Trifolium* still sometimes show and remains of the SS *Beaumaris* can be found off the end of the restricted slipway at the lifeboat end.

The 4th rate man-of-war, *Colchester*, was lost hereabouts by stranding on 16 January, 1704, while en route from Ireland to Plymouth. A large vessel of 696 tons, she had been built in 1674 at Blackwall, River Thames, and carried 54 cannon, a number of which are thought to have been bronze. She is reported to have been carrying a large amount of silver specie. Captain David Wavell and the crew of 170 were all lost.

Somewhere north of the Longships the Sunderland coaster SS *Arnside*, sailing from Birkenhead to Boston with manure, capsized on 13 February, 1914. The first anyone knew of this wreck was when the Sennen Coastguard noticed a small boat in which there were three men, drifting in heavy seas towards Aire Point. Before any help could be given it capsized and all three men were drowned. Despite much wreckage coming ashore, the location of this vessel is unknown.

119   Trifolium   50.55.25N; 05.41.48W. Five lives were lost when this 519-ton iron barque of Gothenburg, Sweden, built in 1875, was thrown ashore on Gwynver Beach, close to Aire Point on 15 March, 1914. Already 16 days on passage from Cardiff to Brazil with coal, she developed a leak and was forced back to Falmouth for repairs. On sailing, she met with a dreadful gale and again started to leak. During the hours of darkness her captain and mate were washed overboard and drowned.

After being driven ashore at 5.30am, the Sennen Cove lifeboat *Ann Newbon* was launched, but was unable to assist because of the low tide. When at 6.40am they fired a rocket line across the rigging in order to establish a breeches buoy, the crew made no attempt to secure it because of heavy seas breaking over her deck. Four men were saved before the barque went to pieces.

120   Beaumaris   50.04.50N; 05.42.00W. The *Beaumaris* was torpedoed on her starboard side by the German submarine *U-53* on 7 February, 1918. Captain Lawther was knocked unconscious by the explosion, and on recovery found that seven of his crew had already left in the port lifeboat and the remaining 29 crew were in the process of lowering the starboard boat. He ordered the Second Engineer to restart the ship's engine and steered for Whitesand Bay, but some 4 miles offshore the crew announced that the ship was sinking. The captain instructed the crew to leave the ship, so that only he and the wireless operator remained on board. Between them, the men then ran her ashore in the bay, stopped her engine

Dive sites in Area 9: Sennen Cove.

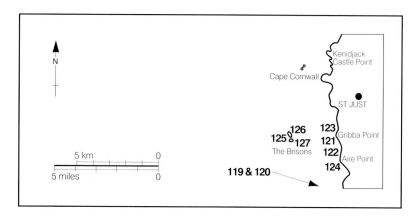

The Royal Navy submarine L-1 at Carn Gloose, south of Cape Cornwall, after going ashore there on 28 March, 1930 (Site 121). She was laid down by Vickers in 1917 as the E-57, and 56 submarines of that class were completed. The L-1 was fitted with two torpedo tubes fore and aft, as well as a 4-inch deck gun forward of the conning tower. Under tow for scrapping at Newport, she broke adrift in a gale and was wrecked. Much of her remains in among the rocks to this day.

and dropped both anchors. The *Beaumaris* broke her back within 24 hours. Salvage has been carried out on the wreck but it is understood much of it still shows in 9m.

The only other access to the coast here is at Cape Cornwall, but as the launching of diving boats is prohibited by the owners it must be considered as a shore dive area. Should you wish to explore the wrecks in the Cape Cornwall, Pendeen Watch and Gurnard's Head area, follow the coast by boat from Sennen Cove or from St Ives harbour. Cape Cornwall has a car park and toilets, but no other facilities. Diving boats may not use the concrete slipway, but this does not prevent shore diving, and it is safe to swim close inshore in either direction. You will find large numbers of rock outcrops and gullies, full of marine life and fish, often with seals basking on the rocks in summer. There is a cliff path leading up to Cape Cornwall and the volunteer Coastguard lookout; the view from Cape Cornwall is spectacular.

121   HM Submarine L-1   50.07.10N; 05.42.08W. Laid down at Vickers Armstrong, Barrow-in-Furness in May 1916 as the *E-57*, the *L-1* was launched after building changes one year later, and at 890 tons and 222ft was considerably larger than the general E-class boats; in addition she carried a 4-inch deck gun, whereas the E-class were fitted only with 12-pounders. On passage from Chatham to Newport, Monmouthshire to be broken up at Cashmore's Yard, the *L-1* broke away from the steam tug *Eastleigh* when off Cape Cornwall during the night of Friday, 28 March, 1930. She drifted ashore inside the Brisons and Inner Greeb Reef, on Penanwell Beach, just below Carn Gloose. The Cape Coastguards reported her ashore, but without crew. When examined three days later she was lying in an exposed position, badly holed and tidal throughout. Lloyd's recommended either her prompt sale or a stripping contract. Limited salvage was carried out after which she was abandoned. Much of the wreck remains, which covers or uncovers as the sand moves.

122   Le Landois   50.06.30N; 05.41.50W. Little remains of this French brig, which went ashore in fog in Penanwell Cove, Carn Gloose on 30 September, 1837, not far south of where the *L-1* lies. However, the story of the wreck is one of the most notorious in Cornwall.

The brig had been intending to enter the Bristol Channel, but mistakenly steered north-east and put *Le Landois* ashore. Her crew of 17 escaped and by early morning the vessel was breaking up in the shallows. Cases of wine, cordial and brandy in jars and casks, thousands of staves in bundles, bales of cotton, cambric and velvet, as well as casks of tobacco lay heaped in the shallows. Many casks of brandy leaked into rock pools and crevices, and news of this bonanza quickly spread among the locals. Houses and farms for miles around emptied as local people clambered down to the beach and fell on the wreck. The Penzance Lloyd's agent and French consul arrived to find at least 1,000 people swarming over the beach helping themselves. An official salvage party was organised, made up mostly of the few law-abiding public present, but the following day when Captain Alexander Sharp and 25 Coastguards arrived on the scene, they faced a drunken mob now estimated to number over 4,000. What the Coastguards were unable to salvage they attempted to destroy, breaking open barrels or upsetting pails, pitchers and buckets filled with wine and brandy. Both sides were determined to get the better of the other, and the Lloyd's agent ordered the Reverend Buller of St Ives to read the Riot Act. One man was arrested for stealing a bundle of staves and sentenced to be hanged, but this was later commuted to transportation for life.

123   Ravenshoe   50.06.20N; 05.42.15W. The wreck of the 3,592-ton steamer *Ravenshoe* lies on Carn Gloose, a small rock-strewn point of land about half a mile south of Priest's Cove. Registered at Cardiff, she was on passage from Lisbon to Barry in ballast to load coal. On 31 December, 1919, 4 miles off the Longships, her engine broke down during the night, and she drifted before a gale towards the shore, narrowly missed the Brisons and went ashore in Penanwell Cove. The Sennen Cove rocket brigade arrived at 6.30am on New Year's Day, and all 26 crew and Captain Vanstone were rescued by breeches buoy. Gales quickly caused the wreck to break up, and today her remains can be found scattered among the boulders in some 9m.

124   Frisia   50.06.00N; 05.42.10W. Very little is known of this wreck, and we have been unable to find anyone who has actually dived on it, but it should be easy to find. A Dutch coaster of Rotterdam, built in 1918, on passage from Swansea to Lisbon with coal, the *Frisia* encountered heavy seas and took on a severe list when her cargo shifted during the night of 28 April, 1919, when off Trevose Head. She

Above: Returning to her home port of Cardiff from Lisbon in ballast, the Ravenshoe broke down off Land's End at 10.15pm on 31 December, 1919 and drove ashore in a gale in Perranwell Cove, near Carn Gloose (Site 123). Her 27 crew were rescued by breeches buoy from the cliff top, and after successive gales drove her further up on the rocks, she was abandoned. This photograph shows ship's stores being landed.

Below: The London registered steamship Datetree drove ashore on the Brisons in dense fog on 25 June 1914, broke her back and was abandoned as beyond salvage (Site 125). All her crew were saved.

Left: The slipway just south of Cape Cornwall.

Below: Old tin mine buildings on the cliffs at Botallack Head.

continued for Land's End, but after rounding the Brisons the list increased to 45 degrees, putting her port side rails underwater. Unable to reach Whitesand Bay, the captain anchored the ship half a mile north of Aire Point in 11m. The crew of 14 took to the ship's boat, which met the Sennen lifeboat and was towed to safety. Two minutes after the crew left the *Frisia* she rolled over on her port beam and sank.

The sea bed in this area is a mass of rock and boulders; locating the wreck with a magnetometer should be relatively easy.

125 Datetree 50.07.15N; 05.43.12W. Visible from Cape Cornwall, ¾ mile to the south-west, lie two very large slate crag islands known as The Brison and Little Brison, which have claimed a number of wrecks. The *Datetree*, a 1,995-ton collier of London on passage from Barry to Brest with coal, was built at Hoboken, Antwerp in 1914, and owned by the Tree SS Company Ltd. On 25 June, 1914, she drove ashore in dense fog at 5.30am and quickly broke her back. Her crew of 18 landed at St Just using their own boats.

The Western Marine Salvage Company of Penzance stripped the wreck of most of her machinery in the 1920s, but her single boiler is still in position among her scattered plating. The wreck makes an excellent dive but should be visited before the heavy weed growth commences, as she lies in shallow water. There is an exceptionally strong tidal current around and through The Brisons, and the site is best visited during slack water neaps.

The remains of the *Datetree* may well be found mixed up with those of the 846-ton German barque *Luna*, sailing from Liverpool to Wellington, New Zealand, with general cargo. Her crew of 17 were all lost. Many hundreds of glass cod bottles – with a pinched neck holding a glass marble – have been found among her wreckage.

126 Devon 50.07.15N; 05.43.30W. Although described as a sailing barge, this 88ft wooden vessel, built at Chatham in 1833, was on passage from Devonport to Falmouth, then Pembroke Dock and Queenstown, carrying valuable government stores and shipbuilding materials when she went ashore. Twelve of the crew of 13 and five passengers were lost.

First Mate William Davis, the sole survivor, made a deposition concerning the loss to the Receiver of Wreck at Penzance. He recorded that the *Devon* rounded Land's End in a west-south-westerly gale, passing 3 miles west of the Longships. Trying to avoid what they thought were sailing vessels, they drove ashore on the Brison Rocks. All the crew and passengers were called on deck, but heavy seas washed away first the boats, then the hatch covers and finally all the people. The Mate saved himself by swimming to The Brison, from where he was rescued.

The wreck lies a little to the south of the SS *Datetree*'s boiler, still on the Little Brison, and among the rocks you will find much evidence of her cargo. Gales often uncover new areas of the wreck, but great care must be taken on the site because of the strong current, which can exceed 2½ knots.

127 Hamlin 50.07.12N; 05.43.15W. The wooden-built, iron-fastened and coppered full-rigged ship *Hamlin* was wrecked shortly before midnight on 17–18 April, 1867, on the two outcrops of The Brisons known as The Bridges. Built at Massachusetts in 1860, she had only recently been purchased by her London owners, and was on passage to London from Cardiff carrying 500 tons of iron slag and dross. She carried a Mr Burfield, who called himself a coasting pilot but was not licensed by any known authority. The weather was thick as they passed the

Longships, the pilot assuming they were some 5 to 6 miles off when breakers were reported ahead and she drove ashore, where she quickly went to pieces.

Little of her hull remains, but fastenings, anchors and cables, and other iron fittings found among the boulders and sand patches probably belonged to her.

AREA 10:

Cape Cornwall to St Ives

Even closer to Cape Cornwall than The Brisons is a reef of rocks just awash at low water known as The Vyneck, about half a mile north-west of Cape Cornwall. There is a wealth of assorted marine life in the many crevices and gullies, as well as the remains of three steamship wrecks, all of which are well worth a visit. Following the coast east towards Zennor Head and Pendeen Watch, there is a set of rocks offshore known as The Wra or Three Stone Oar, which are exposed at low water. There are more wrecks here, particularly of steamships, and nine large vessels can be dived. Further still along the coast, Portheras Cove, Morvah and Grebe Point have all claimed victims in storm and fog, as has Gurnard's Head.

Coastal dive sites

128   Asia   50.07.48N; 05.43.00W. Built at Kiel in 1873, this Danish steamship, registered at Copenhagen, was on passage from Cardiff to Cronstadt carrying a cargo of 1,500 tons of coal. She ran into thick fog when off Trevose Head, and no further sightings of land were made until 10.30am on 31 August, 1889, when she drove ashore on The Vyneck, north of The Brisons. Under Captain Carl Djurson, she carried 21 crew and the captain's wife. Her lifeboats were launched as soon as possible and only two men were lost. The vessel settled in 9m with only her bow and masts showing at low tide. The wreck is reported to have gone to pieces within days of stranding.

As with other wrecks in this area, the *Asia* is heavily weeded and subject to strong tides. She lies at the bottom of a sheer underwater cliff with her bow touching The Vyneck, her stern to the north-north-east. Her propeller and shaft can be clearly seen.

129   Malta   50.08.08N; 05.42.25W. Built in 1865 by Thompson's of Glasgow, the *Malta* was a small, lavishly fitted, Cunard Company liner. She left Liverpool on 14 October, 1889, bound for Italy via Falmouth, with some 2,000 tons of general cargo,

Belonging to the Cunard Steamship Company, the 2,224-ton Malta was on passage from Liverpool to the Mediterranean when she went ashore under Castle Kenidjack in fog on 15 October 1889 (Site 129). Her crew and passengers were all saved, but they lost all their luggage and valuables when the boat carrying it capsized. The cargo included 633 tons of copper, pig-iron, tinplate, herrings and sugar.

19 passengers and 40 crew under Captain Lavis. Off Land's End they met thick fog and proceeded slowly, but they struck the coast within 20ft of a wall-like cliff face, 880yds north of Cape Cornwall, directly under Castle Kenidjack. Two tugs attempted to refloat her, but within a day she had commenced to break up, and was written off.

130 Ixia   50.07.57N; 05.43W. This wreck occurred soon after 4pm on 30 June, 1929, in clear, settled weather and smooth seas. The 2,985-ton *Ixia*, owned by the Stage Line of North Shields, where she was registered, left Swansea for Constantinople carrying coal. She appeared close inshore as she rounded Pendeen Point and Cape Cornwall, but struck The Brisons shortly after. Assisted by the tide she was refloated, then appeared to turn and head for the shore. On finding his ship leaking badly, Captain Holt attempted to save the vessel by deliberately running her ashore, but in so doing struck part of The Vyneck, where she remained fast. Two boats put out to assist. By the time they arrived the starboard rails of the *Ixia* were already underwater, and 25 of the crew were taken off immediately, the captain and officers remaining aboard until 9pm. The wreck broke in two 600yds from the cliff.

As with other wrecks on The Brisons and The Vyneck, weed covers the remains, and care is necessary as there are strong tides. Today the wreck lies against the base of an underwater cliff, about 300m north-north-east of The Vyneck. Her stern lies to the north, her propeller shaft runs north–south and at a break in the reef her bow section and boilers lie in an east–west direction.

131 Glamorgan Coast   50.07.40N; 05.42.35W. This 684-ton steamship was built as the *Channel Trader* in 1913 at Middlesbrough, owned by Coast Lines Ltd

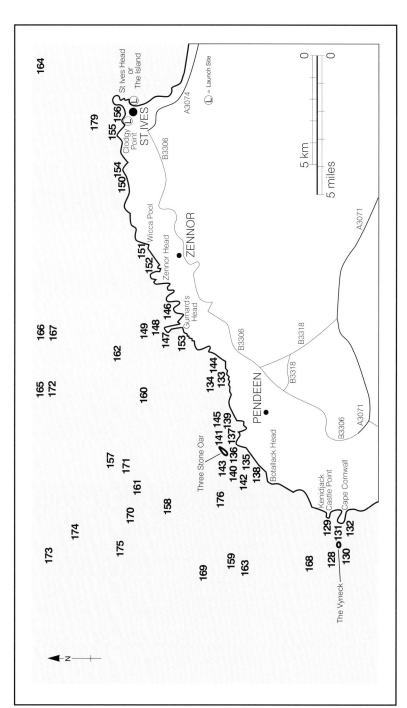

Dive sites in Area 10: Cape Cornwall to St Ives.

and registered at Liverpool. She was creeping around the Cornish coast on her way from Bristol to Penzance with a general cargo, in visibility less than 75ft, when she went aground on North Point, Cape Cornwall, not far from the wreck of the *Malta*. Her crew of 14 and one passenger took to the lifeboats and rowed ashore. She suffered extensive damage when she went aground, with a 6ft gash in her starboard side, and as she settled soon had deep water in every hold.

One of her boilers lies in a gully in about 6m, her engine further inshore, the wreck being very broken and overgrown.

132   Aida Lauro   50.08.08N; 05.42.30W. Almost on top of the wreck of the *Malta* are the remains of this 4,538-ton steel steamship, wrecked 48 years later. Built by Richardson, Duck and Company Ltd, Stockton-on-Tees, in 1923 as the *Radnor*, she later became the Welsh-owned *Treharris* before being sold to Italian owners, who registered her new name at Naples. The ship was carrying cotton seed, ground nuts and linseed from Liverpool to Hull, when she stranded at 1am on 1 July, 1937, about 450ft from the cliff face on Castle Point, under Kenidjack Castle. The vessel broadcast a distress signal, but gave an incorrect location, her true position not being known until the St Ives Coastguard sent men to the scene. The St Ives lifeboat took off two seamen. The remaining 13, including Captain Astrita, took to their boats but stood by the wreck, remaining close to the German salvage tug *Seefalke*, which had been summoned from Mount's Bay. The wreck flooded and there was little hope she would be saved. In fact, when a Salvage Association officer visited her on 4 July, she had already broken in two and salvage was considered impossible, her cargo now entirely saturated.

The wreck makes an excellent dive, despite strong currents, and a drift dive right through this area will take you over several of the wrecks mentioned, none of which is deeper than 12m.

Although on a map or chart Pendeen Watch does not appear as a particularly large or dangerous headland, it has always been notorious for shipwrecks. Those around Pendeen have been mostly colliers engaged in the South Wales coal trade, and 34 such vessels are recorded as having been wrecked, stranded or sunk on the 6 miles of coast between Pendeen and St Ives. There is no access or launching point anywhere along this section of cliff. Should you wish to investigate the area, you must be prepared for a long boat trip from Sennen Cove or St Ives harbour.

133   Gannet   50.10.10N; 05.38.25W. Only the second steamship to be wrecked off Morvah, this 560-ton iron vessel of Liverpool was carrying a general cargo from Liverpool to Antwerp when she met fog off Godrevy Point and went ashore on a ledge.

134   Maas   50.10.05N; 05.38.30W. At 1am on 24 June, 1857, this 168-ton Rotterdam-registered steamship with a general cargo was on passage from Cardiff to Rotterdam when she struck a ledge of rocks 450ft from the cliffs at Morvah, 1 mile east of Pendeen, on the same ledge of rocks as the *Gannet*, where she immediately filled. On 10 July it was reported that several casks of palm oil cargo had been picked up at sea, and that same day she broke in two.

135   William Cory   50.09.45N; 05.40.20W. On the fine morning of 18 September, 1910, workers on the dressing floor below Levant tin mine were astonished to see a large steamer heading straight for the cliffs. She struck heavily, swung round and came to a halt alongside the Enys Rock on the north side, her

Above: Stranded under the cliffs a mile south-west of Pendeen Point, the steamship William Cory struck first a submerged rock offshore in fog. She sank under the Levant mine workings on 5 September, 1910 (Site 135). Much of her cargo of pit-props was washed overboard, but eventually was used in Cornish mines.

Below: The Busby was lost near Pendeen on only her second voyage. She went ashore on 24 June, 1894, was refloated on 16 July, only to go down a mile offshore, just inside the Three Stone Oar reef, seen in the background (Site 137).

stern in the shallows and her bow pointing south-west. Registered at London, this 1,592-ton steamer had left Uleaborg, Finland, for Newport on 27 August, with pit props, including a full deck cargo. Captain St Clair and the crew abandoned ship and rowed into Sennen; later that afternoon only the steamer's poop deck and bridge were visible among a raft of floating timber. At the inquiry, it was established that the steamer had previously struck The Vyneck and, leaking badly, had attempted to reach the shallows of St Ives.

The Cardiff registered and owned Scheldt went ashore about 35yds from the cliff at Pendeen Cove on 23 June, 1890 (Site 136). Although the weather was calm she tore several holes in her bottom plates, and a diving contractor working on the nearby Malta decided that she was beyond recovery, reporting that only moveable gear could be saved.

The wreck lies close up against the cliff, her bow almost touching an offshore rock, which dries at low tide and makes a good marker.

136   Scheldt   50.10N; 05.40W. Built in 1884 and fitted with a two-cylinder compound engine, this Cardiff-registered 707-ton iron steamer was carrying a cargo of coal from Newport, Monmouthshire to Bordeaux when she went ashore in fog near Pendeen Cove on 23 June, 1890. She was visited by a diving contractor from the Liverpool Salvage Association the following day, who reported that only moveable gear could be saved, that her bow lay in 5.2m, her stern in 9m, and that it would be impossible to refloat her. The wreck lies some 120ft from the cliff face.

137   Busby   50.10.08N; 05.40.20W. Built and registered at Stockton-on-Tees, this steel steamship was engaged in general trade with India for her owners Ropner and Company, of West Hartlepool. She had completed only one previous voyage when she left Newport bound for Bombay on 22 June, 1894, carrying 600 tons of coal and an intermediary cargo for Civitavecchia. Steaming down the north coast of Cornwall, intending to pass 5 miles off the Longships, as she cleared St Ives at 10pm visibility became very poor and her speed was reduced to slow ahead. At 11pm the bow lookout saw a brief flash of light ahead as the weather cleared and

Above: Carrying a cargo of coke from Swansea to Antwerp, the Alacrity stranded in thick fog in Portheras Cove, Pendeen, on 13 September, 1963 (Site 139). Attempts to refloat her went on for weeks, but eventually an autumn gale caused her to break up.

Below: Loaded with a valuable general cargo, the Cork-registered SS Umbre left Liverpool in fine weather but met with fog off Cornwall, and on 20 February,1899 steamed at ten knots into the Morvah cliffs, under Greeb Point (Site 145). Her remains joined those of the Busby and Packnam, both lost in the same area.

Captain Sherwood, believing they were near the Longships, ordered full ahead. Breakers were sighted off the port bow, and suddenly the *Busby* was inside the Three Stone Oar Rocks. Although her engine was put full astern, she ran ashore and became fast. The crew were saved by the Coastguard and the port lifeboat.

When the Liverpool Salvage Association began to refloat her a north-westerly gale sent heavy seas over her deck, throwing the 40 salvage men off their feet, while those in her holds were drenched as water fell on them. She was again abandoned and shortly after foundered, leaving only her mastheads visible midway between Pendeen Watch and the Three Stone Oar. On 6 December, divers

Many ships have foundered on the Wra Stones off Pendeen.

recovered part of her stores and equipment, reporting that she lay on a sandy bottom in three pieces, where her remains can still be found.

138   Liberty   50.10.00N; 05.39.55W. The *Liberty* was a Standard-built ship of 1918, launched by Palmers of Hebburn-on-Tyne as the *War Camel*. On completion she was named *Cairndhu*, for the Cairns Line of Dundee, but she was laid up in August 1927. Two further name changes (*Cirndh* and *Styrmio*) later, after World War Two and now named *Liberty* under the ownership of Cia Maritina Internacional, a Liberian company registered at Monrovia, she engaged in the Baltic iron-ore trade. During the evening of 16 January, 1952, the *Liberty* left Newport in ballast for La Goulette, and next day was struggling against a north-westerly gale off Pendeen Watch. The ship suffered falling steam pressure as her elderly engine raced in heavy seas. At 8.30pm, Captain Filinus sent out a radio distress signal for a tug and a lifeboat, and shortly after the *Liberty* drove ashore beam on under the cliffs at Pendeen. The crew of 20 escaped by breeches buoy, rope ladder and lifeboat. There are still many remains of the wreck, some visible at low tide, but only her propeller shaft and bottom plates are recognisable.

139   Alacrity   50.10.00N; 05.39.26W. Another victim of fog, this 554-ton motor vessel, registered at London and built at Goole in 1940, was on passage from Swansea to Antwerp with coke and anthracite dust when she grounded near Pendeen Watch, on 13 September, 1963. Salvage operations to refloat her continued for several weeks, but she broke up in autumn gales, and by Christmas that year her remains had virtually disappeared.

The wreck is in very shallow water, where her scattered remains lie partially buried in sand between the boulders. Parts of the wreck are visible at low tide and the local authorities have made an effort to disperse them as a potential danger to swimmers.

140   Chimu   50.09.50N; 05.35.00W. Coal-laden and on passage from Penarth to Venice, this London-registered steam collier, built as the *Cumbal* in 1900 by the Northumberland Shipbuilding Company, Newcastle, struck the Brisons in fog at 4.55am on 17 August, 1919, and sent out an SOS radio call. Her captain managed to refloat her and headed for the shallows of St Ives Bay, where she could be beached if necessary. As Pendeen Point came in sight the *Chimu*'s bow was almost underwater so she was turned for shore, grounding about a 440yds off Pendeen Cove. By 28 August she had broken in two and was abandoned as a total loss.

141   Ana   50.10.10N; 05.39.00W. Registered at Bilbao, this 392-ton steamship carrying a general cargo between Liverpool and Santander struck the Three Stone Oar reef in fog at 4am on 4 January, 1878. She carried a crew of 22 and 13 passengers, who took to the boats and were adrift for over 7 hours before being picked up by lifeboat. A large number of fishing vessels and Sennen gigs were engaged in salvage operations. Men from the Levant tin mine were employed in salvaging cargo and stores and large quantities of brass pipe and ironmongery were recovered. Having driven ashore under the cliffs, the *Ana*'s remains lie in shallow water.

A wreck site yet to be found outside the Three Stone Oar is the 1,870-ton steamship *Nyanza*, a British-registered iron vessel, which was carrying coal from Greenock to Leghorn when she disappeared during a severe north-north-easterly gale on or about 16 November, 1893. Only one body was found from the crew.

142   Burlington   50.09.30N; 05.41.00W. Built by Doxford and Sons at Sunderland in 1872, the *Burlington* drove ashore in fog on 8 May, 1898, while carrying 1,000 tons of coal from Swansea to Rouen. Captain Butcher and 14 crew had struggled to get the ship down the north coast of Cornwall in bad visibility. She closed on the coast to establish her position, struck the Three Stone Oar reef and was swept ashore on Enys Rock, 880yds south of Pendeen Coastguard Station. Fortunately, weather conditions were good and the crew landed in the cove in their own boats. By nightfall the wreck had sunk and her remains are a short distance north-west of the Enys Rock.

143   Ossian   50.10.15N; 05.40.05W. On 14 February, 1900, at 9am, following a night of violent north-north-westerly gales and a blinding snowstorm, the RNLI Secretary at St Ives received a telephone message about a wreck on the Three Stone Oar. At 9.25am the lifeboat was launched, but to no avail, as all the crew were lost.

It was not until 3 March, 1900, that the occupants of a local boat, using a waterglass, were able to read the name on the ship's starboard bow, which was found only 2m depth. It transpired that this Bristol-registered 160-ton steamer had been carrying coal from Swansea to Tonnay Charente, under a Captain W. Reed and crew of nine.

144   Paknam   50.10.08N; 05.38.30W. The *Paknam* was built at Port Glasgow in 1872 and registered at Saigon. The 700-ton steamship was flying the French flag and carrying coal and cast iron ingots from Glasgow to Le Havre when she struck a rock off Morvah Cliff in thick fog and drove ashore on 13 May, 1895. The pilot and 21 crew landed on Botheras Sand in one of the ship's boats; Captain Offret remained on board overnight, declining to leave his ship until she was at least full of water. The ship was so badly damaged underwater that there was no hope of saving her.

145 Umbre   50.10.10N; 05.39.18W. The 1,312-ton *Umbre* was built in 1898 at Newcastle by Wigham, Richardson and Company, registered at Cork, and fitted with a 195hp, three-cylinder triple expansion engine and two boilers. After she left Liverpool at 6am on 19 February, 1899, carrying a general cargo for Amsterdam and Rotterdam, the weather deteriorated during the night. At 5.55am on 20 February the *Umbre* struck immediately under Greeb Point and shortly afterwards her main deck was submerged. Captain Thomas Stubbs gave orders to abandon ship, and the smaller of her two boats landed safely. Captain Stubbs and those remaining on board were picked up from the *Umbre*'s other boat by a Brixham trawler. The tug *Hercules* arrived off Pendeen with the salvage lighter *Etna*, only to find that the main and lower decks of the wreck had already collapsed, and that the wreck was now only a mass of broken steel.

The wreck lies between the Mozeens and the east side of Pendeen Cove; a boiler and most of her engine block, including her iron propeller and shaft, show above the sand. Her bow section is separate and lies about 150ft to the west.

146 Alexander Yeats   50.11.25N 05.35.48W. This Liverpool-registered 1,589-ton barque was the largest sailing ship ever lost between Land's End and St Ives. Launched in 1876 by Lynch, at Portland, New Brunswick, she was on passage from Holyhead to Devonport carrying deals and pitch-pin. In heavy weather she engaged the services of the tug *Gamecock* off the Smalls in order to avoid going ashore near Milford then, having slipped the tow, headed for Land's End. During the evening of 25 September, 1896, Captain Scott identified the Wolf Rock light, but a south-south-westerly gale got up, driving her north-east past Godrevy Point. The barque's deck cargo shifted and she developed a heavy list to port; throughout that day the Portreath Coastguards kept an extra watch on the ship after she showed signs of distress while 4 miles offshore and the Hayle lifeboat was launched. Shortly before midnight the barque struck under Gurnard's Head, in heavy seas, her 19 crew all being rescued by breeches buoy from the cliff top. Another gale drove the wreck further inshore where she tore her bottom plates open, going to pieces on 12 October.

147 Hickleton   This Hull-registered 490-ton British steamship was in ballast from St Malo to Port Talbot to load coal when her steering gear broke down on 30 August, 1920. She struck the Ebal Rock off Gurnard's Head and with a considerable tide running was swept ashore on the west side at 50.11.35N; 05.36.10W. After drifting, she sank about 150ft offshore in 13m. She was practically new, having been built only a year before at Deklop. A salvage vessel with divers was sent to the scene, who found the wreck entirely submerged, lying on one side with her upper deck to the shore, but so badly damaged that refloating was considered impossible.

148 Lyminge   50.11.40N; 05.37.51W. The *Lyminge* was a British steamer registered at London, built in 1918 by Wood, Skinner and Company, Newcastle, carrying coal between Cardiff and Oporto. She drove ashore in fog at 3.22pm on 19 September, 1931 and broadcast a wireless distress signal, which was picked up by Land's End Radio, reporting that she was off the Lizard, her captain unsure whether he was off the north or south coast of Cornwall! She had in fact struck the

New Brunswick barque Alexander Yeats, of 1,589-tons gross, built in 1876, lost all her sails off Portreath. Having lost her tug she drifted helpless into a small bay just north of Gurnard's Head on 29 September, 1896 (Site 146). This photograph shows her abandoned, after her deck cargo of logs had been recovered. The ship went to pieces on 12 October, only two weeks later.

Ebal Rock off Gurnard's Head, where she badly holed her starboard bow and sank on the west side of the Head, leaving only her stern showing above water. Her crew took to the boats and were saved. Western Marine Salvage was awarded a contract to strip the wreck. She lies in a general depth of 12m, very broken and scattered over a wide area, her engine block and a boiler obvious between Ebal Rock and Gurnard's Head.

149 Traute Sarnow 50.11.28N; 05.35.45W. Built at Flensburg in 1951, this 300-ton, eight-cylinder, oil-engined coaster was carrying anthracite from Cardiff to Ostend when she drove ashore on the east side of Gurnard's Head shortly before midnight on 25 July, 1954. Captain Heinrich Sarnow sounded the ship's siren and fired off a number of distress rockets. All the crew were saved. The vessel broke up in a west-south-westerly gale two days later.

150   Austria   50.12.00N; 05.34.35W. Only 17½ hours out of Penarth, where she had loaded coal for Nantes, this Spanish steamship, registered at Bilbao, ran ashore in fog at 3am on 9 March, 1907. Captain Pedro Goitia thought his vessel was a few miles off the Pendeen lighthouse when suddenly the rocks below Trevassa Cliffs loomed up ahead. The 22 crew panicked when the first ship's boat lowered was smashed to pieces and one of the four men in it was drowned. The remainder of the crew landed on the coast in the second boat. The *Austria* came ashore near Carnelloe Rock, close to the village of Zennor, at 50.11.40N; 05.35.12W.

151   Manu   50.12.20N; 05.34.00W. Another Spanish steamship, the 17-year-old, 2,124-ton *Manu*, built at Sunderland and registered at Bilbao, was carrying coal when she got close inshore in fog, and at one time the crew found themselves surrounded by St Ives crabbers hauling pots in Wicca Pool. Despite the warning shouts of the fishermen, she continued to head for the coast until she struck the rocks beneath the Eagle's Nest on 25 May, 1916. The crew of 24 took to the boats but were ordered to remain within sight of the vessel, while the master remained on board and the mate climbed the cliffs to get help. A tug and several naval patrol vessels attempted to pull the steamship off at high tide but failed. The *Manu* refused to be refloated and soon went underwater. Western Marine Salvage could not attend the wreck for three weeks, by which time she had become a total loss. As with most of the steamship wrecks in this area, she has been torn to pieces by the sea, and only plates and concreted lumps of machinery remain in the shallows.

152   Wilston   50.12.30N; 05.33.25W. Mixed up with the remains of the *Manu* in Wicca Pool are those of the 3,221-ton *Wilston*, a Glasgow-registered steamer, carrying coal from Newport to La Goulette, which drove ashore in Force 10 conditions on 23 January, 1939. That same night the Padstow lifeboat was called out but drove ashore at Gwithian, near Godrevy, badly damaged, having capsized three times, with only one survivor.

Five bodies from the *Wilston* were washed up in Wicca Cove on 29 January, all of which were identified as part of the steamer's crew, and items of equipment were found bearing the vessel's name. The remains of the *Manu* and *Wilston* steamships lie intermixed in the shallows, and it is impossible to identify them as individual ships.

153   Enrico Parodi   50.13.00N; 05.33.15W. This 3,818-ton Italian steamship, registered at Genoa, built by Osborne Graham at Sunderland in 1903 as the *Boscombe*, later renamed *King Edgar* before being bought by the Italian owners, went ashore under Gurnard's Head in thick fog on 23 July, 1916. A salvage crew was already on hand, working on the remains of the SS *Neto* of Glasgow, which had gone ashore only two days earlier some 300yds away and was later refloated and saved. The men stopped work and attempted to save the Italian ship, as she was still afloat from her engine room aft, and that evening the salvage vessel *Lady of the Isles* got her off and commenced the tow to St Ives. Progress slowed as the fog thickened, and at 11pm when it was discovered she had developed a severe leak she was abandoned by the salvage crew, and sank in 12m of water just north of the Carracks, where she lies on a sandy bottom. Her remains lie east–west and are very scattered, salvage work having been carried out using explosives.

154   Bessemer City   50.12.55N; 05.31.20N. The sound of frightened cattle drew Mr Eddy to the cliff edge overlooking Pen Enys Point on 2 November, 1936. From there he saw the masthead lights of a large steamship hard against the cliff. He alerted the Coastguard, who in turn called out the St Ives lifeboat *Caroline Parsons*, which made three trips to the wreck to take off all 33 crew, leaving only Captain Joseph Herman behind. He was rescued later.

The vessel proved to be the New York-registered American steamship *Bessemer City*, which was carrying a cargo of tinned food and zinc ingots from New Westminster to London. She had gone ashore in dense fog at 9.45pm in Brea Cove, where she immediately developed serious leaks in her engine room and broke in two. Much oil was released when she broke up.

The separate halves of the vessel lie at right angles to each other about 70ft apart, and 150ft from the base of Trevalgan Cliff. Her remains lay undisturbed until September 1963 when she was rediscovered by crayfish divers and a large quantity of zinc ingots were recovered.

155   HM ML-498   50.13.10N; 05.29.40W. Although there is no record of any local divers ever having found the wreck of this Royal Navy motor launch, she was one of a trio of fast patrol vessels stationed at St Ives during World War One. On 29 September, 1918, she was driven out of the bay by a north-north-easterly gale, struck Clodgy Point and foundered, the sole survivor being rescued by an army sergeant living at St Ives. The area is an attractive dive site, with offshore rocks and reefs, and it would be well worth either swimming the shallows or using a magnetometer to locate her remains.

156   Alba   50.13.08N; 05.28.42W. The high ground protecting St Ives harbour and approach from northerly and north-westerly gales is known as The Island or St Ives Head. It was here on 31 January, 1938, that two vessels came to grief: the 3,700-ton Panamanian MV *Alba* (previously *Cayuga*) and the St Ives lifeboat *Caroline Parsons*. On passage from Barry Docks to Civitavecchia with coal, in attempting to find shelter in St Ives Bay in the dark, Captain Joseph Horvath mistook his position and ran the ship ashore on rocks known as Carn Everis, just off Porthmear Beach, on the north-west side of the Island. The lifeboat *Caroline Parsons* battled its way around St Ives Head and got alongside the wreck, to find that the 23 Hungarian crew had all packed their suitcases and were expecting to be taken off – baggage and all – in a heavy north-easterly gale! The men were rescued after being told to leave their effects behind, but the weather was so severe they had to lie on the deck of the lifeboat for fear of being washed overboard. A huge sea caused the *Alba* to capsize, while the survivors, lifeboat crew and lifeboat were driven onto the rocks. Five of the *Alba*'s crew drowned, and the *Caroline Parsons* and *Alba* were totally lost.

Offshore wrecks

157   Luxembourg   50.13.20N; 05.39.50W. This British steamship, registered at Leith, was armed with a 12-pounder stern-mounted gun. She was built in 1910 at Port Glasgow and was carrying 700 tons of government stores from Le Havre to

The main slipway in the harbour at St Ives.

Newport, Monmouthshire when at 6.50am on 11 September, 1917, her lookout sighted a floating mine, which was detonated by rifle fire when she was 3½ miles north-east by north off the Pendeen lighthouse. A few minutes later a second mine was seen and the *Luxembourg* just managed to clear it, only for a huge explosion to take place under her bow, as she detonated another mine, which caused her to sink. Her crew got away safely in their own boat and were picked up by the French steamship *Celte*.

158 Kildonian 50.11.30N; 05.42W. The *Kildonian* was a Cardiff-registered 2,118-ton collier, built in 1898 by Pickersgill and Sons, Sunderland. She was carrying iron ore from Santander to Ardrossan when, at 3pm on 29 September, 1917, the track of a torpedo fired by the German submarine *UB-35* was seen, only seconds before it struck, causing the vessel to sink immediately. Although armed with a 12-pounder deck gun, the collier had no opportunity to use it in her defence. As a consequence the master and 13 members of the crew were either killed in the explosion or drowned when the vessel sank, there being no time to lower the boats. Nine men who survived the attack were picked up by the SS *St Chamond*. The wreck lies in 15m.

159 Mary Baird 50.10.12N; 05.43.40W. On passage from Rouen to Newport in ballast, this 1,830-ton steamship, built in 1908 at Rostock as the *Ulla Boog*, suffered a severe explosion on 18 May, 1917, as she detonated a German-laid contact mine. The first lifeboat was lowered with great difficulty and seven of her crew were killed by the mast when it fell across the second boat. The wreck lies in 25m.

160 Unidentified 50.12.12N; 05.38.00W. A small steel steamship wreck, probably a small tanker, lies broken in two, with the stern and midships sections lying upside down, orientated north–south. The detached bow is off to one side pointing south, also inverted, with windlass and anchors visible.

161   Courtown   50.12.30N; 05.41.30W. The *Courtown*, a large steamship of 4,419 tons carrying coal from Cardiff to Montvideo, sank following collision with the SS *La Rochefoucauld* at 6.40am on 27 September, 1924. No lives were lost.

162   Denebola   50.13.15N; 05.37.09W. An ex-German merchant steamship, detained at the outbreak of World War One and taken into British service when she was registered at London, the 1,481-ton *Denebola*, built in 1899, was carrying coal from Swansea intended for Rouen. She was hit by two torpedoes fired by a German submarine on 17 August, 1918. The enemy vessel remained submerged and was never identified. Her 21 crew took to a lifeboat and raft, but two were lost.

163   Bill   50.09.47N; 05.47.02W. The 1,175-ton Norwegian steamship *Bill*, registered at Christiania, was built in 1913 by Bremer Vulkan at Vegesack, and had a 191hp three-cylinder triple expansion engine and other machinery fitted aft. She was carrying coal from Newport, Monmouthshire to Rouen with a crew of 18, when she collided with the SS *Dungeness* of Swansea, and sank 3 miles west by north of Pendeen Watch on 12 December, 1917. The *Dungeness* picked up the crew without loss of life. The wreck lies in a general depth of 49m, with a least depth of 44m, on top of a large rocky outcrop.

164   Madeline   50.20.00N; 05.25.00W. The *Madeline* was a 2,890-ton British steamship, registered at Newcastle, in ballast from Dieppe to Swansea to load coal

The Alba lies stranded on Porthmeor Beach, St Ives on 31 January, 1938, where she became a total wreck (Site 156). The St Ives lifeboat Caroline Parsons went to the rescue of her crew, taking on board all twenty-three men – only to capsize, drowning five of the survivors. The smashed lifeboat can be seen on the rocks.

and armed with a 12-pounder (12cwt) stern gun. She was 10 miles east-north-east of Pendeen Watch, when she was torpedoed on 8 March, 1918. Three men were killed, the remainder of the 26 crew abandoned ship in their own boats; shortly afterwards, a second torpedo struck her. The German submarine responsible, *U-55*, was seen shortly before the *Madeline* was abandoned and a number of shells were fired at the enemy vessel before the steamship sank. The survivors were picked up by a patrol vessel.

165   Skrymer   50.30.00N; 05.38.00W (approx.). Another Norwegian collier, built at Fredrickstad in 1913, registered at Christiania and on passage from Port Talbot to Rouen, the 1,476-ton *Skrymer* was torpedoed by the German submarine *UC-77* off Pendeen on 10 March, 1918. Only four of the crew survived after being picked up from a waterlogged lifeboat.

166   Tryhaug   50.19.15N; 05.35.33W. Built as the *Kjeld* in 1906 and originally Norwegian owned, after assuming British registration at London, this 1,483-ton steamship was carrying vegetables, potatoes, cattle fodder and timber between Belfast and Falmouth when she was torpedoed 10 miles north-east of Pendeen on 22 March, 1918. The German submarine responsible, *UB-103*, had been sighted only seconds before the attack. All but two of the crew of 24 were brought ashore safely. The wreck lies in 30m with her stern broken off, lying orientated north-north-west to south-south-east, on her port side. Her two boilers have fallen out and now lie close to her stern on a sandy and shale sea bed, her propeller and stern tube having been salvaged.

167   Stabil   50.19.00N; 05.36.00W. Very little is known about the loss of this Stavanger-registered 538-ton Norwegian vessel, which was carrying coal from Glasgow to Nantes. When off Pendeen on 30 March, 1918, she was torpedoed and sunk by the German submarine *U-46*. Only two survivors were found, picked up a few hours later from a lifeboat.

168   Liusa   50.07.15N; 05.49.00W. Carrying a general cargo, this 3,603-ton, Barcelona-registered vessel of Spain, built in 1897 at Port Glasgow by Russell and Company, was 6 miles west by south of Pendeen Watch on 12 April, 1918, when she was torpedoed and sunk by the German submarine *UB-74*. Three crew and three passengers lost their lives in the explosion.

169   Elba   50.13.00N; 05.48.00W. This 1,081-ton armed merchant collier was torpedoed by the German submarine *UB-103* on 28 April, 1918, when 6 miles north-west by west of Pendeen Watch lighthouse. Registered at Leith and carrying coal from Cardiff to France with a crew of 20, the torpedo blew away most of her stern, causing her to sink in 3 minutes. Some of the crew took to the lifeboats and rafts, but she went down so quickly that ten of her crew were carried down with the vessel. The survivors were picked up by the SS *Moto* and landed at Barry.

170   Thorsa   50.12.15N; 05.44.00W. The *Thorsa* was built in 1884 by Barclay Curle and Company, Glasgow, and armed with one 12-pounder stern gun. The Leith-registered 1,319-ton steamship was carrying a general cargo from Le Havre to Liverpool, when she sank after the German submarine *UB-103* torpedoed her shortly after midnight on 2 May, 1918. Most of the 15 crew escaped but two men were never found. The wreck lies in 25m.

171   Vasilefs Georgios   50.12.50N; 05.40.00W. This Andros-registered 3,651-ton steamer was in ballast on passage from Le Havre to Barry to load coal when she was torpedoed and sunk by the German submarine *UB-103* on 3 May, 1918, 3 miles north-east of Pendeen. The wreck lies in 20m.

172   Hookroad   50.14.45N; 05.38.00W. The 811-ton collier *Hookroad* was built in 1912 at Workington, had four masts, and was on passage from Penarth to Rouen with a crew of 16 on 9 May, 1918, under Captain F. J. Baxter. Five miles north-north-east of Pendeen lighthouse she sank following collision with the Danish SS *Loly Jensen*, without loss of life.

173   Clan Macnab   50.20.00N; 05.55.00W. This 4,675-ton steamship was in ballast from Plymouth to the Clyde, armed with a 4.7-inch quick-firing stern gun, when she was struck by two torpedoes fired by the German submarine *U-113*. The attack took place 14 miles north-north-west of Pendeen Watch on 4 August, 1918.
   Twenty-three of the crew of 80 were killed, including Captain D. S. Smith. Fortunately, the vessel was in convoy so the survivors were quickly picked up by the Belgian SS *Kasbek*. The men were later transferred to the Royal Navy destroyer HMS *Owl* and landed at Milford.

174   Polesley   50.13.54N; 05.46.00W. Built in 1905 in Glasgow as the *Den of Crombie*, later renamed *Istria* and *Polesley*, registered at London, this vessel was carrying coal from Cardiff to France when, 1 mile north of Pendeen lighthouse, she was torpedoed by the German submarine *UB-88* at midnight on 22 September, 1918. There was only one survivor out of a crew of 43, who later told the authorities that the ship was hit amidships on the starboard side. This sole survivor was picked up by the SS *Fastnet* and landed at Cardiff. Divers who have visited the wreck advise that she lies in 44m, orientated north-east to south-west, and is still upright but now beginning to disintegrate.

175   Christos Markettos   The Italian steamer *Christos Markettos* was built by Ropner and Son, Stockton-on-Tees, in 1892 as the *Glenvech*, later re-named *Cheltonian*, registered at Genoa, was on passage from Bilbao to Newport with a cargo of iron ore on 2 January, 1918, when she was torpedoed and sunk by the German submarine *U-95* without loss of life. The exact position of the wreck is uncertain, as no other vessel saw her sink, but she is believed to be 4 miles north-west of Gurnard's Head, at around 50.13.30N; 05.37.00W.

176   Unidentified   50.10.20N; 05.42.10W (approx.). This is an unidentified wreck lying some 38m deep. The ship carried iron ore; there is a small stern gun still fitted, scattered ammunition, and a shell has been recovered marked with the date 1909, so she is probably a World War One loss.

St Ives to St Agnes

St Ives has a small harbour, which lies in the lee of The Island, and is one of the few havens for sailors on the north coast of Cornwall. The town grew from a tiny fishing hamlet into a busy Elizabethan seaport and has a long history of ship-building, fishing and regular trade with Bristol, Wales, Ireland, France and the Mediterranean. Fishing gave St Ives prosperity until the 1920s and, in its heyday, the town shipped over two million salted pilchards a year to Leghorn, Venice and Naples, a trade that employed two-thirds of its population. There has been a lifeboat station here since 1840.

Within the wide sweep of St Ives Bay, there are offshore rocks, reefs and a lighthouse, as well as the port of Hayle, which is 2 miles south-east of St Ives. Now a sandy, desolate tidal creek, Hayle was once a major outlet for the great copper mines of West Cornwall. In the 1830s Hayle and Bristol were linked by a weekly steam packet service, and when Harvey's iron foundry began building ships as well as mining machinery the port enjoyed a boom, which lasted well into the 1900s. Hayle retained a fleet of steam coasters until the 1920s, including the famous Hain Line, one of the major companies of the late 19th century.

Coastal dive sites

There is a slipway at Porthmeor Beach by the lifeboat station, with a second slipway giving more direct access adjacent to the Seawall Court Hotel. At Porthgwidden Beach another concrete slipway offers access to the sea, and suitable four-wheel drive vehicles can operate on the hard, sandy beach. Toilet facilities are available at the top of the ramp, as is a car park. Parking is allowed on Smeaton's Pier, for a nominal charge, but St Ives is very crowded during the summer, and it is advisable to arrive early. It is not possible to launch boats down the main slipway without the harbourmaster's permission. His office is at the landward end of the new quay.

Opposite: The slipway at Portreath, leading into the outer tidal harbour.

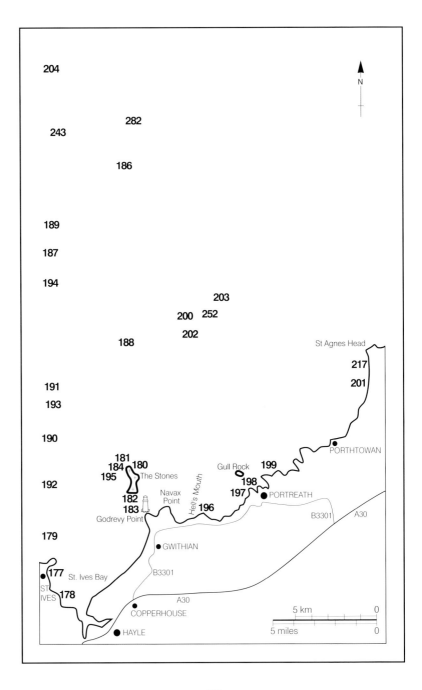

WARNING St Ives harbour is tidal and dries out completely at low water springs; the approaches can be dangerous in rough weather. When a red flag is flying from the mast at the end of the pier, pleasure craft should not attempt to put to sea.

177 Boscawen The 600-ton privateer *Boscawen* was one of the largest of the early wrecks on the rocks at St Ives. Originally the French man-of-war frigate *Medée*, captured by Lord Boscawen in 1744, she was taken into British service as a privateer and renamed. Homeward bound from the Azores, she sprang a bad leak and later the slings supporting her main yard parted, causing it to drop across the ship while there were still 60 sailors working the mainsail. With his ship disabled and severely damaged, Commodore George Walker headed for the Lizard, but a gale swept her past Land's End and she eventually arrived off St Ives, firing her cannon as signals of distress. In an attempt to remain afloat, all her anchors had been jettisoned overboard long beforehand, and she was so deep in the water that it was impossible for her to enter the harbour. As a result she drove on the rocks and broke in two, people from the town wading into the surf to assist the crew. The Commodore remained on board until the last injured man had been handed down into a boat, and only four lives were lost. The vessel broke up in the shallows, depositing her cannon, iron shot and fittings among the rocks.

178 Porthminster Reef or The Carracks 50.12.30N; 05.28.00W. This is a shallow reef only a few minutes from St Ives Pier and slipway, favoured by beginners and snorkellers alike as it has a diversity of marine life, including John Dory, dogfish, lobster, crab, trigger fish and grey or Atlantic seals, in depths ranging from 7 to 13m.

179 Alster 50.13.48N; 05.29.36W. This 709-ton, 200ft Cardiff-registered collier left Swansea for St Nazaire on 16 December, 1885, but ran into thick fog off Trevose Head. She struck the Three Stone Oar Rock off Pendeen Watch and, making water, turned back hoping to reach St Ives. The level of water in the boiler-room soon extinguished her fires and Captain Tregurtha and his 15 crew took to the boats and left the ship to sink approximately 1.5 to 2 miles off The Island. The hull broke into several sections and lies orientated roughly north–south, standing some 3m proud of the sea bed, complete with an anchor and hawse pipe. A spare cast iron propeller is frequently exposed in the sand.

Offshore dive sites and wrecks

180 The Stones, Godrevy Island and the Garland Godrevy Point has parking facilities and it is easy to carry equipment the short distance down to the rocks for shore diving. At the north-east extremity of St Ives Bay is an offshore reef known as The Stones. Godrevy Island is separated from Godrevy Point by a narrow 5m-deep channel.

The Stones have been as great a menace to shipping around St Ives as the Manacles Reef, near Falmouth. The largest and innermost rock, Godrevy Island,

Opposite: Dive sites in Area 11: St Ives to St Agnes.

All that remained of the schooner Sarah Evans after the gale that drove her ashore had moderated. On the left part of her lower hull framing, and on the right part of her keel and auxiliary engine, draped in rigging and anchor cable.

which still carries a lighthouse, lies surrounded by smaller rocks and ledges and is swept by a fierce tide: do not attempt to swim out to Godrevy Island without boat cover. At the northern end of the offshore reef are the Inner and Outer Stones, dominated by a huge wedge-shaped rock, marked by a navigational buoy. Notorious for shipwrecks, it was on Godrevy Island that the sailing ship *Garland* of Topsham was lost on 31 January, 1649, during a great storm. The *Garland* carried the entire personal wardrobe of the Prince of Wales, later Charles II. It took 3 days for the weather to subside sufficiently to allow the rescue of one seaman, a boy and a wolfhound from the island, the only survivors of 60 crew. It is recorded that many valuables were washed ashore around Godrevy, such as coats with gold buttons, drapery and valuable linen, and no doubt the cargo included much specie and other valuables.

Navax Point, on the east side of Godrevy Head, accessible from Pencobben and Fishing Cove, has an interesting range of shore diving in safe, sheltered conditions, provided the wind is not from the north or north-east. The cliffs are steep and boat cover is advisable, but it is possible to reach Hell's Mouth, which holds several modern wrecks.

A St Ives lifeboat disaster took place at Godrevy Point on 23 January, 1939. The St Ives Coastguard had reported a steamship in a dangerous position off Cape Cornwall, and the lifeboat *John & Sarah Eliza Stych* was launched to her assistance. When 1½ miles off Clodgy Point the lifeboat sheered as she came down between seas, and capsized. When she became upright again four of the crew were missing. The lifeboat's engine had shut off, as designed, when she capsized, but all attempts to restart it failed. She then anchored, but the cable parted and as she began to drift across St Ives Bay she capsized again, this time with the loss of the mechanic. With only three crew remaining, as the lifeboat approached Godrevy rocks she capsized for a third time, and on righting only one man remained alive in the boat. Three minutes later the lifeboat crashed onto the rocks, where the sole survivor managed to crawl ashore and alert the authorities.

The wreck was a terrible tragedy for St Ives, particularly as several of the men involved had been in the previous lifeboat accident of 1938. As a direct result, the remains of the lifeboat were burned where they lay and the St Ives lifeboat station was closed until 1940 after World War Two began, when local fishermen pleaded with the RNLI to be able to operate a new boat. In 1940 the *Caroline Oates Aver & William Maine* arrived on station.

The steamship in distress was later found to be the SS *Wilston* (Site **152**), which was lost in Wicca Pool, at Tregerthen Point, with all 32 crew.

181   Nile   50.16.15N; 05.25.36W. The first steamship lost on the Outer Stones, this Irish packet struck at night during a howling gale on 30 November, 1854. Carrying 16 crew and 24 passengers under Captain Moppett, all of whom were lost, this wreck was instrumental in the building of the Godrevy Island lighthouse. Only five years old when lost, the 700-ton screw vessel, belonging to the British & Irish Steam Packet Company Ltd, was considered a very smart vessel, complete with figurehead, bowsprit, three masts and a tall thin funnel. She sailed from Liverpool with a general cargo. It is likely that the *Nile* struck the Stones sometime between 2 and 3am in bad visibility and heavy weather. Fishermen and beachcombers at Portreath were the first to be aware of the wreck, as the cargo was washed ashore. Only one body was recovered. Nearly two weeks later the topmasts of the wreck were found showing just above water, about 1 mile north of the Stones. A week later the wreck broke up. The ship was valued at around £50,000 and insured for almost the full amount, but the cargo was carried at the risk of the shipping company, and represented a huge financial loss.

The wreck lies north-north-west to south-south-east in a general depth of 24 to 28m, with her stern to the north, lying on her starboard side, broken in two amidships, her engine the highest point of the wreck standing 3.5m above the general wreckage. Follow her propeller shaft forward past the engine room, where you will find a spare propeller stowed amidships. No boiler is visible among the wreckage. This is a particularly pretty site with marine life covering the entire wreck, and it is the home of a large shoal of butterfish. As with other wrecks off Godrevy, this is a recommended slack water dive.

182   Geneva   50.15.00N; 05.24.50W. Less than a year old when lost, this 998-ton, full-rigged sailing ship, registered at Quebec, was on passage from her home port to Liverpool when she was lost with all 21 crew on the Inner Stones on 28 October, 1870. She carried a general cargo, including cases of wine, brandy, whisky and beer; and over 50 barrels of wine were landed at St Ives when she began to break up. A wooden wreck, it is unlikely that anything other than her iron and non-ferrous fittings survive, but divers have found much evidence of wreck remains, despite heavy weed.

183   Elsa   50.14.50N; 05.24.30W. Built in Campbeltown in 1882, this 850-ton Glasgow-registered steamship was on passage for Bayonne from Glasgow, carrying coal, when she ran onto the Stones Reef in dense fog and calm conditions on 27 September, 1890. One man drowned, but 14 of the crew abandoned ship, eventually being picked up by the SS *Alice*. Although the *Elsa* went ashore very close to the Godrevy lighthouse, none of the keepers were aware of the wreck, nor had the crew of the steamship heard the lighthouse fog bell. The wreck quickly went to pieces where she lay, and her remains still lie broken and scattered among the boulders.

184 Noorlands 50.15.15N; 05.24.50W. The *Noorlands* (formerly *Salerno* and *Hogland*) was built in 1882 by Osborne, Graham & Company, Sunderland, and registered at Tonsberg. The first indication that the 1,207-ton collier had gone ashore was on 3 May, 1918, when the St Ives Coastguard reported red flares out at sea. The St Ives lifeboat was launched and proceeded to the Stones Reef, where more distress signals guided them to the Outer Stone, where they found the wreck. The lifeboat crew saved the 17 crew and Captain Peterson from their own boat.

185 Jason 50.16.15N; 05.25.45W. A requisitioned vessel of 798 tons, the steamship *Jason* (formerly *Ardanarch*) was launched at Port Glasgow in 1878 but in 1915 was taken over by the Admiralty as a combined collier-cum-ammunition ship. Carrying a crew of 16 under Captain F. J. Baxter, the four-masted vessel collided with the SS *Shoreham* of London, 2 miles north-north-west of Godrevy lighthouse in thick fog, foundering in 22m, north of the Stones buoy on 7 April, 1917.

186 Hampshire 50.23.30N; 05.24.30W. The London-registered 2,597-ton steamship *Hampshire* was on passage from Liverpool to Cardiff on 18 November, 1893, to load coal intended for Genoa, China and Japan. Under Captain Weir, the *Hampshire* had experienced dreadful weather conditions on passage, until eventually a spare length of propeller shaft carried in the afterhold broke its chain lashings, and smashed through the ship's hull. She capsized 2 hours later and there was only one survivor. The steamer sank in an approximate position given as 9 miles north of Godrevy Point.

187 Veghstroom 50.16.00N; 05.35.00W. A Liverpool-registered 1,353-ton vessel, built in 1902 at Rotterdam, the *Veghstroom* was carrying coal from Penarth to Le Havre when she was torpedoed on the starboard side by the German submarine *UC-47* on 23 August, 1917, 7 miles north-west of Godrevy Point. The crew of 29 got into two boats but one of these was dragged under by suction when the ship sank 7 minutes later, drowning five men. Other men thrown into the sea were picked up by the other boat after 30 minutes in the water, and were later rescued. The wreck lies in a general depth of 27 to 30m, north-east to south-west, with her bow to the north-east. Now well broken, her boilers are the highest part of the wreck, standing some 3m proud of the sea bed.

188 Sten 50.19.18N, 05.26.14W. This 928-ton vessel had four previous names (*Juana Nancy, Neva, Aarvak* and *Jan Mayn*), having been built in 1883 by Pearce & Company, Dundee. Registered at London, the *Sten* was on passage from Barry to St Malo carrying 1,000 tons of coal and a crew of 20 when, on 18 October, 1917, she was hit in the starboard side by a torpedo fired from the German submarine *UC-64*, causing her to sink almost immediately. There was only time to launch one boat, which got away with nine men. They managed to pull two more out of the water and attempted to save the captain, but without success. The *Sten* went down within 3 minutes. The wreck lies in a general depth of 20m, 5 miles north of Godrevy Island lighthouse.

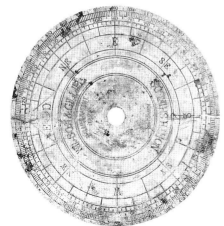

Left: This brass bearing plate from the bridge of the SS Kintuck (Site 189) carries the manufacturers' name.

Below: The small stern gun from the wreck of the St Chamond (Site 192) on the quay at Penzance after being recovered by divers. These defensive weapon were fitted to almost all French merchant ships and were old military weapons, many dating back to 1890 or earlier, fitted to specially made mountings suitable for ships.

189 Kintuck 50.14.20N, 05.31.57W. Having left London for Barry Roads in ballast, sailing alone off the north coast of Cornwall, this 4,639-ton steamship, registered at London and belonging to the China Mutual Steam Navigation Company, suffered a severe explosion in the after-part of the ship on 2 December, 1917. The shock immediately put the *Kintuck*'s engine and steering gear out of action, and she sank. She was abandoned at 3pm by 48 of her crew, leaving the master and ship's officers still on board. They left just before the ship foundered; the men were picked up by the SS *Lutece*. The vessel sank 8 miles north-west by north of Godrevy lighthouse and lies in 26m. Divers who have visited the wreck report that the entire stern is detached from the hull but lies only a short distance away. Armed with a stern gun, wooden boxes containing live brass shells have been found in the sand around her stern.

190 Zone 50.15.20N; 05.29.20W. Carrying a cargo of frozen meat from Las Palmas to Barry, this London-registered vessel was built in 1903 at Sunderland, armed with a quick-firing 4.7-inch stern gun. The *Zone* was attacked on 30 December, 1917, by a single torpedo fired by the German submarine *U-110*. The 41 crew abandoned the ship in their boats at 8.40am and were picked up by an armed patrol trawler.

The wreck lies 3 miles north-north-east of St Ives Head in a general depth of 28 to 32m, and is now very broken, her bow still holding the windlass and anchor cables, her engine and boilers still in their original position. It is claimed that the current owner of the wreck is R. Rogers, of Lyonesse Salvage, but this is suspect as the company is no longer in existence. The *Zone* is one of the most intact North Cornwall wrecks, and her three huge boilers, complete with resident conger eels, still stand on their original beds, while her propeller shaft is complete and still on its bearing blocks. Large shoals of bib and pollack abound.

191 Lutece 50.14.30N, 05.32.00W (unconfirmed). The *Lutece* was a small, 1,346-ton French-registered collier, carrying coal from Swansea to Rouen, when she was torpedoed and sunk without warning by the German submarine *U-4*, 5 miles west of Godrevy Island lighthouse, on 3 February, 1918. It is not known whether there were survivors.

192 St Chamond 50.14.50N; 05.29.54W. The *St Chamond*, another French steamship, built in 1913 at West Hartlepool, was on passage from Glasgow to St Nazaire on 30 April, 1918. She was carrying a general cargo and five railway locomotives, each of about 75 tons, as deck cargo. She was first attacked by gunfire then torpedoed by the German submarine *U-60* and sunk 1½ miles north-east of Clodgy Point.

Although now falling to pieces, the railway locomotives remain on the sea bed in 27m; the highest part of the wreck is the boilers, which stand in 6m. There can be few wrecks around the British Isles where you can descend onto a wreck and then explore the remains of five historic steam railway engines. A small 4-pounder, quick-firing stern gun was recovered by divers in the 1970s. The wreck is always teeming with shoals of bib and ling, which offer tremendous photographic opportunities. This is a slack water dive with a maximum depth of around 30m.

193 Dux 50.15.47N; 05.32.25W. Built in 1904 at Fredrikstad as the *Pollux*, and carrying a cargo of coal from Swansea to La Rochelle, the *Dux* was torpedoed on 8 May, 1918, by the German submarine *U-54*, when 7 miles north-west of Godrevy Island lighthouse. Taking only 3 minutes to sink, it is amazing that the entire crew managed to get away in one boat, which was then ordered alongside the enemy vessel. The crew were made to stand on the submarine's foredeck casing, after which the boat was cast adrift, and they feared the submarine would submerge, leaving them to drown. The German captain kept them there for nearly an hour, before ordering the men to get back aboard. The submarine then made off, but 30 minutes later returned and made a deliberate attempt to ram and sink the boat, after which the enemy ordered the captain of the *Dux* back to the submarine, where he was taken prisoner and ordered below deck. The rest of the crew rowed towards the Cornish coast and were picked up by a patrol vessel. After questioning on board the submarine, the imprisoned captain was released to a fishing boat and taken ashore the following day.

The wreck, orientated east–west, her bow to the west, lies 7 miles north-west of Godrevy Island lighthouse in 29 to 30m, having collapsed on a sandy shale bottom, leaving her engine and boilers upright in the centre of the wreck.

194 Gemini 50.17.44N; 05.36.20W. Launched in 1892 by the Blyth Shipbuilding Company as the *Dingwall*, this Shanghai-registered steamer was flying the Chinese flag when she was torpedoed on the port side amidships, 7 miles north-west of Godrevy Island lighthouse on 20 July, 1918, by the German submarine *U-60*. The steamer was taken in tow by a number of escort naval patrol vessels, who kept her afloat for over 4 hours until she sank. Two firemen in the crew were later found to be missing, presumably killed in the explosion, but the remaining 42 survivors were taken off to St Ives.

The wreck lies in a general depth of 36m, orientated north-north-east to south-south-west, with her bow to the north. Two boilers and engine stand 3m above the sea bed; the ship's bell was found by divers in June 1989.

195 Eleanor 50.15.05N; 05.25.28W (unconfirmed). Unlike most of the other offshore wrecks in this area, this 1,277-ton London-registered steamship sank following a machinery defect on 22 December, 1922. Carrying coal from Barry to Portsmouth, with a crew of 16 under Captain Walters, she was off Pendeen when she developed engine trouble. Distress signals were made, but not one of the many ships in the area stopped to assist because of heavy weather. By now, the *Eleanor* was 8 miles north-west of St Ives, so the local lifeboat was launched to go to their assistance. After rescuing twelve men and Captain Walters, the coxswain of the lifeboat, thinking he had saved the entire crew, was on the point of leaving for home, when three more men rushed out of the forecastle having been asleep below decks. The lifeboat took them off too, leaving the steamer to drift down towards the Stones, where it is believed she eventually sank in approximately 61m, close to Hevah Rock.

196 Secil Japan 50.14.15N, 05.21.40W. This Panamanian motor vessel carrying a general cargo from Aveiro to Liverpool suffered a cargo shift in extreme heavy weather and was blown ashore while attempting to reach St Ives Bay to anchor on 12 March, 1989. The *Secil Japan* broke into three parts very quickly. She was bought for a nominal sum by Colin Martin of Portreath, and a small team carried out extensive salvage over 2 years.

The wreck lies close in under the cliffs and is a very pleasant shallow dive, but sections of steel still lie balanced on boulders and other obstructions; great care is necessary and generally this can be a dangerous dive. The wreck is so close inshore – about 9m – there is no tide to worry about.

197 Ralph's Cupboard and Portreath 50.15.32N; 05.18.20W. Off Carvannel Downs, 1½ miles from Portreath, Ralph's Cupboard is a narrow cove with a deep, rocky fissure leading off a sandy beach. It is the site of a supposed historic treasure ship. There is a local legend that on Christmas Day, 1751, a 200-ton Spanish ship, carrying logwood, indigo, wine, silver specie and bullion, was wrecked in this cove. In 1985 the cove was explored using hand-held metal detectors and a portable magnetometer and a vast number of signals were obtained, many of them very large, suggesting buried iron cannon or shot, but it proved too deeply buried to be uncovered using hand tools. Locals confirm that during changes of sand level, iron cannon are frequently exposed here between boulders on the beach, so the remains of a ship obviously survive.

There are two large car parks, cafés and toilets at Portreath. A miniature and tidal harbour leads to the sea from an inner basin via a waterway, between the granite pier and cliffs. It is possible to launch into the inner harbour from a slipway and leave an inflatable there on moorings, but it is necessary to contact the harbourmaster for permission to do this and there is a fee and be aware that the basin dries at low water. The foundations of a large quay forming an earlier harbour built around 1713 on the western side of Portreath Cove have been revealed and wooden mooring posts, iron mooring rings, a gold guinea of 1739 and an American dollar of 1815 have been found.

198   Escurial   50.15.45N; 05.17.45W. The *Escurial* was a Glasgow-registered, 1,188-ton steamship, carrying coal from Cardiff to Fiume. On 25 January, 1895, she was sighted showing signals of distress by Coastguards at Portreath in very shallow water about 3 miles offshore. The St Ives and Hayle lifeboats were launched and the local cliff rescue team called out. When the St Ives boat reached the open sea the wind was so strong that she was forced to return. The steamship went ashore near Gull Rock, stern first. The Hayle lifeboat was dragged over the sands with great difficulty and was able to save two men who jumped overboard from the wreck but, out of 19 crew under Captain Andrews, 14 were drowned.

The ship's loss was attributed to heavy weather causing her to leak, her bilge pumps having choked on coal dust.The remains of the wreck lie in shallow water only 880yds from Portreath harbour entrance, a little to the east, inside Gull Rock. The bottom is flat sand but large portions of the wreck frequently uncover.

199   Newport   50.15.55N, 05.17.15W. Built in 1897 and carrying a crew of only four, on 27 January, 1930, this 64-ton 50ft coastal collier, fitted with a single mast, her machinery aft, was driven ashore in Gooden Heane Cove (west of Horse Rock, Portreath) in bad weather,. Iron plating and fittings can still be found among the rocks on the beach, but the site is no more than a shallow beach rummage.

200   St George   50.19.30N; 05.21.50W. The *St George* was a 548-ton British steamship, built in 1881 by the London and Glasgow Company and registered at Glasgow. She was fitted with a simple two-cylinder inverted engine of 90hp. On 28 November, 1882, she battled against a north-westerly Force 10 gale on passage from Swansea to Nantes. The heavy tarpaulins covering the after-hatch were washed away and she began to fill. As she settled low in the water, a boat was launched with seven crew, but before the remaining eleven men, including Captain Mackean, could lower the other boat, the ship foundered, drowning them all. She took to the sea bed 525 tons of coal and 100 tons of copper ingots.

The *St George*'s copper cargo was not discovered by divers until August 2002 and some 48 tons were recovered; ingots buried under her coal cargo in the after-hold remain to be found. The wreck has an owner and the only charter boat with permission to take divers there is the *Atlantic Diver* of Newquay, owned by Chris Lowe.

201   Eltham   50.18.05N; 05.14.15W. The Liverpool-registered collier *Eltham* was built in Dublin in 1915 and owned by the Mason Shipping Company Ltd. She was on passage from Swansea to Rouen with coal on 17 November, 1928, when she was seen ashore off Chapel Porth, apparently derelict. Heavy seas were breaking over the wreck and she quickly broke in two. The ship's anchors were stowed and, apart from the hull damage – thought to have been caused after stranding – there was no indication of why she had been abandoned. The fate of the eight crew remains a mystery.

The remains of the wreck lie some 200yds offshore, part buried in the sand, but frequently uncover and often presents a hazard to swimmers and small boats. The *Eltham*'s boiler was still visible in the late 1980s.

202   Bard   50.18.40N; 05.22.06W. This 709-ton Norwegian steamship (formerly the *Jens Meinich*) was built at Christiansand in 1892 and registered at Brevik. She was owned by A/S Furnlumd Company. The ship was torpedoed and sunk without loss of life by the German submarine *U-60* on 11 December, 1917, while carrying coal from Glasgow to Hennebont. The wreck lies in a general depth of 33m, orientated north-east to south-west, but the hull has now collapsed and the highest part of the wreck appears to be the boilers. She has been heavily salvaged but a four-bladed cast-iron propeller is still visible.

203   Buffalo   50.19.20N; 05.18.45W (unconfirmed). An elderly 286-ton Whitehaven collier, built in 1866 by the Thames Iron Works, had loaded a cargo of coal at Cardiff for a port of unknown destination, when she was torpedoed on 19 September, 1918, with the loss of ten lives, including Captain O'Keefe. The wreck lies in a general depth of 30m on a sand bottom and is very broken up.

204   Union Crystal   50.27.00N; 05.34.00W. This 499-ton Malaysian motor vessel, registered at Singapore, built in 1965 by Martin Jansen at Leer, had two previous names (*Majo* until 1972, then *Timrix*). In 1975 her name was changed to *Union Crystal* and she was owned by Sugar Maritime Union Transport Ltd. She was carrying a cargo of salt from Kilroot to Poole when she developed a list in heavy weather, her cargo having shifted, causing her to capsize and founder on 16 November, 1977.

There are no further recommended beach diving sites until you reach Trevaunance Cove, north of St Agnes Head, as Porthtowan and Chapel Porth coves are extensive low-tide sand beaches, ideal for families, swimming and wind surfing, but offering nothing for divers. The cliffs here are very high and unstable, and lifeguard patrols operate during the summer.

AREA 12:

St Agnes to
Trevose Head

This 9-mile stretch of coastline consists of high cliffs from St Agnes Head to Perranporth (or Perran Bay), where there is a 2-mile stretch of sandy beach. However, Perranporth has no slipway or launching facility and the long beach offers nothing for divers apart from general facilities. Then the cliffs continue north-east to Crantock and Fistral Bay, which marks the beginning of Newquay. There are few rocks off this stretch of coast apart from two large outcrops north-east of St Agnes Head, known as Bawden Rocks, and Carter's Rocks off Penhale Point at the south end of Holywell Bay.

St Agnes was once an important outlet for tin and copper, but fell into decay in the 1920s when mining ceased. All that remains of the old St Agnes harbour is a tumble of cut granite blocks in the shallows, among which you can find various remains, some merely by snorkelling.

The access slip and foreshore is privately owned, and it is best to enquire of the whereabouts of the owner before you launch an inflatable boat, as you may be charged a nominal fee. The concrete ramp leading to the beach has a series of steps of about 10cm each. Launching here requires a four-wheel drive vehicle, and you must return to the car park with your trailer and vehicle. Grey seals are a feature of St Agnes, and the cliffs are breeding grounds for gulls, fulmars, guillemots and kittiwakes.

205 Hanover 50.20.05N, 05.10.48W. Probably the most famous of all the treasure wrecks on the north coast of Cornwall, the loss of the packet ship *Hanover* in 1763 caused much excitement at the time as she carried a vast quantity of gold specie and other valuables, the bulk of which was not recovered until 16 months after she was wrecked. Ships of the packet service, which carried mail and valuables as far afield as Malta and the West Indies, were fast brigs armed with up

Opposite: Bedruthan Steps, north of Mawgan Porth.

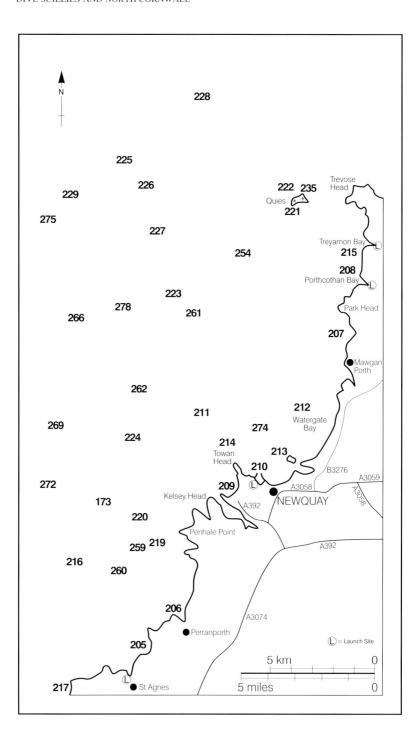

*Right: The wreck of the
Hanover (Site 205) was
identified by the discovery of
the ships bell, bearing its
name, which apart from a
broken hanging tabanacle,
was in pristine condition.*

*Below: A middle-deck lead
scupper strainer plate, found
in the wreck of the Hanover.*

Opposite: Dive sites in Area 12: St Agnes to Trevose Head.

On passage from Iquique to Falmouth, the Dunkirk-registered steel barque Seine was wrecked near Droskyn Head, on Perranporth beach on 28 December, 1900 (Site 206). The wreck was sold, but quickly became engulfed in the sandy beach.

to 14 cannon. These vessels had disciplined crews and 'commanders' rather than captains. They were the equal of small warships or gun brigs, which made an important contribution to communication between Britain and many of its outposts. There were a number of packet vessels named *Hanover*, and that lost between St Agnes and Cligga Head was the third such ship in packet service. She left Falmouth for Lisbon in late October 1763, remained there for two weeks, then sailed for home on 21 November, carrying a crew of 39 and 11 passengers. In addition to mail and dispatches, she carried more than 50,000 Portuguese gold moidas. The overall value of the gold was £67,500, equivalent in 1998 to about £1,822,500. She was also thought to have carried private treasure and diamonds belonging to her passengers valued in excess of 10,000 moidas, worth £13,500 at the time or £364,500 today. Commander Sherburn had no way of knowing that he was to encounter one of the worst south-easterly hurricanes of the century in the English Channel.

The *Hanover* managed to reach England under storm canvas, but in the Channel was blown past the Lizard and Land's End. Some 50 miles off course, the ship sought the shelter of the north coast. When the wind changed it was for the worse, swinging quickly to the north-west, and the crew had no choice but to try to sail north-east, past Gurnard's Head and St Ives; they managed to reach St Agnes as darkness fell on 2 December, 1763. Only three seamen survived, who could give no real account of events other than that the packet drove ashore under the 92m cliffs in the dark.

A reward of 1,000 guineas was offered to anyone who could recover the money or other valuables from the ship, in particular a large iron chest, which contained the main treasure, but nothing was found. A change of sand levels in April 1765 caused the main iron chest, which had remained intact, to uncover and it was sent to London.

The wreck lay forgotten in Hanover Cove, named after the wreck, until 1994, when two Portreath divers relocated her remains. At first they thought they had found the wreck of a man-of-war, as the sea bed was covered in iron cannon. The *Hanover* packet had been armed with only 14 carriage-mounted 8-pounder guns whereas the huge collection they found included cannon of different calibres up to 28-pounder size, which was most confusing. Investors raised sufficient capital for a full excavation programme to begin in July 1997. Huge submersible electric pumps were used to pump thousands of tons of sand out to sea, uncovering a large quantity of the ship's hull structure, more iron cannon and boxes of muskets. After a month the operation was closed down at the instigation of the Archaeological Diving Unit, on the orders of the Secretary of State, who designated the wreck a Protected Site, an order still in force. Litigation followed, and Hydrasalve Ltd appeared in the High Court, obtaining a temporary injunction, but by now the weather had deteriorated and the operation was forced to close down – but not until some 58 iron cannon and a large quantity of shot had been raised.

The wreck remains lie alongside a large rock in the shallows, buried for most of the year beneath 4m of sand. There can be little doubt that a great many gold and silver coins, in addition to personal artefacts, still lie buried in the foreshore awaiting resumption of excavation work.

206 Seine 50.21.05N; 05.09.45W. The 2,185-ton *Seine* was built in 1899 at Rouen and registered at Dunkirk. She had been sailing for 81 days from Iquique to Falmouth for orders, carrying nitrate, when a west-north-westerly gale off Scilly forced Captain Guimper to head for the Bristol Channel. On 27 December, 1900, the clipper came within sight of St Agnes Head. The Perranporth and St Agnes rocket crew realised the ship was in distress and being driven before the wind, and were waiting when she ran ashore just north of Chapel Rock, near Droskyn Head; seven men were landed before the vessel lurched and broke the breeches buoy hawser. Six local youths waded into the sea and threw a line to them, by which means the last five men reached safety. By dawn the vessel lay on her starboard side and went to pieces. Two weeks later the wreck was sold to a Newquay sea captain for £42. Parts of the wreck still uncover on the foreshore following a gale or lowering of the beach level, but this cannot be considered a true dive site.

207 Samaritan 50.29.00N; 05.02.00W. There is little left of this 200-ton wooden brig among the rocks at Bedruthan Steps, but brass candle sticks have been found and her keel occasionally emerges from the sand close to the Samaritan Island, between Queen Bess Rock and Redcove Island, only a short distance north of the cliff stairway. Outward bound for Constantinople from Liverpool, with a valuable general cargo, the brig drove ashore on 23 October, 1846. Only two of the crew of 12 survived. There was much looting by local people as the cargo washed ashore.

208 Sicilia 50.30.40N; 05.01.55W. This 2,129-ton steamship, built as the *Mississippi* in 1871 by McMillan and Son, Dumbarton, was 3 days out from Garston, Liverpool, bound for Barcelona with coal slag when on the night of 1 October, 1895, she encountered a severe gale. By 2am she lay on her beam ends, her pumps choked and boiler fires out. She remained in this position for 16 hours until the Cardiff collier *Caerleon* appeared and took her in tow, but the line soon parted. In the meantime the 28 crew on the *Sicilia* cleared the pumps, lowered the water level and relit her boilers, but the other vessel had no sooner departed than the severe flooding returned. At 3am on 3 October the ship was abandoned to drift ashore 600 yds off Minas Cove, near Porthcothan. The Liverpool Indiaman, the *James Alexander*, was also wrecked here in January 1860.

209   Newquay Town and Harbour   Newquay is surrounded by a number of attractive beaches, none of which have any launching slipways and they are not recommended for diving. There is a small harbour and slipway from which inflatables can be launched easily at high and low water neap tides. However the harbour dries out completely on low springs, when you should launch at least 30 minutes before low tide, making the most of a 1–2m deep scour channel around the harbour wall: a four-wheel drive vehicle is essential. Parking and access from March to October can be difficult, and an early launch is recommended. The only other launching place at Newquay is from a small sandy beach, part of The Ganell, but a four-wheel drive vehicle is necessary.

210   Newquay Old Lifeboat slip   This slip offers probably the only worthwhile shore dive at Newquay, but it should only be attempted 2 hours either side of high water. Enter the sea from a small, sandy bay to the right of the slipway and exit on the slip only if there is no swell. There is safe shallow diving down to 12m near the headland; rock gives way to sand and off the slip there are walls, gullies and caves. Little Fistral beach offers parking and shore diving is easy from the opposite side of the headland.

The Hemsley I, built in 1916, was on passage from Liverpool to Antwerp for breaking when she went ashore in Fox's Cove, west of Treyarnon Bay, in dense fog and a gale on 12 May, 1969 (Site 215).

Right: Trescore Island.

Below: The 1883 builders' nameplate from the wreck of the SS Whinfield (Site 221), which was found loose in the mass of collapsed steel forward of her bridge superstructure.

211   Syracusa   50.26.25N, 05.06.42W. This 1,243-ton Hamburg steamship was carrying coal from Newport to Naples when she suffered a shift in her cargo during a gale on 6 March, 1897. The Newquay lifeboat, *Willie Rogers*, put out but was defeated by huge seas. At 11pm three flares were shown by the ship, then nothing more was seen until daybreak, when her topmasts were seen sticking up out of the sea, close inshore.

The wreck lies 330yds off Towan Head, in 35m. It is 25m to the top of the boiler lying within the hull; a smaller third donkey boiler lies off to the port side. The *Syracusa*'s prop shaft can be followed to a four-bladed propeller, which lies detached, flat on the sea bed. The most intact part of the wreck is her bow section.

212   Poll Texas   50.26.396N; 05.04.676W (GPS). Poll Texas is a rock pinnacle about half a mile from Porth Island and just over 1 mile from Newquay Harbour. The top of the pinnacle lies in 12–14m and drops off to 18m. The north side of the rock shelves gradually but the south side is near vertical, covered in fan coral.

213   Milky Rough   This reef lies 325ft off Porth Island, Newquay, at a depth of 12m. This interesting dive offers long, deep gullies running right through the reef.

214   Towan Head Reef   50.26.010N; 05.06.231W (GPS). This is a large reef with many pinnacles and some sheer faces. There is abundant marine life.

The 264-ton schooner Petrel, of Leith, was on passage from Leghorn to Belfast on 9 December, 1886. She was carrying a valuable cargo of cut marble when she was driven stern first into Wine Cove, in Treyarnon Bay, where she went to pieces. Parts of a timber wreck have been located in the shallows. The marble cargo of the Petrel was of sufficient value for a salvor to provide two steam-driven traction engines on the cliff top. Uusing a wood boom as a crane, these enabled the company to recover the blocks. The lower photograph shows shows a block in mid-air, and men at work on the wreck preparing the remaining marble for lifting. The salvaged marble was later sold to a monumental mason at St Austell.

215   Hemsley I   50.31.24N; 05.01.45W. *Hemsley I* was built for the Admiralty in 1916 by the Tyne Iron Steamboat Company Ltd as the *Scotol*. Following a long career working in the Mersey and Manchester ship canal, this 1,178-ton London-registered ship was sold for breaking at Antwerp. She set off on her final voyage from Liverpool in April, but in fog and a southerly gale went ashore under the high cliffs; the crew escaped by clambering onto the rocks and up the cliffs.

The wreck was partially salvaged in the shallows, but parts of her hull still show above the surface at low water, and her engine room machinery and fittings lie scattered across the sea bed on a very rocky bottom.

North of Park Head is Trescore Island, which lies a little to the south of Porthcothan, where there is a possible launch site off the B3276 Newquay–Padstow road. Inside the island there is evidence of a shipwreck, as small clay tiles are scattered in the sand, and two large caves are worth exploring. At the back of one of them is a large hole through to the clifftop. The road continues to Treyarnon and Constantine Bays.

Offshore dive sites and wrecks

216   Kynance   50.22.00N; 05.15.10W. When some 12 miles off St Ives Head at 5.30pm on 3 May, 1875, this 327-ton Falmouth-registered collier encountered thick fog and collided with the Greek SS *Ithaca* – although the identity of that ship was not known until it was later arrested after entering Wapping Dock at Bristol, still bearing scars of the accident. The *Kynance* was struck just abaft her foremast rigging, destroying her lifeboat and davits, the bow of the other vessel cutting well into her side. The *Ithaca* backed off, then carried on her course, paying no attention to signals and cries for assistance. With only one small boat remaining intact, the twelve crew got into it but were forced to leave their belongings behind. The *Kynance* sank nine minutes after the collision.

217   Prestige   50.18.34N; 05.14.02W. This composite motor 284-ton mine-sweeper, built in 1944 and 128ft long, was repurchased by the Royal Navy in 1953 for conversion to a degaussing vessel, but the work was never completed and she was sold in 1958 for disposal. Under tow of the MFV *Micalen* for Milford Haven, she met with a north-westerly gale on 7 December, 1960, well out to sea from the Bawden (Man and His Man) Rocks, and foundered. There was no one on board at the time. The wreck lies about 880yds south of St Agnes Head; her bow, engine and general wreckage lie close in below the cliffs in about 4.5m.

218   Rossmore   50.24.45N; 05.14.15W. The 627-ton coaster Rossmore, built in 1907 at Port Glasgow, was a Cardiff-registered, Portreath-owned collier. She was on passage from Hayle to Barry in ballast on 25 March, 1941, when she was bombed and sunk by German aircraft off Kelsey Head, when 12 miles north-east of Godrevy light. Of her crew of ten, six were killed; the collier went down in 37m on a sandy sea bed.

219   Harriet Shiel   50.23.00N; 05.11.00W (unconfirmed). Very little is known about this 352-ton Dieppe-bound small collier of Liverpool. She disappeared off Perran Bay during a severe northerly gale on 26 October, 1886, with all hands.

Wreckage identified as belonging to her was washed ashore on Perran Sands. It is generally believed that she sank off Penhale Point.

220   Sandfly   50.24.30N; 05.10.30W. Carrying 60 tons of sand from Hayle to Llanelli, this small 33-ton coaster developed a severe leak and sank west of Kelsey Head on 25 September, 1920, leaving 4.5m of her mainmast showing above water. The crew took to their boat and landed safely at Newquay.

221   Whinfield   50.32.43N: 05.03.18W. The *Whinfield* was built in 1883 by the Tyne Shipbuilding Company Ltd at Newcastle and fitted with a two-cylinder compound engine. She carried a crew of 19. This 1,468-ton Newcastle-registered vessel, carrying a cargo of iron ore between Decido and Cardiff, encountered heavy fog on 24 April, 1901, and Captain T. Gorvin lost his way and drove ashore. The ship was abandoned and the survivors were picked up by a pilot boat. The wreck is very broken, lying scattered among large rocks in 10m, only her boilers identifiable.

Two large islands and several smaller rock outcrops 1 mile west from Trevose Head, named the Quies, offer excellent diving, as they hold the remains of two steamships and several sailing vessels. They are easy to locate, lie surrounded by 18m of water, and offer a wide variety of fish life and marine growth, particularly cup anemones.

222   Runswick   50.32.43N; 05.03.18W. Another steamship wreck lies only a short distance from the *Whinfield*, on the north-east side of the Quies. Though registered at London, the *Runswick* was on charter to the Italian government and carrying a cargo of coal from Newport to Barry Roads and then to Italy when she was torpedoed by the German submarine *UB-109* on 18 April, 1918. She was taken in tow by patrol vessels but later drifted ashore on the outer Quies. The crew of 33 abandoned ship and were rescued. The wreck lies in a maximum depth of 21m. Although broken, large sections complete with winches remain, and one of the two boilers now stands on end protruding some 5m above the wreck. Ownership of the wreck is currently vested in Mr N. Cavill of Newquay. This is a scenic dive, but avoid diving here on spring tides or in ground seas.

223   Jackal   50.30.00N; 05.08.00W. The exact location of this 181-ton paddle steamer is unknown. Built in 1881 by Thomson's at Glasgow, she was on her way to Falmouth when she disappeared south-west of Trevose Head on 26 November, 1881. The steamer was seen by the Trevose Coastguard on the morning of 25 November heading south, but next morning the St Agnes Coastguard lookout reported she had turned round and was heading back up channel, but in no apparent distress. Two days later identifiable wreckage was found ashore under Trevose Head, but the bodies of the nine crew and Captain Downer, who had accompanied Livingstone on several African voyages and was familiar with the African coast, were never found.

224   Indus   50.28.00N; 05.08.00W. The 2,486-ton *Indus* was built in 1884 by Gourlay Brothers at Dundee, and was carrying coal from Cardiff to Dieppe and Tenerife, 6 miles south-west of Trevose Head on 14 October, 1886. She lost a foreward hold bilge plate in heavy weather, filled and sank. The crew of 31 under Captain Robert Leslie, and one passenger, all escaped in a lifeboat.

225 City of Bristol Location unknown. This 796-ton Dublin-registered iron steamship, carrying coal from Swansea to Rotterdam and a crew of 18 under Captain J. Moran, disappeared on 29 September, 1898. One of her boats was picked up off Trevose Head and bodies of some of the crew were washed ashore near Linney Head. Her bridge structure drifted down as far as the Wolf Rock, but where she sank is a mystery: it is unlikely that she has been found.

226 White Rose Location unknown. Another mystery wreck off Trevose Head, this 2,691-ton Liverpool-registered steamship was carrying a general cargo from Boulogne to Llanelli when she foundered on 20 March, 1920, following collision offshore with the British SS *Fantee*. Her crew were saved.

227 Bratto 50.31.45N; 05.08.00W (unconfirmed). Built in 1890 at Sjotorp, Sweden, the ship carried four different names during her 30-year career (*Glasbruk III*, *Express*, *Express I* and *Bratto*). She was registered at Newcastle. Loaded with china clay taken on board at Penzance, destined for Preston, she met heavy weather and was forced into Hayle harbour. She sailed before the weather settled and again experienced heavy weather off Trevose Head, where she developed a serious leak and her engine room had to be abandoned. Her signals of distress were seen by the SS *Woodburn*, on passage for Genoa, who took off the crew of eight and Captain Hart on 25 November, 1920. The abandoned steamship, whose machinery was in the aft part of the vessel, was still afloat when last seen, and may have drifted some distance before sinking.

228 Sturdee Rose 50.35N; 05.05.00W (unconfirmed). This Liverpool-registered steamship was loaded with coal taken on board at Garston and destined for Plymouth when she took on a heavy list on 15 November, 1945. She had already developed a bad leak and when this worsened her crew of ten took to the ship's liferaft. Captain Alcorn was below decks searching for distress flares when she went down by the head and he drowned. The liferaft was blown seaward and the survivors were unable to attract the attention of any of the ships they could see on the horizon. For 8½ days they remained adrift, and six had died of exposure when they were picked up 30 miles off Waterford.

229 Humbergate 50.33.00N; 05.11.30W (unconfirmed). On 2 October, 1963, this 200-ton Hull-registered motor vessel was on passage for Bristol. In heavy weather, she developed a severe list when her cargo of granite chippings shifted. It was obvious she would capsize, so the crew of five under Captain George O'Brien took to their liferaft. Fortunately the wind blew the raft steadily towards the shore and they landed near West Pentire, in Porth Joke Cove, near Newquay.

AREA 13:

Trevose Head and Padstow

Only one of the beaches between Newquay and Padstow is suitable for diving or launching and if you intend to dive in this area you are recommended to base your activities on Padstow. It is also possible to launch a large inflatable at Trevone Bay, but you will need the help of a four-wheel drive vehicle, as there is no slipway. There are facilities (shop, café and toilets) on the beach.

230   Padstow   This historic fishing port, 2½ miles up the Camel Estuary, dates back to the 6th century and in the days of sailing ships was North Cornwall's most successful seaport. Trade declined as ships became bigger and the river became difficult to navigate because of silting. Across the port's mouth, reaching from Hawker's Cove to Daymer Bay, stretches the infamous Doom Bar, a natural sand bank, which has caused the loss of more than a hundred ships; it is notorious for its ability to change position, and the channel to and from Padstow shifts frequently and unpredictably. There is a road from Padstow to Trevose Head, where a lighthouse stands 75m above the sea. This whole area is a mixture of very steep cliffs, rock and low-tide sandbanks.

   The entrance to Padstow Bay is dominated by two headlands: Stepper Point to the south and Pentire Point and its offshore islands to the north. Stepper Point is such a prominent headland that in the 1800s work began to lower the height of the cliff, and many thousands of tons of granite were removed. The project took so long that it was eventually overtaken by the development of steam-powered ships, and abandoned.

   There is an ideal launch site near the harbourmaster's office, with adjacent parking, public toilets, pubs, shops and cafés. There is also an inner harbour, reached via lock-gates, open either side of high water, which is available for larger live-aboard diving vessels. Permission of the harbourmaster must be obtained

Opposite: The lighthouse on Trevose Head.

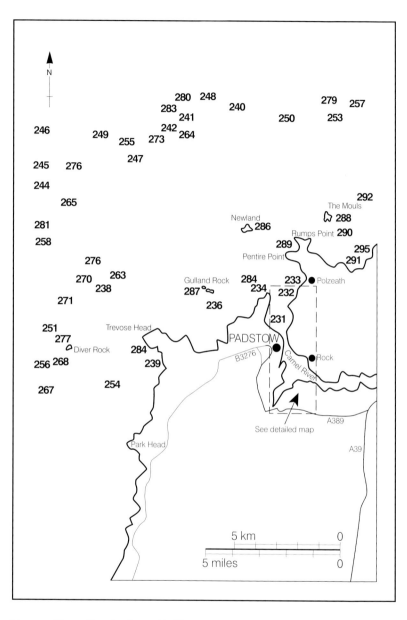

**Above: Dive sites in Area 13, Trevose Head and Padstow.
For a detailed map of the marked area see page 165.**

before launching from either slipway, and you should be aware that Padstow is very tidal, the estuary drying out at low water. Familiarise yourself with the dangers of the Doom Bar. There is a third concrete slip near the sailing club compound, at the start of the Camel Cycle Trail and car park. The port is well served with chandlers, outboard engine repair and spares, marine engineers and a museum with many displays concerning local shipping and shipwrecks.

Modest river dues must be paid by all craft navigating the Camel within the port limits upstream of a line from Stepper Point to Pentire Point. Launching fees, dictated by engine capacity, are reasonable and payable to the harbourmaster's office. Call the Padstow harbour office (tel. 0841 532239 or 0841 532052 if out of hours), the berthing master (tel. 0841 533228) or the Shore Bosun (tel. 0841 532079), as appropriate.

Coastal dive sites

231 HMS Whiting   50.33.12N; 04.56.15W. This Royal Navy armed schooner of 14 guns, built by Arrow in 1812, was sent into the Irish Sea to catch smugglers, but when she met fog Lieutenant John Jackson decided to put into Padstow. Unfamiliar with the area, and without a pilot, he put the ship ashore on the Doom Bar, and all attempts using anchors and sail to get her off failed. All the ship's guns were thrown overboard but at high water it was found she was leaking badly and she was eventually abandoned as a total wreck. Her crew of 50 and most of her stores were landed, but the wreck capsized and became a navigational hazard. Eleven years later a sandbank had formed around the wreck, which threatened to block the main channel; eventually a Captain Joseph Odgers managed to refloat her using dockyard pontoons. Although nothing of the hull remains, several iron cannon became exposed on the Bar at low spring tides in the 1980s and a number have been recovered.

232 HMS Medea   50.33.58N; 04.55.48W. The 540-ton vessel, then called *M-22*, was built by Raylton Dixon at Middlesbrough in 1915 as an M-class coastal monitor and armed with a 9.2-inch and a 3-inch gun. In 1919 the *M-22* was converted into a minelayer and given the name *Medea* from 1925, being sold out of service to Cashmore Shipbreakers Ltd, Newport, Monmouthshire in December 1938. She was on passage under tow of a tug with a four-man towing crew when she broke loose off Trevose Head on 28 January, 1939, during a hurricane. She drove ashore on Greenaway Rocks, where one man was washed overboard and drowned, but the other three were saved by breeches buoy. The old monitor was scrapped where she lay, and today rusting wreckage and a large concrete post mark the double bottom and hull plating of the wreck.

233 Immacolata   50.34.25N; 04.55.30W. This Italian brigantine, on passage from Corfu to Falmouth with a cargo of bones, missed stays on entering Padstow Bay and was stranded close to the Doom Bar on 26 September, 1875. The lifeboat *Albert Edward* put out and took off her crew, but overnight she dragged and went ashore at Polzeath, where she went to pieces, leaving wreckage strewn the length of the beach.

The *Immacolata*'s bell was recovered and hung in the tower of St Enodoc church. When taken down in 2000 for new iron work to be installed it was found that the embossed name on the bell was *Sahel* and not *Immacolata* as everyone had expected. This was probably her previous name, and the matter is still being investigated.

234 Favourite   50.34.05N; 04.57.10W. This 1,039-ton American full-rigged ship, in ballast from London to Cardiff, her home port Boston, USA, was the largest sailing ship lost on Stepper Point. A north-north-westerly Force 11 hurricane drove her into a cove named Butterhole, behind Stepper Point, on 25 October, 1859, drowning all 36 of the crew, including Captain Wilson. The *Favourite* was one of 26 vessels lost in the area the same day. She went ashore on the rocks directly under the daymark marking the entrance to the estuary. Pieces of copper found by divers here probably belonged to the ship as she was copper-sheathed and fastened.

Offshore dive sites and wrecks

There are many offshore reefs, pinnacles, islands and rocks to explore off Padstow's estuary. Within 1½ miles of Stepper Point and Pentire Point – themselves well worth a shallow dive – you will find Gurley Rock (3m in 12m); Chimney Rock (2m in 13m); The Hen (5m in 13m); Tom's Rock (7m in 15m) and the Roscarrock, which breaks surface in 16m. A little further out are Mouls Island, Newland Island and Gulland Rock. Deeper still, the Inner and Outer Gulland Reefs lie in 26m and 33m respectively. West of Trevose Head are the Quies Rocks, with many shipwrecks, and Diver Rock (14m in 30m), which is further out and has a wreck almost next to it.

235 Royal Albert   50.34.15N; 05.04.20W. On the Quies Rocks, west of Trevose Head, in addition to two steamship wrecks lie the remains of the 1,437-ton *Royal Albert*, an iron full-rigged ship from Liverpool, which was carrying a general cargo from Calcutta to Liverpool on 16 January, 1866. She carried goods insured for £160,000, a huge sum at that time. At first it was thought that having struck the rocks she had got off and sunk in deep water, as there was no sign of Captain Davies or his 34 crew. It was not until July 1866 that remains of the vessel were found among the rocks,. and much cargo was also recovered. What happened to the crew remains a mystery, as weather conditions when the ship struck were not severe.

236 Devitz   50.33.55N; 04.59.45W. Another large sailing vessel lost in the approach to Padstow Bay was the Prussian sailing vessel *Devitz*, in ballast for Cardiff from Cork. An early report stated that the hull of this ship, of 500 to 600 tons, was seen 880yds inside the Gulland Rock where she sank on 19 March, 1869, with the loss of Captain Grouon and all twelve crew. Part of the wreck was washed

Opposite: Detailed map of the Camel estuary at Padstow.

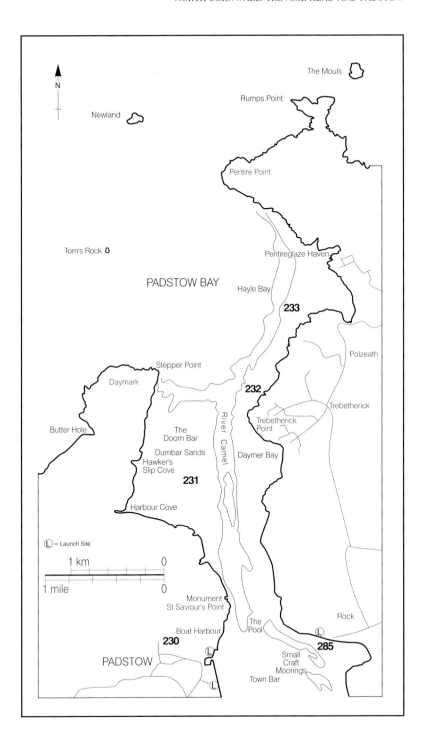

N

The Mouls

Rumps Point

Newland

Pentire Point

Tom's Rock

Pentireglaze Haven

PADSTOW BAY

Hayle Bay

233

Polzeath

Stepper Point

Daymark

232

Trebetherick

Butter Hole

Trebetherick
Point

River Camel

The
Doom Bar

Dumbar Sands

Daymer Bay

Hawker's
Slip Cove

231

Harbour Cove

Ⓛ = Launch Site

1 km   0

1 mile   0

Monument
St Saviour's Point

Rock

The
Pool

Boat Harbour

Ⓛ

285

230

Ⓛ

Small
Craft
Moorings

PADSTOW

Town Bar

Ⓛ

ashore in Trevose Bay. The location of this wreck is speculative, and presumably lies between Gulland and Gurley Rocks, in a general depth of 25m.

237 Galatea 50.40.00N; 05.12.00W (unconfirmed). This 353-ton Swansea-registered barque was carrying coal from Swansea to Cape Town when she collided with the SS *Edendale* of Sunderland on 5 December, 1880. As the weather was fine, there was no obvious reason for the accident except for negligence on the part of the steamship's officers, which bore down on the sailing ship at full speed, cutting into her port side and deck level with her foremast shrouds. Captain James and twelve crew got away by boat.

238 Countess Evelyne 50.35.00N; 05.05.00W (unconfirmed). During the afternoon of Saturday 13 May, 1893, this 864-ton Cardiff-registered steamer, laden with iron ore taken on board at Bilbao for Cardiff, ran into patches of dense fog. Although her speed was reduced to dead slow ahead and her siren sounded at regular intervals, at 11.20pm she collided with the Dublin-registered SS *City of Hamburg*. The impact appeared so slight that those on board the Irish vessel were totally unaware that they had damaged another ship. Captain J. Evans of the *Countess Evelyne* ran forward on the main deck to see what had happened, but only just had time to jump onto the bow of the other vessel before his ship sank beneath him. The First Officer managed to scramble out through the hole made in the side of the ship, reporting that she sank in less than 1½ minutes. He and the captain were the only survivors of a crew of 16 and eight passengers.

239 E. S. Lancaster 50.32.44N; 05.02.23W. In ballast from Newhaven to Cardiff, where she intended to load coal, this 294-ton collier, registered at Cardiff and built in 1890, struck Dinas Head on the west side of Trevose Head at 3am on 11 October, 1894, and foundered. Some of the crew of twelve, under Captain T. Kelly, landed at Trevose Head in their own boat, leaving the masts of their ship just showing above water. The remains of the vessel lie in some 11m very broken and scattered among dense kelp weed.

240 Labarrouere 50.45.40N; 04.58.30W (unconfirmed). On passage from Cardiff to St Nazaire carrying coal, this 1,173-ton Cardiff-registered steamship, built in 1880 by Palmers & Company at Newcastle, was steaming in calm conditions with a smooth sea, but towards dawn it became dark with heavy drizzle. At 6.30am, without warning, the ship was struck a terrific blow on the port side between her mizzen mast and stern. The vessel involved was never seen, but investigation revealed it was almost certainly the schooner *Western Maid*, which also sank. The *Labarrouere* foundered within an hour of the accident, but all the crew managed to escape. The six crew of the *Western Maid* were also saved.

241 Drumcree 50.40.48N; 04.59.50W. The Chief and Third Officers were on the bridge of this Liverpool steamship on 18 May, 1915, on passage from Barry to Port Arthur in ballast, when they saw the track of a torpedo only 300ft away, as they were 11 miles north by east of Trevose Head. The explosion amidships destroyed the *Drumcree*'s engine room, the radio room and accommodation areas. No distress signals could be broadcast as the ship's radio equipment was destroyed, but the SS *Ponto* pulled alongside and took the *Drumcree* in tow. However, a second torpedo struck the *Drumcree*'s stern and she began to go down. Captain

A. Hodgson and the 36 crew took to the boats and were picked up by the *Ponto*, which got away safely.

242   Dumfries   50.45.12N; 05.01.25W. Built in 1905 by W. Dunford & Sons at Sunderland as the *Carthusian*, this 4,121-ton vessel was carrying coal from Cardiff to Leghorn, when she was torpedoed at 11am without warning on 19 May, 1915. She immediately took a heavy list to starboard. A patrol trawler, HMS *Kudos*, which had witnessed the attack, went alongside and took off the 54 crew. The wreck lies in a general depth of 35m, but her current condition is uncertain.

243   Armenian   50.27.30N; 05.32.45W. The *Armenian* was the largest merchant ship lost off the north coast of Cornwall. The 8,825-ton liner, built by Harland and Wolff, Belfast, in 1895 belonged to F. Leyland & Company, registered at Liverpool, was torpedoed and sunk 20 miles west of Trevose Head on 28 June, 1915. She was on passage from Newport News, USA, to Avonmouth carrying 3,000 army mules destined for the war in France, and 162 crew. The German submarine *U-24* was seen approaching the liner on her port bow when still about 3 miles distant. Captain Trickery at once altered course to put the enemy vessel astern, but the difference in their respective speeds allowed the submarine to overhaul them quickly and commence to shell the vessel. After a 30-minute chase the liner was so badly damaged she was forced to stop her engine and the crew abandoned ship. No sooner had they got clear than the enemy fired two torpedoes into the stationary ship, and she sank with all 3,000 mules and a cargo of general military stores. Nine of the crew and 20 cattle attendants were killed, 14 others wounded.

Few divers have visited this site, but it is understood that she lies upright in 84m, with five boilers obvious, animal bones everywhere and many huge rectangular portholes still fitted. The wreck presents a huge target on an echo-sounder, side-scan sonar or magnetometer.

244   Magda   50.32.00N; 05.16.30W (unconfirmed). Built at Port Glasgow by R. Duncan & Company in 1905, the *Magda* carried the previous name *Darry*. This Norwegian steamship, registered at Tonsberg, was carrying coal from Port Talbot to Rouen when she was captured by the German submarine *U-27*, 8 miles west of Trevose Head. Her crew was forced to abandon ship, after which she was sunk by gunfire.

245   Sverresborg   50.34.00N; 05.18.00W (unconfirmed). The *Sverresborg* was torpedoed on the same day as the *Magda*, by the same German submarine, the *U-27*. This Bergen-registered Norwegian steamship was carrying coal, loaded at Barry and destined for Le Havre, and apparently sank without loss of life.

246   Ministre Beernaert   50.52.00N; 05.31.00W (unconfirmed). Owned by Cie Royale Belgo-Argentine and built by the Northumberland Shipbuilding Company at Newcastle in 1907, this 4,205-ton Antwerp-registered Belgian steamer, formerly *Graciana*, was torpedoed and sunk by the German submarine *UB-24*. Fitted with a three-cylinder triple expansion engine of 372hp, served by three boilers, she went down without loss of life.

247   Essonite   50.38.45N; 05.04.06W. This Glasgow-registered steamship was built in 1904 by Scott and Sons at Bowling and had an overall length of 53m with an 8.56m beam. She was on passage from Caernarfon to Rochester, carrying a cargo of stone on 1 February, 1917, when, 3 miles north-north-west of Trevose Head, she was torpedoed and sunk by the German submarine *U-55*, with the loss of ten of her crew.

248   Diligent   50.45.45N; 04.58.30W (unconfirmed). Unlike the majority of wrecks lying off Padstow, this 2,184-ton Sunderland-registered steamship was lost when she collided with the French SS *Marquise de Lubersac* on 12 April, 1917, when 12 miles north-north-east of Trevose Head. She had been carrying a cargo of government stores on passage from Santander to Troon with a crew of 24.

249   Plutus   50.41.24N; 05.07.12W. Built as the *Holland VII* in 1910 at Campbeltown, this 1,189-ton steamship was in ballast from Rouen to Barry Roads where she intended to load coal for a return passage. When 9 miles north-north-west of Trevose Head on 24 April, 1917, she was hit by a single torpedo fired by the German submarine *UC-47* at 4.30am. The survivors were picked up by an Admiralty patrol trawler. The wreck lies in a general depth of 35m, upright, but her stern has completely collapsed.

250   F. Heradia   50.35.35N; 04.55.25W. Built in 1871 at Glasgow by Aitken and Mansel this steamship had served under two previous names (*Saga* and *Moringen*). Registered at Christiansand, the *F. Heradia* was carrying coal from Barry to Le Havre when she got close inshore in dense fog on 25 April, 1917, struck the Mouls Rocks east of Pentire Point and, while attempting to reach the shallows of Padstow Bay, sank at Rumps Point. All the crew escaped. At high water she lay completely submerged.

251   Warnow   50.33.00N; 05.11.30W. Built as the *John Readhead* in 1883 by J. Readhead & Company South Shields, the 1,593-ton vessel's name was changed when sold to the Warnow Steamship Company Ltd, South Shields, although she remained registered at Dundee. She was sailing under Admiralty sealed orders from Penarth carrying a cargo of railway components, intended for use by the army in France. When 6 miles west of Trevose Head on 2 May, 1917, she was hit by a torpedo fired by the German submarine *UC-48* at 3am, her deadweight cargo causing her to sink very quickly. She took with her the captain and 13 crew, leaving the Chief Officer and five men clinging to the keel of an upturned boat. The submarine then surfaced and stopped alongside the survivors, asking them questions about the name of their ship and her cargo, but they refused to give any details. A request to the Germans to assist them in turning the lifeboat over met with no response and the enemy vessel made off. The survivors were in the water for almost 2½ hours before being rescued. The wreck lies in a general depth of 30m.

252   Jeanne   50.19.30N; 05.18.45W (unconfirmed). Although lost well down the coast towards St Agnes Head, the only location for this wreck is given as 16 miles south-west of Trevose Head. She foundered on 9 August, 1917, after collision with the Norwegian SS *Echo*, while carrying coal from Swansea to Nantes.

253   Wisbech   50.43.30N; 04.53.00W. This 1,282-ton steamship registered at Newcastle, was 12 miles north-east of Trevose Head when she was torpedoed in her engine room on 14 August, 1917. Nothing was seen of the German submarine *UC-51*. Two men were killed in the explosion and the survivors escaped. The wreck was identified in September 2002 by her patent coal cargo.

The Medea was built by Raylton Dixon in 1915 for the Royal Navy as the M-22 coastal monitor, and was fitted with a single 7 inch turret gun as well as two 3 inch guns. She was converted to a minelayer in 1919, and re-named in 1925 when converted to a mining tender for the HMS Vernon torpedo school. She was sold out in 1938 to Messrs Cashmore for breaking, and was under tow of the tug Scotsman when she broke adrift off Trevose Head, and drifted onto the rocks at Trebetherick. She could not be refloated and was abandoned; parts of her remain in the shallows to this day (Site 232).

254 Poldown 50.31.35N; 05.05.05W. The 1,370-ton London-registered steamship *Poldown* (formerly *Hawk* and *Pellworm*), built in 1904 at Fevig, was carrying 1,700 tons of coal from Penarth to Boulogne when she detonated a mine on 9 October, 1917, which blew off her entire bow. The crew of 18, under Captain Watson, escaped. The wreck is said to lie in 18m.

255 St Croix 50.42.00N; 05.16.30W (unconfirmed). Built in 1913 by Bremer Vulkan, at Vegesack, her machinery fitted aft, the 2,530-ton Norwegian steamship *St Croix* was carrying pulpwood from Gothenburg to Pasajes on 12 December, 1917. She was torpedoed and sunk by the German submarine U-60 when 13 miles north-west of Trevose Head.

256 Ingrid II 50.31.30N; 05.14.00W. The *Ingrid II*, formerly *Hazelmere*, was carrying coal from Barry to Boucan for her Norwegian owners when she was torpedoed and sunk by the German submarine *U-60* on 19 December, 1917, apparently without loss of life. The wreck lies on the sea bed 6 miles off Trevose Head in 35m.

257 Townley 50.50N; 04.48W. Although armed with an 18-pounder stern chaser gun, this 2,476-ton Newcastle-registered collier proved no match for the

German submarine *U-46*, which sent her to the bottom 18 miles north-east of Trevose Head on 31 January, 1918. In ballast from Devonport to Barry Roads to load coal, she was struck by a torpedo on her port side abeam of the boiler-room. One of the 24 crew was killed in the explosion but the 23 survivors got away in a lifeboat.

258   Cavallo   50.36.00N; 05.10.00W. The *Cavallo*, carrying coal from Swansea to Odda and armed with a 12-pounder, 12cwt stern gun, was hit by a torpedo on the port side on 1 February, 1918. Captain Bradley ordered his crew of 28 to abandon ship and they took to two boats, but three men were lost. The *Cavallo* was the fifth victim of the German submarine *U-46* during its patrol in the Bristol Channel, and its second steamship victim in 24 hours, the enemy having sunk the *Townley* only the previous day in the same area. The wreck lies in a general depth of 35m.

259   Cristina   50.22.20N; 05.11.48W. Unarmed, since she was Spanish, registered at Bilbao, and hence neutral in World War One, this steamship (formerly *Cadiz II* and *Kiora*) was built in 1903 at Cadiz. She was on passage to her home port from Port Talbot with coal when she was torpedoed and sunk without warning by the German submarine *U-55* about 15 miles south-west of Trevose Head on 10 March, 1918. She went down in 30m without loss of life.

On 20 April, 1924, the Lowestoft-registered steam fishing drifter Smiling Throu' drove ashore at night on Trevone beach, south of Trevose Head. The Padstow lifeboat Arab was called out, but finding the vessel abandoned, its crew having rowed their boat into Padstow, they returned empty handed. Attempts to refloat the trawler failed, and she became a total wreck.

260 Petersham 50.25.05N; 05.17.42W. Built in 1899 by Richardson, Duck & Company at Stockton as the *Clinton*, this 3,381-ton London-registered steamship was carrying iron scrap from Bilbao to Glasgow when she sank following collision with the Spanish SS *Serra* at 11pm on 5 May, 1918. The colliding vessel picked up the crew. The collision took place 10 miles west-south-west of Trevose Head, and the wreck site was positively identified by the finding in 1988 of the ship's bell, which had "*Clinton*, Hull" roughly scratched on its surface.

The wreck lies in a general depth of 40m and is upright but partly collapsed. Fitted with a stern chaser gun, there are a number of empty shell cases loose and in boxes scattered around the stern.

261 Tagona (Position not known). The *Tagona* was taking a cargo of iron ore loaded at Bilbao to Glasgow when she was torpedoed amidships at 10am on 16 May, 1918, by the German submarine *U-55*, 5 miles west-south-west from Trevose Head. There was no warning of the attack and the enemy vessel was never sighted. The captain and eight crew were killed in the explosion. Thirteen survivors were picked up from their own lifeboats by a patrol motor launch. The ship had been armed with a 12-pounder, 12cwt stern gun, and shell cases in boxes have been found among her wreckage dated 1906–14. The wreck lies in a general depth of 50m on an even keel but split down the middle. She is very broken and much of the plating is covered in cargo. Orientated north-east to south-west with her bow to the south-west, her two boilers and engine stand 4m above the sea bed. The wreck was heavily salvaged in the 1970s when a condenser and gun were removed, and both engine-room telegraphs and a bell were recovered at a later date. The site is still worth diving, however.

262 Mefjord 50.28.00N; 05.11.00W. The *Mefjord* was a 720-ton Norwegian steamship, built in 1914 at Christiania and registered at Skien. She was carrying coal from Newport to Rouen when she was stopped by the German submarine *UC-64* on 23 May, 1918. The crew were given the opportunity to abandon ship in their own boats and, once clear, the enemy torpedoed their vessel, causing her to sink 7 miles west-south-west of Trevose Head. The position of the wreck is uncertain. With so many war losses in the area, until the wreck is found and identified her location is doubtful.

263 Saphir 50.34.27N; 05.04.26W. Torpedoed and sunk without loss of life by the German submarine *U-94*, this 1,406-ton, Haugesund-registered Norwegian steamship was carrying coal from Barry to Bayonne when attacked 1½ miles north-north-west of Trevose Head on 25 May, 1918. She was fitted with a 132hp, 3-cylinder triple expansion engine driving an iron propeller. The wreck lies in 36m in a rock gully, her stern collapsed to starboard, the remaining parts of the wreck having gone flat. Brass condenser tubes lie scattered across her remains. There are very few fishing nets caught on the wreck, the highest point being her two boilers. It is possible to swim into part of the stern superstructure.

264 Brisk 50.45.51N; 04.59.27W. Another Norwegian war loss, this 1,662-ton steamship was carrying patent coal fuel in blocks when she was torpedoed and sunk by the German submarine *U-82* on 7 June, 1918. As far as is known, the wreck has never been identified and therefore her location is uncertain, other than that she was lost 13 miles north-east of Trevose Head. With an overall length of 268ft and a beam of almost 40ft, and having two boilers, she will make a considerable magnetic target, lying in a general depth of 40m.

265 Hunsgrove 50.36.00N; 05.11.00W. Built in 1913 by the Newport News Drydock and Shipbuilding Company, USA, as the *Lorenzo*, this London-registered vessel was carrying coal from Cardiff to France when she was torpedoed on 8 June, 1918, 6½ miles north-west of Trevose Head, by the *U-82*, the same German submarine that had sunk the *Brisk* the previous day. Three men were killed in the explosion; Captain Kirkwood and the remaining 37 crew escaped.

266 Saima 50.29.05N; 05.23.00W. The 1,147-ton London-registered steamship *Saima* was built in 1914 at Bergen and was on passage from Rouen to Barry to load coal when she was torpedoed on 8 June, 1918. Captain W. Nelson was among 16 men lost; five survivors were picked up by a trawler.

The generally accepted position for the attack was 10 miles west of Trevose Head, but her exact position is still uncertain. The third victim in two days of the German submarine *U-82*, the wreck is believed to lie in a general depth of 35m.

267 Anna Sofie 50.31.42N; 05.08.05W. *Anna Sofie* (formerly *Vera*, *Anargyros* and *Theologos*) was built in 1896 by Ropner and Sons, Stockton. Like the *Saima*, this 2,577-ton London-registered steamship was in ballast heading for Barry Docks when she was torpedoed on 23 July, 1918, by the submarine *U-55*. She carried a crew of 29 under Captain J. E. Martin; all but one of them escaped. The survivors watched the steamship go down when 4 miles west of Trevose Head, in a general depth of 45m. She settled alongside a large reef and is difficult to locate, but two large boilers and a spare propeller still lie in the wreck.

268 Portugal 50.32.00N; 05.07.00W. Very little is known about this Antwerp-registered Belgian steamship, which was in ballast from Le Havre to Newport, Monmouthshire when she was torpedoed and sunk by the German submarine *U-113*. Captain Godderis and his 23 crew all got away safely in their own boats, and watched their ship sink between 3 and 4 miles west-north-west of Trevose Head. The *Portugal* has rarely been dived, but has been confirmed to lie in 35m at low water.

269 Onega 50.27.03N; 05.14.18W. The 3,636-ton *Onega* was registered at New York, having been built at Belfast by Harland & Wolff. She had carried five previous names (*British Queen*, *Obdam*, *McPherson*, *Brooklyn* and *Luckenbach*). This 401ft steamship, carrying a cargo of pit wood from Bordeaux to Swansea, was 38 years old when she was torpedoed and sunk 9¾ miles south-west of Trevose Head on 30 August, 1918. The *Omega* lies in approximately 30m on her port side and is very broken; a short section of the bow is reasonably intact and stands some 3m high. The finding of the ship's bell in 1978 gave a positive identification. The sea bed here is gravel on rock with many long gullies and this is an excellent dive.

270 Brava 50.34.16N; 05.06.30W (approx). Built in 1893 as the *Togo*, this 3,184-ton iron steamship was registered at Lisbon. She was sailing under the Portuguese flag, carrying pit props from Bordeaux to Cardiff, when she was torpedoed by the German submarine *UB-125* on 3 September, 1918, 4 miles north-west of Trevose Head. Details of the attack are confused as the submarine sank the

SS *Lake Owens* immediately after attacking the *Brava*, leaving 44 survivors from both vessels in a number of lifeboats awaiting rescue. They all survived.

Both wrecks lie in 53m only 880yds from each other; on the *Brava* empty shell cases lie scattered among crockery.

271   Lake Owens   50.33.30N; 05.06.35W. *Lake Owens* was built in 1918 by the Great Lakes Engineering Works and registered at Ecorse, USA. The 2,308-ton steamship was in ballast from Nantes for Barry Roads to take on coal when she was torpedoed some 3 miles north-west by west of Trevose Head on 3 September, 1918. Five of her crew of 29 were killed in the explosion.

The stern of this wreck is very impressive, upright but listing to starboard. It still holds a huge emergency steering wheel, her stern gun and many boxes of shells. The rest of the wreck is flat until the bow section, which sits upright and intact. In the centre are boilers surrounded by crockery. The wreck is at a general depth of 53m and considered one of the best deep dives in the area.

272   Acadian   50.25.10N; 05.15.58W. The sole survivor of the *Acadian*, a Canadian steamship registered at Montreal with 25 crew under Captain George Green, told the authorities that on 16 September, 1918, she was steering a straight course at 8 knots when a torpedo struck her. It was later found out that the enemy vessel was the German submarine *UB-117*. The ship sank 11 miles south-west by west of Trevose Head. The only survivor remained on a raft for almost 24 hours before being rescued. The wreck lies in a general depth of 38m.

273   Madryn   50.38.11N; 05.01.08W. The *Madryn* was built in 1916 by Osbourne, Graham & Company at Sunderland, and registered at Newport, Monmouthshire. She was a non-commissioned Admiralty 2,244-ton collier and armed with a 3.5-inch stern gun. On 16 September, 1918, she was carrying coal on passage from Penarth to Devonport with a crew of 23 under Captain J. T. Harris when, 5 miles north-north-east of Trevose Head, she was torpedoed by the submarine *U-82*. The entire forward part of the vessel was was blown away and she sank in 10 minutes; the crew escaped.

274   Lavernock   50.28.00N; 05.05.00W (unconfirmed). The *Lavernock* was built in 1888 at Palmers Shipbuilding Company Ltd and registered in Cardiff. The 2,406-ton steamship was carrying iron ore from Bilbao to Glasgow, Newcastle, when she was attacked by the submarine *UB-117* on 17 September, 1918, when 5 miles south-west of Trevose Head. There were only two survivors out of a crew of 28. The explosion caused the vessel to sink almost immediately.

275   John O'Scott   50.32.00N; 05.16.00W. This 1,235-ton steamship was built in 1906 by Wood-Skinner & Company Ltd, Newcastle, and registered at Newcastle. On 18 September, 1918, she was on passage from Barry to Dover as a non-commissioned Admiralty collier and when 9 miles west by north of Trevose Head she was attacked by the same submarine that sank the *Lavernock*. Despite the fact she was armed with a 12-pounder, 12cwt stern gun, her gunners never had a chance to use it. There was one survivor of a crew of 19.

276   Kalmia   50.35.00N; 05.05.00W (unconfirmed). This Milford Haven-registered 184-ton steel fishing trawler was built in 1898 by J. Duthie & Sons, Aberdeen. She struck submerged wreckage off Trevose Head, resulting in a serious

The remains of the Sphene, off Port Quin (Site 292).

leak, and foundered before she could reach Padstow. It appears that this wreck has never been found.

277   Claretta   50.32.30N; 05.07.00W (unconfirmed). Built in 1896 at Workington, this relatively small 500-ton steamship had been built as the *Brest Rock*, and was on passage from Cardiff to Granville with coal when she sank following collision with the British SS *Borderland* on 31 August, 1930. The vessel was 3 miles west of Trevose Head at the time, the accident taking place in dense fog. The crew were picked up and taken to safety.

278   Shoreham   50.30.00N; 05.15.00W (unconfirmed). Built in 1914 at Dublin Dockyard, this 805-ton collier sank following collision with the French SS *Annik* on 31 August, 1930, in thick fog. The *Annik* picked up survivors. Although the collision supposedly occurred 5 miles west of Trevose Head, the *Shoreham* remained afloat for 3 hours and drifted a considerable way from the original accident scene.

279   Empire Otter   50.40.00N; 04.51.00W. Launched in 1920 by the International Ship Building Corporation, Pascagoula, USA, the 4,670-ton tanker *Empire Otter* (formerly *Torino* and *Amsco*) was part of a large fleet of vessels built by the US government that were made available to the Ministry of Shipping at the beginning of World War Two. Carrying a cargo of crude oil from Southampton to Avonmouth, the steamship detonated a mine that was almost certainly part of a British minefield and sank. The wreck is believed to lie in a general depth of 20m.

280   Svint   50.40.36N; 04.57.12W. Built in 1925 by Skiens Verksted A/S at Skien, the 1,174-ton *Svint* (formerly *Hovland* and *Skagatind*) was on passage from Workington to Plymouth with coal, carrying a crew of 17 on 10 July, 1941. When 7 miles north-west of Kellan Head, Port Quin, she was sunk by German aircraft. The wreck lies in a general depth of 36m, upright but partially collapsed, her machinery aft.

281   Tregor   50.34.54N; 05.10.12W. The *Tregor* was built in 1936 at Groningen and registered at Cardiff. Carrying 230 tons of flour in bulk from Avonmouth to Hayle, this 222-ton coaster was abandoned by her crew of six after being attacked by German aircraft in the Bristol Channel. She was taken in tow for Padstow, but foundered 2½ miles from the land and 6 miles off Trevose Head. She went down in 35m and is said to lie reasonably intact and upright on the sea bed.

282   HMS Warwick   50.26.42N; 05.22.47W. The 1,300-ton *Warwick* was a First World War destroyer, 300ft by 29ft and armed with four 4-inch guns, one 2-pounder, five Lewis guns and six 21-inch torpedo tubes. She was escorting a convoy of merchant ships when torpedoed at 20 February, 1944, by the German submarine *U-413*, when 20 miles south-west of Trevose Head. There was a huge explosion as her stern magazine exploded, blowing the ship in two before sinking in 54m. Three officers and 64 naval ratings were killed; Commander D. Rayner and 93 men escaped using inflatable liferafts dropped by the RAF. The two halves of the wreck lie some distance apart on the sea bed, and the site is designated a War Grave.

283   Ezra Weston   50.40.02N; 05.01.31W. This is a particularly worthwhile dive, as among the 5,800 tons of military stores carried by this 7,191-ton American ship was a full deck cargo of army vehicles. Built in 1943 by the New England Shipbuilding Corporation, Portland, she was on passage from Avonmouth to Falmouth, one of ten vessels under escort as part of the convoy EBC-66. She was torpedoed by the German submarine *U-667* (Lange) well below the waterline. Captain E. W. Larrabee headed for the coast some 7 miles away, but the ship sank 2 hours later. All the 71 crew escaped. The wreck lies in 30m and is frequently visited by diving groups who report that although partly collapsed, her deck cargo can still be explored.
   The wreck lies in a general depth of 55m, her two halves some 1320yds apart. Although partly collapsed, he deck cargo can still be explored. The wreck of the *Regina* lies next to the bow section, but the two wrecks should not be explored in one dive.

284   Arthurtown   50.34.10N; 04.57.30W. Built in 1936 in the Netherlands, this 527-ton vessel was registered at London and on passage from Southampton to Ardrossan when she ran aground on the rocks under Trevose Head in fog during World War Two. She backed off and sank in 17m, when 295 degrees, 1,600ft from Stepper Point daymark. She had been carrying a cargo of scrap iron, including many old petrol and diesel engines, which still remain within her hold, making her an easy target to locate using a magnetometer.
   The wreck lies north-east to south-west with her bow to the north-east and her single 20mm anti-aircraft gun has been removed and placed on display in the Charlestown Shipwreck Centre. The *Arthurtown* makes an interesting dive as she sits upright with her main hold intact, packed solid with scrap iron and steel; her diesel engine stands upright in the stern and most of the wreck has collapsed.

285   Rock Village   Opposite Padstow harbour is an alternative boat launch site at Rock. The village has spread along the waterfront at Padstow and has few facilities, but has recently become popular with young people. The Mariners Inn is almost opposite a concrete slipway to the beach, which can take four-wheel drive vehicles; there is a launching fee. This is an ideal site from which to explore the offshore Newland, Mouls and Gulland Rocks, as well as Pentire Point, Rumps Point and the sheltered coastline reaching east to Port Quin.

286   Newland Rock   Newland Rock is a large island 880yds north-west of Pentire Point. The south side offers shallow water but the north-east side drops quickly to large gullies in 30m. This is best dived at slack water but makes for an excellent drift dive. Grey seals are often found here and as underwater visibility is frequently greater than 24m this is an excellent area in which to photograph marine life, as the fish here are seldom disturbed.

287   Outer Gulland   This is a large reef 3 miles north of Stepper Point, with lots of pinnacles and drop-offs. It is a favourite area for local divers.

288   Roscarrock Rock and the Mouls   Roscarrock Rock is an outcrop covered at high water and the Mouls a large island 440yds off Rumps Point, an area that experiences strong tides but offers a scenic dive. Beware of tourist boats, particularly if you are underwater, as they go very close in to the island and sometimes fail to keep clear of boats with diving flags.

289   Rumps Point and Maria Assumpta   50.35.42N; 04.55.18W. The remains of the last three-masted sailing ship to be wrecked in the west country lie close under the cliff in shallow water, only a short distance north-east of Rumps Point. The oldest working sailing ship in the world at the time, built in 1858, the ship was returning from a two-week refit in Gloucester Docks and visits to Bristol and Swansea on 30 May, 1995. She sailed close inshore as she was approaching the River Camel estuary leading to Padstow, when both her diesel engines failed, and with no time to raise a sail she was swept onto the rocks where she went to pieces, with the death of three of her crew of 15.

The wreck lies in 1 to 15m and consists of smashed up timbers and remains of hull fittings, electric drills and crockery. Full details of the wreck can be found in Padstow's Municipal Museum.

The remains of a small French trawler, consisting of a few steel plates and part of her engine block, lie in shallow water around 7m on the Seven Souls Rocks.

290   Unidentified galleon   50.35.45N; 04.54.10W. There is an unidentified early wreck, believed to be Spanish, near Galleon Rock. Four bronze cannon dated 1620, lead shot and iron stirrup mountings for guns have been found.

291   Unidentified East Indiaman   50.35.10N; 04.52.45W. It is believed that an East Indiaman, possibly named *Thornton*, was lost on the set of rocks known as the Screamers west of Doyden Point. A large ship's bell, believed to be late 18th century has been recovered, along with various iron and non-ferrous fittings, but nothing to help identify the wreck or the period in which she was lost. These remains were recovered from the sand outside the rocks fronting the cliff, and it is possible further remains lie buried.

292 Sphene 50.36.165N; 04.53.214W. Built at Montrose in 1920 as the *River Tawe*, this 815-ton steamship, registered at Glasgow, was on passage from Barry to London with coal on 5 February, 1946. In heavy seas and poor visibility she struck the Mouls and the crew escaped in a single boat before the *Sphene* went down in Port Quin Bay.

The wreck is covered in fishing net and lies in a general depth of 22m. She is well broken, but her two boilers and machinery stand proud of the wreck, and the propeller and shafting are easily identified. While exploring you may come across a machinery builder's nameplate inscribed W. Beardmore & Company Ltd, Glasgow.

To reach Port Quin and Port Isaac take side roads to St Minver, where you join the B3314 and follow signs to Port Quin.

Port Quin to Boscastle

Port Quin has a car park but no toilets, shops or inn. Refreshments are available at the Stable Tea Rooms. The 20ft concrete slipway is privately owned and a notice states "No launching", but with permission dive boats can be launched here. The foreshore makes an ideal safe point from which beginners and snorkellers can beach dive, exploring Kellan Head outside the harbour, as there little or no tide, or the Cow & Calf Rocks, which offer a shallow, safe diving area with lots of marine life.

Continue to Port Isaac on the coast road or, if you are towing a boat or trailer, on the B3314 then B3267, which will take you to Port Isaac and Port Gaverne, as the coast road is very narrow. The recommended route will bring you into Port Isaac through Trewetha, past a public car park and toilets; the town has good facilities. There is a large concrete slipway giving easy access to the water. You will have to launch your boat then return to the car park with your vehicle, but it may be possible to leave a trailer on the beach – ask at one of the shops or the RNLI station. A second, smaller, slipway stands alongside the main public slip, but is reserved solely for use by the inshore lifeboat: don't block it. Two granite jetties encompass the harbour, which dries at low tide, but it has a hard sand bottom suitable for four-wheel drive vehicles. Boats can only be launched with the permission of the harbourmaster (tel. 01208 880607) and on payment of a fee. You are recommended to telephone in advance during summer months.

Coastal sites

293 James C. Bell 50.35.42N; 04.50.00W. This 602-ton wooden barque left Liverpool on passage for Bombay with a cargo of coal, but was forced to return the following day after loosing some of her sails. On passing down St George's Channel she met with heavy weather. On 5 March, 1868, the starboard bilge pump ceased

Opposite: Divers on the beach at Port Gaverne.

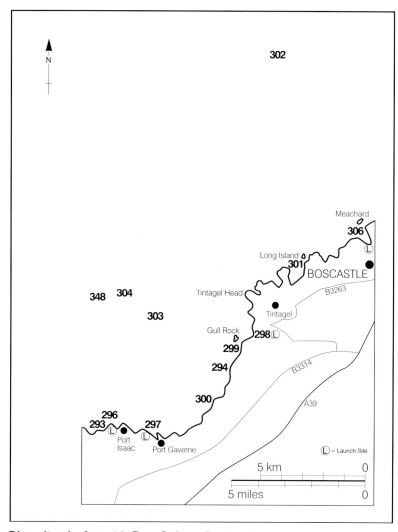

Dive sites in Area 14: Port Quin to Boscastle.

to work, and the crew decided that the vessel was unseaworthy. Though heading for the Welsh coast, wind forced the barque towards Cornwall. Later that day the crew of 17 lowered the boats and rowed for Port Isaac. Abandoned, the ship drove ashore on the rocks at Pine Haven, where she went to pieces. Whether or not anything of her remains is uncertain, but she was a large vessel so there may be some timber or iron to be found.

294   Woodleigh   50.37.25N; 04.46.20W. Very little is known about this 2,664-ton steamship, as she went ashore in fog on 28 August, 1917, nearly 3 miles north-east of Port Gaverne, at a time when newspaper reporting was restricted. Registered at Whitby and in ballast from Boulogne to Barry Roads to load coal, she had been built in 1894 by J. L. Thompson & Sons of Sunderland. There is only one known photograph of the wreck, showing her hard ashore under the 200ft cliffs, and therefore any remains are likely to be very scattered and lying in shallow water. There are a number of big caves on this stretch of coast worth exploring.

295   Skyopelos Sky   50.35.15N; 04.52.25W. On passage from Garston to Algiers with lubricating oil in 40-gallon drums, this Piraeus-registered Greek 2,776-ton motor vessel developed a severe list when her cargo shifted in heavy weather, and then suffered complete engine failure. Unable to anchor, she drove ashore at night 1,000ft south-south-west of Droyden Point. The stern remains in shallow water, well broken, and is frequently completely covered by sand.

296   Castor I   50.35.42N; 04.50.10W. By coincidence, the last two strandings in this area were both caused indirectly by engine failure. The 500-ton, 147ft *Castor I* (formerly *Nordpol, Stella Nova, Santaelena, Tor Ireland, Neugraben* and *Newgraben II*) was under tow, in ballast from Londonderry to Par to load china clay, during a severe northerly gale. She broke adrift, going ashore on the headland to the west of Port Isaac harbour entrance on 26 November, 1980, and capsized against the rocks. The crew of twelve survived.

297   Port Gaverne   Adjoining Port Isaac to the east is Port Gaverne, which is a recommended launch site for a club inflatable. The small slipway is 20ft wide and leads off the main road onto a sand and gravel beach. There is a small launch fee (contact the harbourmaster, John Wild), but you can get a boat into the water at any state of the tide with a bit of effort.

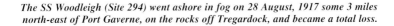

The SS Woodleigh (Site 294) went ashore in fog on 28 August, 1917 some 3 miles north-east of Port Gaverne, on the rocks off Tregardock, and became a total loss.

181

Above: Built as the Baltic Star in 1961, the MV Skopelos Sky (Site 295) went ashore just west of Doyden Point, Port Quin on 18 December, 1979.

Below: For many years this lifebelt from the wreck of the Iota (Site 301) marked the grave of Cantanese Domenico, the 14-year-old cabin boy.

298 Trebarwith Strand   The next possible launch site northwards is Trebarwith Strand, about 9 miles by road. There are plenty of facilities here, including a car park opposite public toilets. There is no slipway, just two concrete steps and a short area of flat rock leading directly to the sandy foreshore. The most suitable time to launch is probably 2 hours either side of high water. On the whole this is not a good place to launch, but a boat dive around Gull Rock, which lies just offshore, is recommended. In a maximum of 20m it offers a very pretty drift dive; the area is tidal, but you are likely to see sunfish and small octopus in summer, and a profusion of fish, seals and cup anemones.

299 Sarah Anderson   50.38.45N; 04.45.50W. *Sarah Anderson* was a large sailing barque carrying a cargo of manganese ore from Coquimbo to Fleetwood when she was wrecked in this area. She anchored near Port Isaac in a dismasted condition on 17 October, 1886, in better weather conditions no doubt the lifeboat would almost certainly have reached the wreck and saved the 13 crew and one passenger, sailing under Captain William Puxley. The barque sank halfway between Trebarwith and Gull Rock and there were no survivors. The wreck lies some distance offshore in 10 to 12m on a flat sandy bottom, swept by a strong tide.

300 Lynx   50.36.25N; 04.47.10W. Built in 1869 by Backhouse & Dixon, Middlesbrough, the *Lynx* was fitted with a 38hp two-cylinder compound engine and carried three masts. The Cardiff-registered 174-ton steamship was in ballast on passage from Portreath to Port Talbot when she was brought to anchor 3 miles off Port Isaac on 1 October, 1899, in a north-north-westerly gale. Her engine had stopped owing to the failure of her circulating pump. A lifeboat rescued the crew of seven and Captain T. J. Crothers. The ship was driven ashore on the rocks at Bound's Cliff, some 3 miles east of Port Isaac, and became a total wreck. A very strong tide sweeps this rough coast, and with no access from the clifftop the site can only be reached by sea.

Offshore dive sites and wrecks

301 Iota   50.40.28N; 04.44.20W. A 1,000-ton Italian iron barque was carrying patent coal fuel from Cardiff to Trinidad with a crew of 12 under Captain Vinceza Mazzella when she was driven ashore in a gale in Bosiney Cove, on Lye Rock Island. Most of the crew jumped on the rocks and were rescued by breeches buoy. The wreck's timbers remain and copper fastening pins uncover from time to time; artefacts are still recovered in the shallows among the rocks and weed.

Of the five offshore steamship wrecks in this area, all except one sank unseen and with the loss of all hands; the location of all five is speculative until divers find sufficient evidence to identify them.

302 Alliance   50.46.00N; 04.45.00W (unconfirmed). No one saw this Cardiff-registered 942-ton steamship go down, lost with all 16 crew. She left Cardiff for St Nazaire carrying a cargo of coal on 4 December, 1884, and disappeared. A number of offshore contacts have been established using a magnetometer, but have not yet been identified.

303 Depute Gaston Dumesnil 50.39.00N; 04.51.00W. This 2,400-ton steamer was sailing from Penarth to Rouen, having loaded coal at Barry Docks for the French government. Lifebelts, bodies and wreckage were seen by local people in the bay of Port Isaac floating in the direction of Tintagel Head on 6 November, 1921, but nothing is known about the circumstances under which she sank.

304 Vervande 50.40.00N; 04.48.00W. The *Vervande* (formerly *Kilfinny*, *Kenrhos*, *Heljo* and *Horsia*) was built in 1918 by Cochrane and Sons at Selby. While carrying 450 tons of scrap iron from Southampton to Swansea, the 793-ton Norwegian steamer, registered at Mandal, was attacked and bombed by German aircraft when 10 miles west by north of Tintagel Head on 20 March, 1942. Although armed, she was sent to the bottom. The 16 crew and two DEMS gunners were saved.

Boscastle to Morwenstow

Tintagel Head offers interesting drift diving with overfalls, and at Tintagel Haven a number of caves are frequented by grey seals.

Boscastle has a deep, fiord-like harbour, which wriggles inland to a cluster of restored granite buildings. There is a car park on the south side of the road before you reach the harbour and various facilities in the town. Always difficult to enter from seaward, unless it is very calm, the harbour is one of the few havens on this long stretch of coast. Consisting of an inner and outer harbour, the best slipway of two available is that on the north side at the head of the inner harbour, but you must launch within 2 hours either side of high water, as the harbour dries out completely. You should call at the harbourmaster's office (F. Silford, tel. 01840 250453; the office is next to the NT office) in order to obtain advice, permission to launch, and pay the fee. No vehicles other than those owned by local fishermen are allowed on the quay or jetty on the south side of the harbour. Boscastle is an excellent point from which to explore this section of the north coast and there are splendid coastal walks either side of the harbour along steep cliffs, and an Iron Age promontory fort on the Willapark headland. There is said to be the remains of an East Indiaman wreck off Willapark.

The small village of Morwenstow, which has only a track leading to the coast, is part of Devon and the northerly limit of this guide. There is no access to the foreshore along the stretch of cliffs at Lower and Higher Sharpnose Points other than by boat from Bude.

306 Penally Point   There is an interesting shore dive just outside the harbour at Boscastle at Penally Point, easily reached from the track and steps on the outer harbour wall on the north side. Here there is a cave or blow-hole, 60 to 80ft long, with a dog-leg, which goes right through Penally Point from the harbour to the open sea and in calm weather is a safe shallow tunnel dive, after which you can swim round the headland back to the harbour entrance. As the tunnel is always completely flooded, a heavy swell can cause ear pressure problems, so beware.

307 Londos   50.42.25N; 04.40.50W. The *Londos* was built in 1860 by Richardson Duck & Company of Stockton and fitted with a four-cylinder compound engine of 45hp and one boiler. The London-registered 283-ton steamship was

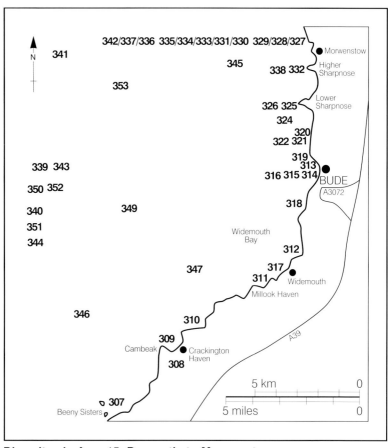

Dive sites in Area 15: Boscastle to Morwenstow.

sailing from Cardiff to Poole carrying a mixed cargo on 14 November, 1891, when there was a fire on board when she was 10 miles off Hartland Point. The fire had started in the engine room but spread quickly; the crew of seven under Captain W. Fryer, fearing an explosion, took to the boats and landed at Compass Point, Bude. After drifting all day the burning ship went ashore 1½ miles north-east of Boscastle under Beeny Cliff, just clear of the Beeny Sisters Rocks. After going ashore the wreck discharged what was left of a hundred barrels of fuel into the sea and as each cask of petroleum touched the water it burst into flames. The wreck lies very broken up on the foreshore on Beeny Beach.

308 Crackington Haven   Crackington Haven is a large sandy beach, dominated by Pencannow Point and the Cambeak; there is safe snorkelling among the rocks at the Cambeak end at high water, but nothing here for divers. It is just possible to launch here at high water in calm conditions, but it is a soft foreshore with no slipway.

309 German E-boat and the Eugenie   50.44.20N; 04.38.55W. In December 1946 the surrendered German E-boat *No. 89*, after being sold by the British government, was on passage from Portsmouth to Milford Haven for breaking when she broke adrift. She drifted until she went ashore on the north side of the Cambeak, where attempts were made to get her off the rocks but she was too badly damaged, and broke up in the winter gales. Parts of the wreck, including her engines, remain high on the foreshore but covered by the sea at high water.

The remnants of the Prussian full-rigged ship *Eugenie*, of Danzig, are also here. She was carrying patent fuel from Swansea to Barcelona when she ran ashore on 1 February, 1865, after developing a serious leak. The 16 crew under Captain L. Brockish abandoned ship.

310 Thyra   50.45.00N; 04.37.10W. Built at Sunderland as the *Sarah Wascoe* in 1856, this 334-ton Danish barque was carrying a cargo of coal and bricks from Burry Port to Stockholm when she ran into a severe gale. She was sighted from the land on 26 October, 1896, flying signals of distress, and the lifeboat was launched. The crew of nine under Captain Schou were taken off and the vessel left abandoned. She eventually drifted ashore on the rocks at Cleave Strand 1 mile north-east of Pencannow Point. The ship's anchors and cables are said to remain in the shallows, together with broken building bricks.

All that remains of the German E-boat No. 89 today on the beach at Crackington Haven is one 10-cylinder petrol engine, gear box and propeller shaft and a few pieces of steel and aluminium.

Above: Boscastle harhour.

Below: The bay and breakwater at Bude.

311 Millook Haven Millook Haven is a great place for shore diving as it is very rocky, with a maximum depth of 10 to 12m, with easy access at high water. Monkfish are frequent visitors to the cove, and the tide here is manageable. Only very limited parking is available, however.

312 Widemouth Bay There are many tourist facilities at Widemouth Bay, but the bay is composed of sand and many shallow reefs exposed at low water, making it almost impossible to launch a boat. Bude Haven should be used instead.

313 Bude Haven Bude makes an excellent base should you wish to explore the northern end of the Cornish coastline. A canal feeds the lock that isolates the basin from the sea, built in 1825 to allow the transportation of calcium-rich sea sand inland for agricultural use. There is no outboard engine service here, chandlers, dive-shop or source of air recharging. However, there is an excellent museum (tel. 01288 353576) on the quay, where you can learn about Bude's maritime history and shipwrecks. The collection includes the figurehead of the *William Tapscott* (Site **318**), a 1,593-ton barque of Boston, USA, which went ashore off Maer Cliff on 20 March, 1888 and went to pieces. While exploring around the entrance to Bude Haven, which includes the breakwater, Chapel Rock and Compass Point, it is worth remembering that three large full-rigged ships were wrecked against the breakwater or close by, and iron fittings or copper fastenings are still to be found.

314 Bencoolen The *Bencoolen* was a 1,415-ton barque, classed as an East Indiaman, and was carrying a general cargo from Liverpool to Bombay on 21 October, 1862. She was found to be making 3ft of water in 24 hours, but Captain W. Chambers refused to turn back. Severe gales brought the ship ashore near the entrance to Bude harbour.

315 Kishon The 507-ton barque *Kishon* of North Shields was in ballast from London to Appledore on 7 November, 1890, when she got into difficulties and accepted the services of the steam tug *Australia*. Off Trevose Head the towing hawser parted and weather conditions prevented it being reconnected, so that the *Kishon* was left at the mercy of a north-westerly gale. She drove ashore on the ridge of rocks stretching out from the end of Bude breakwater, from where all eight crew and Captain Duthrie were saved by breeches buoy.

316 Capricorno The last of the three sailing ships wrecked near Bude was the 1,000-ton Austrian barque *Capricorno*, which was under tow but left helpless in a gale, so that she drove ashore on Bude breakwater on 28 December, 1900. A total of twelve out of the 14 crew lost their lives.

Coastal diving sites

317 County of Sallop 50.46.55N; 04.33.55W. This 2,164-ton steamship, registered at Liverpool, was in ballast from Le Havre to Swansea when she drove ashore in north-north-westerly Force 8 winds on 10 March, 1892. The state of the sea prevented the lifeboat from being launched but Captain Evan and the 27 crew were rescued by breeches buoy. Salvage divers reported that the wreck's entire engine bed and boilers had shifted to starboard and that bottom hull plates and 50ft of her keel were missing. The remains lie scattered on the foreshore.

318   Villasandino   50.49.25N; 04.33.30W. Under the cliffs at Efford Beacon are the remains of this 1,820-ton Spanish steamship, which was lost on 28 February, 1925. After sailing from Ayr, Scotland, for Bayonne, with a cargo of coal, the *Villasandino* (formerly *Amaya Julio*) experienced very heavy weather and when 30 miles west of Lundy Island her condenser broke down. Signals of distress were hoisted and shortly afterwards a heavy sea threw her over to port, causing her cargo to shift, leaving the ship listing heavily. The tanker *British Chancellor* made four attempts to take her in tow, but without success. The tanker finally took off the crew and the *Villasandino* was abandoned to drift; the wreck is now 440yds south of Bude breakwater, past Compass Point.

Although very broken, the *Villasandino*'s two boilers, bow section and plating can be found in 8m; her bow inshore stands separate from the rest of the wreck, her rudder and propeller showing 3m above the sea bed on a rocky bottom.

319   William Tapscott   Location unknown. This American full-rigged ship of 1,524 tons, on passage from Rio de Janeiro to Cardiff in ballast, was wrecked in strong winds on 29 March, 1888. Captain Alexander Hume and his crew of 19 got away in their own boat. The wreck lies north of Bude, 880yds offshore from Crooklets Beach and various remains have been found. There are also scenic reef dives 2 miles due west from Bude Haven where there is a mass of rose coral in 30m.

320   Northcott Mouth   Northcott Mouth is a long sandy beach, but has no launching facilities. A number of wrecks have been blown ashore here but there are unlikely to be any identifiable remains.

321   Belem   50.50.55N; 04.33.30W. The 260ft *Belem* was registered at Lisbon and had been built at Flensburg in 1890. The 1,925-ton steamship was on passage from Gibraltar to Newport with iron ore to load coal when she drove ashore in dense fog on 20 November, 1917, very close to where the collier *Woodbridge* had spent a month ashore in April 1915 before being refloated and saved. Efforts were made to get the *Belem* refloated, but without success.

322   Arwenack   50.50.50N; 04.33.25W. The *Arwenack* was a small steam tug of Falmouth, built in 1911. She was found ashore on the rocks at Northcott Mouth on 31 January, 1920, very close to where the SS *Belem* had gone ashore two years earlier. The indications were that she had been under tow and broken adrift.

323   Nettleton   The *Nettleton*, a 2,413-ton steamship, was lost in fog on 2 February, 1916, 880yds off Steeple Point, close to Duckpool Beach. The stretch of shore between Lower Sharpnose and Knap Head has many wrecks: the SS *Cambalu* (see Site **331**); the SS *Eilanus* (see Site **330**), the SS *Sjofna* (see Site **329**), the SS *Uppingham* (see Site **333**) and the SS *Welbury*.

324   Miura   50.51.15N; 04.33.25W. The *Miura* was a Cardiff-registered 274-ton fishing trawler, built of steel in 1916 at Smith's Dock Company Ltd, Middlesbrough. She was fitted with a 67hp three-cylinder triple expansion engine, fed by one boiler. She went ashore at midnight in heavy seas on 29 March, 1927, after her engine had

The iron donkey-engine, her windlass, anchor chain and copper hull fastening pins from the full-rigged sailing ship William Tapscott (Site 319), can still be seen underwater some half mile off Crooklets Beach, north of Bude. She was lost in 1888, and is shown in this painting under full sail.

become disabled and her radio put out of action. Homeward bound from 12 days' fishing off the Isles of Scilly, she drove ashore on Mevachurch Point. Her crew of twelve all jumped overboard but only five reached shore. The wreck lies in the shallows at the bottom of the cliff.

325 Newton 50.54.05N; 04.34.05W. This Hartlepool-registered 914-ton steamship, built in Newcastle in 1883, was on passage from Bremerhaven to Cardiff in ballast when she ran into thick fog off Cornwall. Captain Nicholas Keen managed to find his way up the Bristol Channel but, with visibility down to less than 15m, the *Newton* ran ashore at Lower Sharpnose Point on 21 March, 1886, and then drove into the cliffs. The crew of 18 clambered off the ship as she broke up. Her remains lie scattered among the large boulders at the base of the shallow cliff.

326 Voorwaarts 50.53.10N; 04.34.05W. This 2,801-ton steamship was registered at Genoa; soon after leaving Cardiff with a cargo of coal she developed a bad leak and Captain Pittaluga ordered his crew of 22 to abandon ship. Twelve men and the captain left in two boats, but both capsized, drowning all the occupants. The nine men who had remained on board stayed with the ship until she drifted close in to the Cornish coast, where they anchored. The Newquay lifeboat was launched and took off the nine survivors. The steamer was later taken in tow, but 15 miles south-west of Lundy the towing hawser parted and she was abandoned, going ashore on Lower Sharpnose Point, where she became a total loss.

Above:The 491-ton barque Kishon, bound from London to Appledore where she was to refit, drove ashore on the rocks at Bude on 7 November, 1890. (Site 315). Her crew were saved by breeches buoy.

Below: Thick fog caused the 916-ton SS Newton to get off course and end up on the rocks at Higher Sharpnose on 21 March 1886, where her 18 crew jumped ashore over the rocks, leaving the vessel to go to pieces (Site 325).

The Voorwaarts (Site 326) was a 2,801-ton Italian-owned ship that leaked to the point her crew commenced to abandon ship, but when 13 drowned as two lifeboats capsized, the remainder stayed with the vessel. Taken in tow, she broke adrift, going ashore on Lower Sharpnose Point. Her remains survive in the shallows.

327 Cornelia 50.57.20N; 04.32.48W. This London-registered 214-ton steamship left the River Thames with a cargo of coal-tar on 18 February, 1868. As she rounded Land's End, she met with a succession of gales and when approaching Lundy ran into fog. On 24 February, 1868, she ran ashore on Nabor Point, close to Gull Rock.

328 Avonmore 50.56.05N; 04.32.55W. The 1,158-ton *Avonmore* was built at New Brunswick in 1867 and registered in Bristol. The full-rigged wooden ship was sailing from Cardiff to Montevideo with coal when she encountered a severe gale off Sharpnose and Captain Corfield ordered all three of her masts to be cut down.

The effort to reduce windage and save the vessel was wasted as she parted her cables, drove ashore and became a total wreck. Seven of the 22 crew were washed overboard and drowned. A breeches buoy was rigged on the cliff, which brought nine survivors ashore; six men were left on deck and did not escape. The only remains you are likely to find are iron fittings, ballast blocks and copper from sheathing and fasteners.

329 Sjofna 50.56.35N; 04.32.55W. The *Sjofna* (formerly *Phoenix* and *Kongsaa*) was built in 1918 at Gouderak. Carrying a full cargo of china clay in bags loaded at Fowey for Larne, the 619-ton ship drove ashore in dense fog on 23 November, 1944. All the men on board were rescued. The remains of the wreck are mingled with the remnants of 600 tons of cast iron, which had been in the holds of the SS *Eilanus*, lost here in 1936.

330 Eilanus 50.56.30N; 04.33.00W. The *Eilanus* was built in 1917 at Hardinxveld, and had a three-cylinder steam engine and single boiler located aft. The *Eilanus* (formerly *Aldegonde* and *Wyke Regis*) left Blyth on 2 June, 1936, discharged a cargo of coal at Dunkirk, then proceeded to Le Havre where she took

The small dry-cargo coaster Empire Grove was in ballast between Hayle and south Wales to load coal, when she went ashore in fog near the Longpeak on 8 October, 1941 and broke up (Site 335).

on board 800 tons of scrap metal. On passage for Briton Ferry she ran into thick fog off Trevose Head and went ashore just off Knap Head on 15 June. Her crew of ten, including Captain Griffiths, took to the boat and managed to get ashore at Marshland Mouth. The wreck quickly went to pieces, her cargo mingling among the rocks with iron plates from the SS *Cambalu*.

331 Cambalu 50.56.20N; 04.33.00W. The *Cambalu* was built in 1920 by Day, Summers & Company Ltd at Southampton, with her machinery and boiler aft. Another victim of fog, this 496-ton Liverpool steamship was on passage from Plymouth to Mumbles in ballast when she ran ashore at Knap Head in dense fog on 30 January, 1933. Her crew of nine and Captain Crowther took to their boat and were picked up by lifeboat. The wreck lay on rocks close to the high water mark and was so badly damaged that she was abandoned as a total loss.

332 Caledonia 50.56N; 04.33W. This Arbroath registered brig of 200 tons had a crew of ten under Captain Peters. She had loaded wheat at Odessa for Falmouth, had called at Constantinople, and was on passage for Gloucester when caught off the north Cornwall coast by a severe north-west gale. She drove ashore on the shallow reefs just north of Sharpnose Point on 8 September, 1842 and quickly went to pieces with only one survivor, Edward le Dain of Jersey. Her figurehead, a Scottish maiden armed with a sword and shield, still stands in Morwenstow churchyard about a mile inland and the incident has been immortalised in Jeremy Seal's book *The Wreck at Sharpnose Point*.

333 Uppingham 50.58.20N; 04.32.10W. This 2,203-ton London-registered steamship developed engine trouble when off Bude, and after setting auxiliary sail she put about for Lundy where Captain Lilley and his 27 crew hoped to find shelter. Before she could reach the island the ship's engine failed and she drifted back onto the rocks near Longpeak on 23 November, 1890.

334 Flora 50.58.45N; 04.32.05W. The *Flora* was registered at Amsterdam and in ballast from her home port to Swansea under Captain Stuit, carrying a crew of 19, when she drove ashore in fog on 3 April, 1915, near the Longpeak, 1 mile south of Hartland Quay. There were suggestions that the *Flora* was running contraband for the Germans during World War One, and the crew were arrested by the military on suspicion of supplying oil fuel to enemy submarines. The wreck broke up, making the salvors' task easier, but much of her remains among the gullies of the foreshore.

335 Empire Grove 50.58.45N; 04.32.06W. A Tudor Queen type dry cargo coaster built by Pimblott & Sons Ltd, Northwich, this 321-ton vessel carried her six-cylinder oil engine aft and had a single hold and two masts. On her maiden voyage from Hayle to Cardiff in ballast, the coaster drove ashore in fog on 8 October, 1941, and became a total wreck near the Longpeak, hard up against the cliffs.

336 Mousse le Moyec 51.01.12N; 04.31.30W. Although registered at L'Orient, this 2,038-ton steamer was sailing under the British flag, having been taken over by the Ministry of Shipping at the start of World War Two. Built in 1921 and in ballast from Plymouth to one of the South Wales ports to load coal, she went ashore in fog under St Catherine's Tor, south of Hartland Point on 6 December, 1940, during a north-westerly gale. Her engine had broken down and she could not be restarted.

337 HMS Saltburn 50.58.45N; 04.32.06W. One of 119 Hunt-class minesweepers built for the Royal Navy in 1917–18, this sweeper was completed by Murdoch & Murray, Glasgow on 9 October, 1918. Under tow of a tug for breaking at a Welsh scrapyard, she broke adrift off Hartland Point and, with no one on board, her engine disabled, drifted down onto the Longpeak and became a total wreck.

338 Lowlands 50.53.45N; 04.34.00W. Built as the *Newton* in 1883, this Hartlepool-registered 915-ton steamer was on passage from Bremerhaven to Newport, Monmouthshire in ballast to load coal. She lost her way in dense fog and a west-north-westerly wind, going ashore on the rocks near Morwenstow, on Sharpnose Point Rocks, on 21 March, 1886, where she eventually went to pieces. Her crew of 18 under Captain N. Keen were all saved.

Offshore dive sites and wrecks

339 City of Vienna 50.50.00N; 04.45.00W (unconfirmed). One of many steamships lost offshore between Boscastle and Bude, this 4,672-ton steamship of Dublin was carrying a cargo of sodium and coal from Swansea to Rotterdam when she sank following collision with an unidentified steamship on 8 November, 1900. Captain P. J. Cunningham and 19 of his crew were lost, there being only one survivor.

340 N. Verberckmoes 50.48.00N; 04.45.00W. The *N. Verberckmoes* was a 1,353-ton French steamer, built at South Shields in 1890, by J. Readhead & Sons, and fitted with a three-cylinder triple expansion engine with two boilers. Sailing from Swansea to Dunkirk, her home port, she was carrying coal when she was captured by the German submarine *UC-51*, and her crew forced to abandon ship, after which she was torpedoed and sunk.

341 Rewa 50.55.35N; 04.59.59W. The 7,308-ton *Rewa*, built in 1906 by Denny Brothers, Dumbarton, was registered at Glasgow and had a single screw powered by three steam turbines linked to one shaft, generating 850hp. She was sailing from Salonica to Avonmouth as a hospital ship with 279 wounded, 80 medical staff and 207 crew under Captain Drake. When 17 miles north-west of the Cambeak on 4 January, 1918, she was torpedoed amidships on the port side without warning by the German submarine *U-55*. She sank quickly and, except for four men killed in the explosion, all 14 boats holding the wounded managed to stay together and the men were all rescued. The wreck lies in 57m and is almost the furthest wreck offshore in the Sharpnose area.

342 Northfield 51.01.00N; 04.49.00W (unconfirmed). Another typical collier sailing alone, following the coast in an attempt to avoid enemy submarines and British minefields, this 2,099-ton steamer, built in 1901 at Newcastle, was carrying coal from Glasgow to Devonport Dockyard with a crew of 27. She was probably torpedoed, as a huge explosion beneath the vessel on 3 March, 1918, caused her to sink almost immediately, taking 15 crew to the bottom. The others escaped by lifeboat. As far as is known, the wreck has not yet been found; the most reliable

*After going ashore near Knap Head, the rusting bow section of the Cambalu (Site 331)
was joined by that of another Liverpool coaster Eilanus (Site 330), on 15 June, 1936,
and sections of both wrecks still lie close together in the shallows.*

source puts her at 11 miles west-north-west of Knap Head, another quotes 15 miles
south-west of Lundy and another 25 miles south-west of Lundy.

343 Dalegarth Force 50.50.00N; 04.44.00W. Built in 1914 by the Dundee
Shipbuilding Company Ltd, the *Dalegarth Force*'s three-cylinder triple expansion
engine and single boiler was mounted aft. Registered at Whitehaven, she was on
passage from Treport to Barry Roads in ballast carrying a crew of 13 when she was
torpedoed on the port side on 18 April, 1918. There were eight survivors, who were
rescued from the sea. One war report suggests that the enemy submarine
responsible was *UB-86*; another account suggests she was attacked by a second
submarine, the *UB-73*, at the same time.

344 Gregynog 50.47.00N; 04.43.15W. A Sunderland-registered 1,701-ton
steamer, the *Gregynog* was built in 1899 by S. P. Austin & Son, Sunderland, her
machinery manufactured by J. Dickinson, Sunderland. This vessel was torpedoed
on the starboard side and sank on 18 April, 1918. Three of the crew of 22, including
Captain Way, were killed; the survivors escaped by lifeboat.

345 Rimfakse 50.54.46N; 04.35.50W. Carrying 1,600 tons of iron ore from
Bilbao for Cardiff, sailing under the Norwegian flag, this steamship was torpedoed
and sunk by the German submarine *U-60*.

The Liverpool-registered steamship County of Salop went ashore on Widemouth Beach (Site 317) at 4pm in atrocious weather conditions, a force eight gale and heavy snow, on 10 March, 1892. The Bude lifeboat was taken over land to the site on its carriage, but the weather proved too rough to launch. The crew were saved by breeches buoy.

346   Girdleness   50.45.39N; 04.41.12W. Built in 1905 by Ropner & Son, Stockton-on-Tees, this vessel (formerly *Blacktor*, *Rockabill* and *Grelisle*) was sailing with a crew of 35 and cargo of patent coal, loaded at Swansea. The submarine *U-60* torpedoed her, killing two men, on 2 May, 1918. The survivors got away and were later picked up by minesweepers. The wreck lies in 32m on a sand and shale sea bed, with a least depth of 27m, which is to the top of her engine block. The vessel was heavily salvaged to non-ferrous metals in the 1970s and as a result is very broken and scattered.

347   Saint Georges   50.46.50N; 04.37.50W (unconfirmed). Built in 1891 by Craggs & Sons, Middlesbrough, her machinery by Gourlay Brothers, Middlesbrough, the *Saint Georges* (formerly *Patrator* and *Cirages Français*) was registered at Oran and sailed under the French flag. She was torpedoed and sunk by the submarine *U-60* on 17 July, 1918.

348 Milly 50.40.34N; 04.51.33W. The *Milly* was on Admiralty service as a non-commissioned collier, in ballast from Brest to Barry to load coal on 6 September, 1918. Sailing alone on a zigzag course, in an attempt to evade German submarines, the track of a torpedo was sighted when only 90m away. It was later established that it had been fired by *UB-87*. Two men drowned; the others were rescued. The wreck lies in a general depth of 47m, and her stern gun was lifted from the wreck in 1991 by members of Loughton BSAC Diving Club. After restoration, it was mounted outside the Golden Lyon Inn at Port Isaac.

349 Dimitrios 50.49.05N; 04.41.00W. When approximately 4 miles west-north-west of Bude Haven, this 1,916-ton Greek-owned steamship, registered at Piraeus and carrying china clay from Par to Runcorn, developed a serious leak. On 5 September, 1920, following distress rockets being fired by the ship, the crew were rescued by lifeboat. The *Dimitrios* sank in a general depth of 37m.

350 Vervande 50.50.00N; 04.50.00W. The *Vervande* was a Norwegian steamer, registered at Bergen, carrying coal from Cardiff to Las Palmas. She disappeared off Bude during a terrible gale on 25 March, 1927. At an inquest into the discovery of five bodies washed ashore at Widemouth Bay it was decided the ship had probably gone down off Boscastle. The corpses were Norwegian sailors, but it was difficult to make any positive identifications. As the wreck has not been found, it seems that she is one of the marked wrecks on Admiralty Chart No.1156, or else her remains lie offshore undetected.

351 Elna E. 50.46.00N; 04.44.00W (unconfirmed). Carrying patent coal fuel in blocks, this Bergen-registered Norwegian steamship was on passage from Cardiff to Plymouth with a crew of 17 when she detonated a mine and sank off Crackington Haven on 16 March, 1941, with the loss of one crewman.

352 Botne 50.50.00N; 04.48.00W. The *Botne* was built in 1922 at Holens Verks, Larvik. A small, 991-ton steamer, she was in ballast from Shoreham to Newport when she was in a collision 8 miles west-north-west of Bude Haven on 3 September, 1941, and abandoned to sink.

353 Brabant 50.53.30N; 04.41.30W. While on passage from Hayle to Port Talbot in ballast, this 15-year-old Dutch motor vessel, registered at Terneuzen, was bombed by German aircraft when 5 miles west of Higher Sharpnose on 13 June, 1942. She was attacked at 11.30pm but her DEMS gunners put up such a fight with Lewis guns that the enemy was unable to sink her until 12.10am the following day, when she was abandoned without loss of life. The wreck lies in a general depth of 18m, upright but partially collapsed.

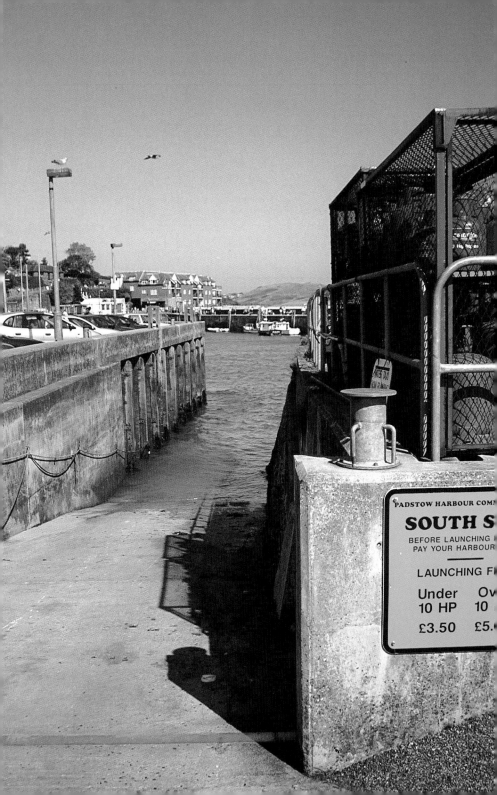

PADSTOW HARBOUR COMM

SOUTH S

BEFORE LAUNCHING
PAY YOUR HARBOUR

LAUNCHING F

Under   Ov
10 HP   10

£3.50   £5.

APPENDIX 1:

Dive services

Air stations, dive shops and diving schools

Bill Bowen, Albert Pier, Penzance (tel. 01736 752135).

Bude Haven Sub Aqua Club. Air to 300 bars by arrangement with Stuart Locke, Thursday evenings only at St Stephen's Hill Garage, Launceston (tel. 01566 773838).

Cornish Diving and Watersports, Bar Road, Falmouth, Cornwall TR11 4BN (tel. 01326 311265; fax 01326 313178; email: cdsdiving@aol.com; www.cornishdiving.uk).

Dive Action Diving Centre, Unit 2c Treskewes Industrial Estate, St Keverne (tel. 01326 280719).

Dive Newquay, David Dowling, Alexandra Rd, Porth, Newquay TR7 3NA (tel./fax 01637 853953; e-mail davidsara@13fs.freeserve.co.uk). BSAC and PADI. Offers air and nitrox courses to all standards, equipment sales and servicing with air to 300 bars, mixed gas and 02 for rebreathers. Based within the grounds of the Paradise Cove Hotel but independent, with heated indoor swimming pool for training, and other facilities. Hire boat *Pressure Seeker* available (see Boats for Charter or Hire, below).

Dive Newquay North Cornwall, Alexandra Road, Newquay (tel. 01637 853953)

Dive St Ives, 25 The Wharf, St Ives (tel. 01736 799229)

Hainault Hotel, Tower Road, Newquay (tel. 01637 851415). Air to 300 bars.

Opposite, the south slipway at Padstow is adjacent to the harbour office.

Haven Scuba School, 16 Penhale Gardens, Fraddon, St Columb (tel. 0870 744 3180; www.havenscubaschool.com).

The Isles of Scilly Wildlife Trust (rear of the Hugh Town Dairy), Carn Thomas, St Mary's (tel./fax 01720 422153). Offer shallow-water conducted snorkel tours with all equipment provided, to view underwater marine life around St Mary's. Includes surface briefing with charts of marine species prior to commencing a tour and information available regarding wildlife, flora and fauna around the islands. Book in advance as tours are not available every day, and the equipment and number of suits available is limited.

Koolair Diving, 45 Polwhele Road, Newquay TR7 2SJ (tel. 01637 872449; mobile 07855 262899; www.koolairdiving.com.uk). Air to 300 bars, equipment rental.

Lyonesse Scuba Centre, Unit 3C, Trewellard Industrial Estate, Pendeen, Penzance TR19 7TF (tel. 01736 787773; e-mail mark@lyonesse.co.uk; www.lyonesse.co.uk).

Seaways, Seaway House, Commercial Road, Penryn (tel. 01326 375544; fax 01326 375401). Air to 300 bars, servicing and sales.

St Martin's Diving Services – Tim and Viv Allsop, Higher Town, St Martin's (tel. 01720 422848; e-mail Tim.Allsop@ukgateway.net). In addition to being BSAC Diving School No. R81, which offers courses from a 3-hour introduction to diving, to a recognised qualification to British Sub Aqua Club standards, involving a 4- or 5-day course, St Martin's Diving Centre offers a wide choice of wreck and reef diving, including some of the best drop-offs in the country, to shallow diving for the less experienced or photographers, accommodation arranged. Snorkelling safaris and snorkelling with seals are arranged, which can be a 3-hour trip including RIB ride, with all equipment and an instructor. Beginners find these very rewarding. Large or small groups are catered for. The Centre has the 35ft fully equipped diving hard boat *Morvoren*, and a 21ft RIB for charter, whether for diving, media support or television camera crews. Equipment hire and sales, air to 300 bar cylinders recharged by arrangement. Accommodation arranged.

Undersea Adventures, 15a Cuxhaven Way, Longrock Industrial Estate, Penzance TR20 8HZ (tel. 01736 333040; www.undersea.co.uk; email team@undersea.co.uk).

Underwater Centre – Jim and Lena Heslin, Gunner Rock, Jackson's Hill, St Mary's (tel. 01720 422595). Dive boat: *Moonshadow*, Lochin 33, fully equipped and licensed, fitted with easy entry diving ladder. Available for diving charters to groups or individuals and operates every day in the season except Saturdays. Visits any of the wrecks in Scilly or spectacular diving sites. Cylinders and weight belts available for hire, air cylinders for recharging can be left outside the Underwater Centre, Porthmellon Industrial Estate by prior arrangement, and collected next morning. Surface diving support for media and television. Accommodation arranged.

Underwater Safaris – Mark Groves, "Nowhere", Old Town, St Mary's (tel./fax 01720 422732; mobile 07747 615732). Offers organised boat dives to wrecks and reefs for suitably qualified divers; snorkelling with grey Atlantic seals, with tuition as required by a qualified instructor; and exhilarating high-speed RIB tours of the islands suitable for all the family. These tours last about 2hrs and visits are made to wreck sites, areas with seals and sea birds, and to uninhabited islands. Equipment is provided for all activities and is also available for hire or sale. Accommodation arranged.

The Man of War shop, situated near the Rachabite slipway on St Mary's, is a treasure trove of marine artefacts, coins, books and souvenirs.

For the family on the Isles of Scilly

Buccabu Bike Hire – Sean Lewis, The Strand, St Mary's (tel. 01720 422289). Modern bike hire for all ages, including infant carriages. Helmets available.

Horse and pony riding – Tracey Guy (tel. 01720 423269, mobile 07768 198106). Conducted horse and pony rides around the islands for all ages. Helmets provided.

Isles of Scilly Windsurf & Sailing Centre – Richard Mills, Porthmellon Beach, St Mary's (tel. 01720 422060 and 423399; fax 01720 422037) and Pentle Bay/Old Grimsby, Tresco (tel. 01720 424919). Sailing, windsurfing and kayaking centre whose qualified instructors can develop beginners or the more experienced to RYA Level III. A comprehensive range of dinghies and day boats is available to explore the islands; alternatively, take part in a watersports activity day, which includes an introduction to sailing, windsurfing, kayaking and the thrills of power boating. Watersports Feasts for families, and Windsafaris – exclusive off-island adventures for all ages – are also offered. There are sailboards, sit-on kayaks and surf skis for hire, including wetsuit and buoyancy aids. Individuals, schools and groups are welcome to join any of the above activities.

Outdoor Adventure – Isles of Scilly – Murray and Susan Hodgson, Avalon, Porthloo, St Mary's (tel. 01720 422641; e-mail murray@wiosh.fsnet.co.uk). Canoeing, climbing, abseiling, orienteering and sailing. All sessions last 2–3 hours, morning, afternoon or evening, one whole day counting as two sessions (10am to 4pm). All technical equipment is provided and activities are led by a qualified coach.

Engine maintenance, inflatable boats and chandlers

Bay Marine Engineering, Unit 4, Chough Close, Tregoniggle Industrial Estate, Falmouth (tel./fax 01326 378087; www.suzukimarine.co.uk).

Challenger Marine, Freemans Wharf, Falmouth Road. Penryn TR10 8AS (tel. 01326 377222; fax 01326377800; e-mail challengermarine@btinternet.com).

Robin Curnow, Commercial Road, Penryn TR10 8AG (tel. 01326 373438).

Explorer Marine, Bradfords Quay, Wadebridge (tel. 01208 815211).

Inflatable Boat Service Ltd., Unit 8a, Kernick Industrial Estate, Penryn (tel. 01326 377600).

R. and M. Kirkwood, Hendra Farm, St Tudy, Bodmin (tel. 01208 841365).

Padstow Boatyard, A. J. Marine, South Quay, Padstow (tel. 01841 533114).

Polar Bears Diving Equipment Ltd., Unit B1–2, Pennygillam Way Industrial Estate, Launceston (tel. 01566 773654).

Sea Com Electronics, Falmouth Marina, North Parade, Falmouth (tel. 01326 210031).

Seacat Marine and Leisure, Unit 1–2, Fishers Garage, Wadebridge (tel. 01208 812508).

The Workshop, Nigel Cottage, The Parade, Mousehole (tel. 01736 810784).

C. Jenkins, Southard Engineering and Chandlers, Thorofare, Hugh Town, Isles of Scilly (tel. 01720 422539).

Boats for charter or hire

Isles of Scilly licensed boat hire. Contact Mike Hicks and Son, Trenemene, McFarland's Down, St Mary's (tel. 01720 422541).

Atlantic Diver, a fast Offshore 32, fitted out with a large heated cabin, oven and hot water. Range 60 miles. Contact Chris Lowe (tel. 01637 850930; mobile 07860 927833; www.atlanticdiver.co.uk).

Jekaro, 23ft, available for 20 miles offshore, north and south coasts of Cornwall. Tel. 01637 872449.

Jo-Adlin, a large, fast RIB, fitted with a wheelhouse, is licensed for twelve divers to MCA Code 2 for 60 miles. It cruises at 25 knots and is operated by Haven Scuba School, a PADI 5-star development centre, based in Falmouth. Tea, coffee and packed lunches are available on request. There is also a dive shop and compressed air on site. Contact Jackie Baker, Dive Centre co-ordinator (tel. 01326 210296 or 01726 861771; www.havenscubaschool.com).

Katrina Thompson, 62ft charter liveaboard, fully equipped for twelve divers, based at Penzance for summer months, 2- to 5-day trips to the Isles of Scilly; 86 tons, sleeps 12, 4m Avon safety boat (tel. 01752 691219; mobile 07720 168514).

Kool Air Diving, Open all year, 23ft RIB will take up to eight divers up to 20 miles offshore; MCA Cat.5. Air to 300 bars. Contact Robert Newton (tel. 01637 872449; mobile 07855 262899).

Maureen of Dart, this 67ft wooden vessel accommodates twelve divers in addition to its owners. Operates out of Dartmouth. Five cabins, all with central heating and wash basin. Long weekend and weekly guests have full board. Air compressor with nitrox available in custom mixes as an optional extra. A 15ft inflatable with a 20hp outboard engine is carried as a tender (safety) boat. Contact Mike or Penny Rowley, 23 Lower Fairview Road, Dartmouth. TQ6 9EE (tel./fax 01803 835449; mobile 07860 571012; e-mail mvmaureen@deepsea.co.uk).

Our Unity, 40ft, licensed for 12 divers, North Devon and Lundy from Ilfracombe. Tel. 01271 883051).

Pressure Seeker, 26ft, RIB, 20-mile range offshore, visiting wrecks, coastal sites, reefs and offshore sites. Contact David Dowling (tel./fax 01637 853953).

Samuel Irvin, a Cygnus 33 hard boat operating out of Dartmouth, visits the Isles of Scilly on a regular charter basis. Fully equipped to MCA Cat 2 requirements; colour video wreck finder; 30-mile range radar; two DGPS systems; plotter to record dive marks. Two VHF radio sets (one a new DCS system with automated distress facility); auto-pilot; 180-mile cruising range; power winch for anchor recovery; side screens for weather protection. Contact: Ian Noble, Mill Poole House, 7 Market Street, Dartmouth, Devon TQ6 9QE (tel: 01803 834598; mobile 07780 970803; e-mail iannoble@tesco.net).

Triton Diving, 19ft, Humber Destroyer RIB, licensed for eight divers, individual or groups, up to 20 miles from Hayle harbour. Fitted with proton magnetometer, DGPS and echo sounder. Operates seven days a week, all year round; diving cylinders provided, also compressed air and nitrox fills (tel. 01209 613055; www.tritondiving.co.uk).

Local diving clubs

A.L.P. Subaqua Association (1695). Falmouth.

Budehaven BSAC (715). Meets at Launceston Sports Centre Pool on Fridays at 9.30pm.

Cowethow Mor BSAC Special Branch (1135).

Falmouth Dolphins (1402). Meets at the Odd Fellows Inn on Wednesdays at 8pm.

Fowey SAA. Meets at the Fowey Hotel on Thursdays at 9pm.

HMS *Seahawk* (Special Branch BSAC).

Just Divin' (1501). Plymouth.

Kernow Association of Sub-Aqua Clubs.

Lanlivet SAA Branch.

Looe BSAC (1631), now South-East Cornwall Sub-Aqua Club. Meets at the Jolly Sailor pub at West Looe on Wednesdays at 8pm.

Mid-Cornwall BSAC (885). Meets at Polkyth Recreation Centre on Wednesdays.

Newquay and District BSAC (1619). Meets at Whiteacres Holiday Park.

Padstow BSAC (1535).

Peninsular BSAC (1036). Meets at Carn Brea Leisure Centre, Camborne, on Tuesdays at 7.30pm.

Penzance and District BSAC (116). Meets at the Club House on Albert Pier on Thursdays.

RAF St Mawgan BSAC Special Branch (288).

St Ives BSAC (1610). Meets at Carn Brea Leisure Centre, Camborne, on Saturdays at 8am.

Tolgus BSAC (778). Meets at Carn Brea Leisure Centre Camborne on Thursdays at 8.45pm.

Truro Duchy Divers (1541). Meets at Truro Swimming Pool on Mondays at 9pm.

Diving assistance

If your club or group wants general advice about a particular site or area, the following individuals or organisations are willing to assist:

Tim Allsop, St Martin's Diving Services (BSAC/PADI School), Higher Town, St Martin's (tel. 01720 422848; e-mail Tim.Allsop@ukgateway.net).

Isles of Scilly Wildlife Trust Snorkel Tours, Trust Office, Carn Thomas, St Mary's (tel./fax 01720 422153).

Jim and Lena Heslin, Underwater Centre and Scillonian Diving Services, Gunner Rock, Jacksons Hill, St Mary's (tel. 01720 422595).

Richard Larn, Tamale, Buzza Hill, St Mary's (tel./fax 01720 423679).

David McBride, Porthloo Workshops (tel./fax 01720 422455) or Schiller, Pilot's Retreat, Church Road, St Mary's (tel. 01720 423162).

Other useful numbers

BSAC technical support department (tel. 0151 350 6262; e-mail technical@bsac.com).

Divers Alert Network (DAN) (emergency tel. 01224 585747 or non-emergency tel. 0797 0821 1222).

Regional and area BSAC coach. Contact Maxine Smith, 28 Pitman Court, Gloucester Road, Bath BA1 8BD (tel. 01225 311103; e-mail southwest.coach@bsac.com).

APPENDIX 2:

The Diver's Code of Conduct

Divers must at all times adhere to the BSAC code of conduct. It is reproduced here with the kind permission of the British Sub-Aqua Club, and has been extracted from the BSAC *Safe Diving Practices* booklet, available from BSAC Headquarters.

The Diver's Code of Conduct

More and more people are taking to the water. Some for recreation; some to earn their living. This code is designed to ensure that divers do not come into conflict with other water users. It is vital that you observe it at all times.

Before leaving home

Contact the nearest British Sub-Aqua Club Branch or the dive operator local to the dive site for their advice. Seek advice from them about the local conditions and regulations.

On the beach, river bank or lakeside

1. Obtain permission, before diving in a harbour or estuary or in private water. Thank those responsible before you leave. Pay harbour dues.

Opposite: The rocks and foreshore between Peninnis Inner Head and Porth Cressa Bay.

2. Try to avoid overcrowding one site, consider other people on the beach.

3. Park sensibly. Avoid obstructing narrow approach roads. Keep off verges. Pay parking fees and use proper car parks.

4. Don't spread yourselves and your equipment since you may upset other people. Keep launching ramps and slipways clear.

5. Please keep the peace. Don't operate a compressor within earshot of other people – or late at night.

6. Pick up litter. Close gates. Be careful about fires. Avoid any damage to land or crops.

7. Obey special instructions such as National Trust rules, local bye-laws and regulations about camping and caravanning.

8. Remember divers in wet or dry suits are conspicuous and bad behaviour could ban us from beaches.

In and on the water

1. Mark your dive boats so that your Club can be identified easily. Unmarked boats may become suspect.

2. Ask the harbour-master or local officials where to launch your boat – and do as they say. Tell the Coastguard, or responsible person, where you are going and tell them when you are back.

3. Stay away from buoys, pots and pot markers. Ask local fishermen where not to dive. Offer to help them recover lost gear.

Pendeen lighthouse.

4. Remember ships have not got brakes, so avoid diving in fairways or areas of heavy surface traffic and observe the "International Regulations for the Prevention of Collisions at Sea".

5. Always fly the diving flag when diving, but not when on the way to, or from, the dive site. Never leave a boat unattended.

6. Do not come in to bathing beaches under power. Use any special approach lanes. Do not disturb any seal or bird colonies with your boats. Watch your wash in crowded anchorages.

7. Whenever possible, divers should use a surface marker buoy.

On conservation

1. Never use a speargun with an aqualung. Never use a speargun in fresh water.

2. Shellfish, such as crabs and lobsters, take several years to grow to maturity; over-collecting in an area soon depletes stocks. Only take mature fish or shellfish and then only what you need for yourself. Never sell your catch or clean it in public or on the beach. Don't display your trophies.

3. Be conservation conscious. Avoid damage to weeds and the sea bed. Do not bring up sea-fans, corals, starfish or sea urchins – in one moment you can destroy years of growth.

4. Take photographs and notes – not specimens. Shoot with a camera not a speargun – spearfishing makes fish shy of divers. Never spearfish wrasse or other inshore species since once an area is depleted of such fish, it may take a long time for them to re-colonise.

On wrecks

1. Do not dive on a designated wreck site. These are indicated on Admiralty Charts and marked by buoys or warning notices on the shore nearby.

2. Do not lift anything which appears to be of historical importance.

3. If you do discover a wreck, do not talk about it. Pinpoint the site, do a rough survey and report it to the BSAC Archaeology Adviser or the Council for Nautical Archaeology who will advise you.

4. If you do not lift anything from a wreck, it is not necessary to report your discovery to the Receiver of Wreck. If you do lift, you must report.

5. If your find is important, you may apply for it to be designated a protected site. Then you can build up a well qualified team with the right credentials and proceed with a systematic survey or excavation under licence without outside interference.

Don't Let Divers Down – Keep To The Diver's Code

APPENDIX 3:

Further reading

A Century of Images. Cowan. 1997. Andre Deutsch Ltd, London. ISBN 0 233 98992 7.

Admiral Shovell's Treasure and Shipwreck in the Isles of Scilly. McBride. P. & Larn, R. 1999. Tor Mark Press, Redruth. ISBN 0 9523971 3 7.

Advisory Committee on Historic Wreck Sites – 2002. Lists all designated wreck sites, with map.

A Sea Miscellany of Cornwall and the Isles of Scilly. Gills, R. 1968. Harvey Barton of Bristol Ltd.

British Merchant Ships sunk by U-boats in the 1914–1918 War. Tennent, A. J. 1990. The Starling Press Ltd, Newport. ISBN 0 9516314 0 3.

British and Commonwealth Merchant Ship Losses to Axis Submarines, 1939–1945. Tennent, A.J. 2001. Sutton Publishing Ltd, Stroud, Gloucester. ISBN 0 7509 2760 7.

British Vessels Lost at Sea 1914–18. (HMSO, reprint). 1977. Patrick Stephens, Cambridge. ISBN 0 85059 291 7.

British Vessels Lost at Sea 1939–45. (HMSO reprint). 1977. Patrick Stephens, Cambridge. ISBN 0 85059 267 4.

British Warship Losses in the Age of Sail. Hepper, D. J. 1994. Jean Boudriot Publications, Rotherfield. ISBN 0 948864 30 3.

BSAC Wreck Register – the West Country. No. 1. Butland, W. E. & Siedlecki, J. K. 1985 and 1987.

Castaway and Wrecked. Cowan, R. 1978. Duckworth & Co. ISBN 0 71561145 3.

Opposite: The coastguard tower on Telegraph Hill, St Mary's.

Cornish Lights and Shipwrecks. Noall, C. 1968. D. Bradford Barton, Truro.

Cornish Shipwrecks – the South Coast. Larn, R. & Carter, C. 1969. David & Charles. ISBN 7153 4289 4.

Cornish Shipwrecks – the North Coast. Carter, C. 1970. David & Charles, Newton Abbot. ISBN 0 7153 4796 9.

Cornish Shipwrecks – the Isles of Scilly. Larn, R. 1971. David & Charles Ltd, Newton Abbot, Devon. ISBN 0 7153 4976 7.

Cornwall's Lighthouse Heritage. Tarrant, M. 1990. Twelveheads Press, Truro. ISBN 0 906294 20 7.

Cornwall's Maritime Heritage. Kittridge A. 1989. Twelveheads Press, Truro. ISBN 0 906294 15 0.

Deep Sea Treasure. Williams, M. 1981. William Heinemann Ltd. ISBN 434 86660 1.

Excavation of HMS Association. Rogers, R. Lyonesse Salvage Company Ltd, Isles of Scilly.

HMS Association – Sank 1707. Mace, M. Scillonian Diving Service, Isles of Scilly.

HMS Colossus. Morris, R. 1979. Hutchinson & Co. Ltd. ISBN 0 09 134660 6.

Island Treasure. Morris, R. 1969. Hutchinson of London.

Lloyd's War Losses, the First World War. Lloyd's of London Press Ltd. 1989. ISBN 1 85044 314 9.

Lloyd's War Losses, the Second World War. Lloyd's of London Press. 1989. ISBN 1 85044 217 7.

Portreath – Some Chapters in its History. Tangye, Michael. 1984. Dyllansow Truran, Croft Prince, Mount Hawke, Truro. ISBN 0907566 88 X.

Ships, Shipwrecks and Maritime Incidents Around the Isles of Scilly. Edited by Larn, R. 1999. Isles of Scilly Museum Publication No.3. ISBN 0 9523971 4 5.

Shipwreck. Fowles, J. & Gibson, F. 1974. Jonathan Cape. ISBN 0 224 01053 0.

Shipwreck Index of the British Isles, Vol. 1. Larn, R. & B. 1995. Lloyd's Register of Shipping. ISBN 0 980528 88 5.

Shipwrecks around Land's End. Larn, R. & B. 1992. Tor Mark Press, Redruth. ISBN 0 85025 307 1.

Shipwrecks at Land's End. Larn, R. & Mills, E. 1970.

Shipwrecks of Great Britain and Ireland. Larn, R. 1981. David & Charles, Newton Abbot. ISBN 0 7153 7491 5.

Shipwrecks of the Isles of Scilly. Larn, R. 1993. Thomas & Lochar, Nairn, Scotland. ISBN 0 946537 84 4.

Shipwrecks on the Isles of Scilly. Gibson, F. E. 1967. Armorel Studio, Isles of Scilly.

Shipwrecks – St Ives to Bude. Larn, R. & B. 1990. Tor Mark Press, Redruth. ISBN 0 85025 324 1.

Sunken Treasure. Williams, M. 1980. Cassell Ltd. ISBN 0 304 30502 2.

The Cita – Scillies own "Whisky Galore" Wreck. Larn, R. & McBride, D. Shipwreck and Marine, Charlestown. 1997, 1998 and 2001. ISBN 0 9523971 0 1.

The Cruel Cornish Sea. Mudd, D. 1981. Bossiney Books. ISBN 0 906456 09 6.

The Dutch East Indiaman Hollandia wrecked on the Isles of Scilly in 1743. Cowan, R. & Z. 1975. International Journal of Nautical Archaeology, Vol. 4, No. 2, reprint of pages 267–300.

The Savage Sea. Gibson, F. 1987. Armorel Studio, St Mary's, Isles of Scilly.

The West Country and the Sea. Parker, D. 1980. Longman Group Ltd, London. ISBN 0 582 41181 5.

The Wreck of the Torrey Canyon. Gill, C., Booker, C. & Soper, T. 1967. David & Charles, Newton Abbot.

Treasure Trove Islands – the Scilly Isles. Morris, R. (author & publisher) Admiral Benbow, Chapel Street, Penzance.

Valhalla, the Tresco Figurehead Collection. National Maritime Museum. 1984. ISBN 0 905555 77 5.

Westcountry Shipwrecks. Behenna, J. 1974. David & Charles, Newton Abbot. ISBN 0 7153 6569 X.

Wreck and Rescue Round the Cornish Coast. Vol. 2. Noall, C. & Farr, G. 1965. Bradford Barton Ltd, Truro.

Wrecks of the Isles of Scilly. Boulay, J. du. Mariner's Mirror reprint, Vol. 45 No. 4 (1959); Vol. 46 (1960).

Acknowledgements

The compilation of such a comprehensive, detailed and accurate guide would not have been possible without the assistance, co-operation and guidance of many people, most of whom are divers. The authors are grateful to everyone who has assisted in the book's production; their knowledge and help will lead to the greater enjoyment of underwater expeditions and exploration by the many thousands of divers who visit the area each year.

The authors especially wish to acknowledge and thank the following: Chris Lobb, Mid Cornwall Sub-Aqua Club, for his outstanding assistance, general comments and knowledge of the north coast of Cornwall; Colin and Judith Ingram, Bude BSAC; Kevin Heath of the Orkney Islands; Ken Dunstan of Cornwall; Tim and Viv Allsop of St Martin's; Mark Groves of St Mary's; Murray and Susan Hodgson of St Mary's; Richard Mills of St Mary's; Sean Lewis of St Mary's; Roy Graham of St Mary's; Terry Parsons of St Mary's; Jim and Lena Heslin of St Mary's; Mike Brown of St Mary's; Mike Rosse of Devon; Frank Gibson of the Isles of Scilly; Richards & Sons of Helston; Studio St Ives; Clive Carter of Penzance; John Davies of Truro; The *Western Morning News* of Plymouth; World Ship Society; Malcolm Henchley; Peter Jones of East Sussex; Mike Stevens of Bodmin; David Dowling of Newquay; Chris Lowe of Newquay; Bridget Larn of Scilly; and Sarah McBride of Scilly; V.M. Roffe of Ermington, Devon; S. Watts, Maritime Officer, St Mary's; J. Penhaligon, Harbour Master, St Mary's; M. McCarthy, Berthing Master, St Mary's; and the late Roland Morris of Penzance.

All the colour photographs of the North Cornwall coast were taken by Roy Smallpage, except for the view of Boscastle on page 188, which was taken by Richard Larn.

The following photographs were kindly supplied by:
Clive Carter: pages 125 (top), 182 (foot), 197
Colin Ingram: pages 191, 193
Daily Telegraph: page 70

Opposite: The river at Boscastle at low tide. There are slipways on both sides.

Edwin Mills: page 156 (top)
George Ellis: page 169
Gibson's of Scilly: pages 38, 40, 49, 51, 55, 57, 71, 77, 95, 105, 113, 115, 120, 123 (both), 124, 152
Mark Groves: page 25 (top and foot)
Kevin Hunkin: page 174
London Express Pictures: page 105
M. McCarthy: page 170
Malcolm Henchley: page 182 (top)
Peter Jones: page 187
Richards & Sons: page 129
Richards Brothers: page 156 (foot)
Studio St Ives: pages 125 (foot), 133
Western Morning News: pages 88, 154.

All the other photographs reproduced in this book were taken by the authors or are from their collections.

Index

The bold numbers in parentheses are dive site numbers.

219